IMPLIED POWERS OF THE UNITED NATIONS

IMPLIED POWERS OF THE UNITED NATIONS

RAHMATULLAH KHAN

VIKAS PUBLICATIONS
DELHI — BOMBAY — BANGALORE

© Rahmatullah Khan, 1970

PRINTED IN INDIA

AT THE OXFORD PRINTCRAFT INDIA PVT. LTD., 68 SCINDIA HOUSE,
NEW DELHI-1, AND PUBLISHED BY MRS. SHARDA CHAWLA, VIKAS
PUBLICATIONS, 5 DARYAGANJ, ANSARI ROAD, DELHI-6

To

DR. NAGENDRA SINGH

ACKNOWLEDGEMENTS

I AM INDEBTED to Dr. Wilfred Jenks, Mr. Oscar Schachter, Professor Quincy Wright, Professor Louis Sohn, Professor Leland Goodrich, and Professor Louis Henkin, with whom I had valuable discussions on the subject. The completion of this work would not have been possible without a grant by the Indian School of International Studies to cover the expenses to go to Switzerland and the USA for six months on a field research programme.

My gratitude goes in full measure to Dr. Nagendra Singh who, in spite of his official preoccupations, supervised my work and gave me great encouragement. And to Dr. R. P. Anand who patiently went through the whole manuscript and gave valuable suggestions, I owe an everlasting debt. Special mention must be made of the very kind interest shown in my work by Dr. M.S. Rajan, the Director of the Indian School of International Studies.

Also, I feel greatly obliged to Mrs. Virginia Walker and Mr. Michael Cummins of the UN Legal Library at the Headquarters, Badr Kasme of the *Palais des Nations* UN library at Geneva, and to the Librarian, Mr. Girja Kumar, Mrs. Andrade, Mrs. Shaukat Ashraf, Mrs. Chaya Devi, Miss Shanta Sehgal, Miss Usha Dhingra, and Mr. Ansari of the ICWA Library without whose gracious assistance this work would have been incomplete. I am grateful to Miss Lakshmi Devi for conscientiously preparing the index for the book.

PREFACE

THE STARTING POINT for the present enquiry was the famous International Court of Justice declaration regarding the powers of the United Nations in the *Reparations case*. The Court had pronounced in that case that the Organization must be deemed to have those powers which, though not expressly provided in the Charter, are conferred upon it by necessary implication as being essential to the performance of its duties.

That strikes one as an epoch-making opinion. For, the general run of thinking among jurists and international legal scholars till that time was that international organizations as creations of sovereign States for specific purposes had only those limited powers conferred on them, nothing above and beyond them. Any other interpretation, it was believed, would have a restrictive effect on State sovereignty, which was inadmissible without the State's consent. The *Lotus* ruling of the Permanent Court of International Justice lent support to that argument. The Court in that case had said that "the rules of law binding upon States . . . emanate from their own free will" and that "restrictions upon the independence of States cannot therefore be presumed."

In point of fact, however, the ruling was not revolutionary at all. International organizations had come to be recognized as possessing international personality independent of their member States. State practice bears ample testimony to that fact. As far back as 1920, the Swiss Government had recognized the international personality of the League of Nations in the *modus vivendi* drawn up between the organization and the Swiss authorities guaranteeing certain privileges and immunities considered hitherto as the sole attributes of sovereign States. The International Labour Organization, the International Institute of Agriculture, the International Telecommunication Union, the Universal Postal Union, etc., likewise, were either expressly recognized in their headquarters agreements or in actual practice to possess international personality and an independent identity. The post-World War II practice also confirms this practice. The headquarters agreement and the conventions concerning privileges and immunities of the UN and other Specialized Agencies make specific mention of the juridical personality of these organizations. Some of them had such a provision incorporated in their constituent instruments themselves.

Moreover, the PCIJ itself had occasion to pronounce upon the jural personality of the ILO and was called upon to say whether such concept could be used to stretch the orbit of the organization's functions over and above the specified field of operation. The Court had found such unexpressed authority to "legislate" admissible so long as the activities could be assimilated to the express provisions by implication.

The doctrine, therefore, of implied powers of international organization was not a startling innovation in the international jurisprudence. What warrants careful consideration is the International Court's brave attempts at balancing on the tight-rope between a liberal interpretation of the functions and powers of international organization and a restrictive interpretation of the duties and obligations of sovereign States.

The shifting shades of emphasis that the Court supplied on the nature and conditions of implied powers in the successive advisory opinions concerning the competence of the UN make an interesting study. It is indeed a vast sweep from the *Reparations* dicta that the Organization must be deemed to have "necessary powers by implication as being essential to the performance of its duties" to the *Expenses* pronouncement, "(s)ave as they have entrusted the Organization with the attainment of these common ends, the member States retain their freedom of action." But these rulings have built-in legal auto-limitations, and are susceptible to political checks and balances. This is the main burden of Part I of the study.

In a further passage of the *Reparations* Opinion the Court expressing its views on the quantum of the rights and duties of the UN as distinguished from those of a State, had affirmed: "Whereas a State possesses the totality of international rights and duties recognized by international law, the rights and duties of an entity such as the Organization must depend upon its purposes and functions as specified or implied in its constituent document and *developed in practice.*" (ICJ *Reports*, 1949, 180. Italics added.) This brought the whole range of functions and powers that the Organization exercised in the course of practice under the cover of legality. It was felt, therefore, that sufficient attention had to be paid to accretion of powers through usage and practice, and an effort must be made to probe into the legal bases for the same. It is indeed a fascinating study to see how the Organization spread its functions and powers onto the twilight zone that separates express authority from specific prohibition. Any attempt, however, to cover the whole gamut of powers invoked or envisioned that could cleanly be subsumed under this category would have been an unwieldy task. On the other hand, spotlighting such areas as would bring out the complexities and limitations, which at the same time could be considered legal, it was felt, would be a more valuable contribution. Two areas, viz. peace-keeping and treaty-making (Chapter 2 and Chapter 3), were selected as being the most illustrative of the expansive scope of powers by implication of the Organization. The issue of expulsions, forced withdrawal, etc. (Chapter 4), was considered to be an apposite venue to project the complexities that the doctrine is likely to run into in the event of its application to goals not measuring up to the ideal. The chapter on admissions (Chapter 5) has been included as revealing the availability of abundant discretion in spite of the finite limits and the exhaustive criteria expressly provided for in the constituent instrument.

The law of internal administration which forms the subject-matter of the next chapter would appear on the surface unrelated to the central thesis. But one can see very easily the thread of argument in the part that the doctrine of implied powers is not a double-edged sword, that the General Assembly can invoke the doctrine to establish an administrative tribunal with judicial powers but that it cannot draw upon the same source for appellate authority.

The writer is fully aware of the need to emphasize the legal and political limitations of the doctrine which, when transformed into the doctrine of institutional effectiveness, raised a storm of criticism from both scholars and the statesmen, and which failed to serve as the legal solution to the financial crisis of the UN.   The partial paralysis which the Organization suffered at the 19th General Assembly session had, after all, to be cured by readjustments of political positions.   It occurred to the writer, therefore, that any assessment of the powers of the UN cannot afford to ignore the political and legal objections to its constitutional competence.   The objections range from a rather sweeping remark that the Afro-Asian States in the General Assembly were forcing the Organization to take irresponsible positions to specific charges of unconstitutionality in particular cases.   In the latter category can be subsumed the British Prime Minister Harold Wilson's charge that the UN has been passing "irresponsible resolutions" in the case of Rhodesia "leaving us [Britain] to do the dirty work." (*The Times*, London, 2 November 1968.)   Eminent scholars, like Professor C. G. Fenwick, have also cast serious doubts about the constitutional competence of the UN in the case of Rhodesia (*AJIL*, Vol. 61, 1967, pp. 753-5).   In a study of the UN handling of the Kashmir problem, the present writer found that the Security Council was guilty of a kind of *suppressio veri* and *suggestio falsi*.*   The constitutionality of a whole range of UN resolutions, again, from those on South West Africa to the ones designed to end economic disparities of nations have at one time or the other been challenged.   The role of the Secretary-General in cases like the Congo has been subjected to severe criticism on legal and political grounds.

This raises the fundamental question of the effect of unconstitutional acts by international organizations.   Work in this field has been done by Professor R. Y. Jennings and Professor E. Lauterpacht in a theoretical framework.   Part III of the book, therefore, is devoted to an examination of the problem of nullity of unconstitutional acts of international organizations.

New Delhi   RAHMATULLAH KHAN

Kashmir and the United Nations, Vikas Publications, Delhi, 1969.

CONTENTS

PART I: DOCTRINE

PART II: PRACTICE

PART III: CRITIQUE

PART ONE

DOCTRINE

CHAPTER 1

DOCTRINAL ASSESSMENT

EVERY ORGANIC INSTITUTION in the course of its existence is
bound to face a situation where a certain exercise of power or
function becomes necessary to effectuate the general purposes
for which it is created, though its constitutive instrument does
not expressly provide for such a specific power or function. The
question then arises if the institution has an implied power to
embark upon that activity. The answer to this question depends
upon several factors, such as the intention of the parties creating
the institution, the scope of its objectives and purposes, the ambit
of its expressed powers, the historical background, the need for
adapting to changing times, and so on. Also, it depends upon
its legal personality.

National courts in various countries have evolved what has
come to be called the doctrine of implied powers by a liberal
interpretation of the provisions of the Constitutions to suit the
genius of their peoples and governments. Thus, for example, in
the United States Constitution, where the Federal government's
powers are enumerated, the remaining being reserved for the
constituent States, the accretion of power to the Federal government
through liberal interpretation of the relevant provisions has been
maximum. Chief Justice Marshall's dicta in the celebrated case,
McCulloch v. *Maryland* (1819), remain a touchstone on which the
constitutionality of all federal functions is judged even today:

> We admit, as all must admit, that the powers of the government
> are limited, and that its limits are not to be transcended. But
> we think the sound construction of the Constitution must allow
> to the national legislature that discretion, with respect to the
> means by which the powers it confers are to be carried into
> execution, which will enable that body to perform the high

duties assigned to it, in the manner most beneficial to the people. Let the end be legitimate, let it be within the scope of the Constitution, and all means which are appropriate, which are plainly adapted to that end, which are not prohibited, but consist with the letter and spirit of the Constitution, are constitutional.[1]

In the Canadian and Australian Constitutions where there is a double enumeration of powers, this doctrine has minimal application. The accretion of power in these countries is limited to ancillary and incidental fields. In the Indian Constitution, where there is an exhaustive treble enumeration of powers, the doctrine, according to the Supreme Court, has no relevance at all.[2]

The idea of attributing to international organizations powers by implication—over and above those specified or expressed—received an authoritative *imprimatur* from the International Court of Justice in the *Reparations* case. The issue in that case, a *cause celebre* in the law of the UN, was whether or not, in the absence of express authority in the Charter, the UN could espouse a claim on behalf of its employee who suffered a serious injury (fatal in this case) in the service of the Organization. Recognizing a large measure of international personality as evidenced in the Charter and developed in practice, but refusing to equate such personality to that of a State or super State, the Court affirmed emphatically: "Under international law, the Organization must be deemed to have those powers which, though not expressly provided in the Charter, are conferred upon it by necessary implication as being essential to the performance of its duties."[3]

In fact the doctrine of implied powers of international organization was in gestation for a long time. As early as 1946 the UN was called upon to assume certain responsibilities for which no specific authorization was to be found in the Charter. The example that comes immediately to mind is the Free Territory of Trieste.

---

[1]4 Wheat, 316.

[2]See *State of West Bengal* v. *Union of India*, AIR, 1963, Supreme Court, 1241, 21 December 1962; especially Justice Subba Rao's dissent, 1274.

[3]ICJ *Reports*, 1949, p. 182.

FREE TERRITORY OF THE TRIESTE CASE

Article 2 of the Permanent Statute of the Free Territory of Trieste, which was annexed to the 1947 Italian Peace Treaty, provided:

> The integrity and independence of the Free Territory shall be assured by the Security Council of the United Nations Organization. This responsibility implies that the Council shall:
> (*a*) ensure the observance of the present Statute and in particular the protection of the basic human rights of the inhabitants;
> (*b*) ensure the maintenance of public order and security in the Free Territory.

The Statute also authorized the Security Council to appoint a Governor, who would have the status of the Council's representative. The Governor was to have extensive administrative and legislative powers.

Following a request by the Chairman of the Foreign Ministers[5] for adoption of the responsibilities entrusted thus, the matter came up for discussion in the Security Council at its 89th meeting. A few delegates had grave doubts over the constitutional basis for the assumption of such responsibilities by the Council. It was pointed out that the Charter provides no specific authority to enable the Council to undertake such governmental functions or to assure the integrity and independence of a State. The Australian delegate challenged the Council's competence in the following terms:

> ... Chapter V of the Charter contains the general powers and functions of the Security Council and it is further stated in Article 24, paragraph 2, that specific powers granted to the Council for the discharge of its duty to maintain international peace and security are laid down in Chapters VI, VII, VIII, and XII. Chapters VIII and XII are not relevant to the present

---

[4] Annex VI, Treaty of Peace with Italy, 10 February 1947, *United Nations Treaty Series*, Vol. 3, p. 187.

[5] UN Doc. S/224/Rev. 1 dated 12 December 1964, *Security Council Official Records*, 2nd year, Supp. No. 1, Annex 1.

case. Turning to Chapters VI and VII, we find that neither of these chapters authorizes the Council to give any general guarantee of integrity and independence to a particular territory. It is only in the particular circumstances referred to in those chapters that the Council acquires and can acquire jurisdiction. Before the Council may act, there must be a dispute or a situation which might lead to international friction or give rise to a dispute or a threat to the peace, or a breach of peace. These powers of the Security Council, under the Charter, operate independently of any peace treaties drawn up by the Council of Foreign Ministers, and they operate in respect of all territories, including Trieste.

The proposals now before the Security Council, however, are to the effect that the Council should accept various new responsibilities and, in particular, the responsibility of assuring the integrity and the independence of the Free Territory. The acceptance of such responsibilities is clearly not authorized by the Charter.[6]

On the other hand the Secretariat, which was called upon to clarify the constitutional position in a legal memorandum,[7] gave its opinion that the words "primary responsibility for the maintenance of international peace and security," coupled with the phrase, "acts on their behalf" constitute a grant of power sufficiently wide to enable the Security Council to approve the documents in question and to assume the responsibilities arising therefrom.

The documents of the San Francisco Conference were invoked by both the sides to buttress their arguments. The Australian delegate referred to the rejection by the Conference of a move to incorporate in the Charter a territorial guarantee similar to that of Article 10 of the League Covenant.[8] Whereas the Secretariat memorandum referred to the unanimity of opinion expressed in

---

[6] *Security Council Official Records*, 89th meeting, pp. 6-7.

[7] *Ibid.*, 91st meeting, pp. 44-5.

[8] Article 10 of the Covenant of the League of Nations expressly stipulated the obligation of the members "to respect and preserve as against external aggression the territorial integrity and existing political independence of all members of the League."

the 14th meeting of Committee III/1 at San Francisco, to wit, that when the maintenance of peace and security is at issue, the Council should not be regarded as limited by specific Charter provisions, other than the fundamental principles and purposes found in Chapter 1.[9]

However, a majority believed that in spite of the lack of specific provision in the Charter enabling the Council to assume such responsibilities, Article 24 was broad enough to embrace the desired power. As additional props the French and the US delegates referred to the expectations of the world community;[10] and the UK and Columbian delegates warned about the undesirability of creating a bad precedent by fearing to assume such responsibility.[11] The consensus was that the Council should act on the basis of the spirit of the Charter, rather than on a definite provision. At the 91st meeting itself the Council approved the Annexes embodying the status of Trieste, thereby accepting "the responsibilities devolving upon it" under them.[12]

Strangely this unorthodox assumption of power by the Security Council did not provoke comparative comment in the academic circle, with the exception of an article by Professor Hans Kelsen.[13] In a very forceful analysis Kelsen maintained that the Organization in general lacked authority to guarantee the integrity and independence of the members and that there was no provision which authorized it to enter into international arrangements of that nature. More specifically, the Security Council was simply incompetent to assure the integrity and independence of a State and that "[t]here

[9]See Doc. No. 597, III/I/30, *Documents of the United Nations Conference on International Organization, San Francisco*, United Nations Information Organizations, London, New York, 1945 (hereinafter cited as UNCIO Docs.), Vol. II, p. 393.

[10]*Security Council Official Records*, 2nd year, 89th meeting, pp. 15-6 (France), p. 11 (US).

[11]*Ibid.*, pp. 9-10 (UK), p. 18 (Columbia).

[12]*Ibid.*, p. 60, by a vote of 10-0-1 (Australia).

[13]Hans Kelsen, "The Free Territory of Trieste under the United Nations," *Yearbook of World Affairs*, Vol. 4, 1950, pp. 174-90. The lack of concern could perhaps be attributed to the fact that the Security Council never assumed the actual powers because of the parties' inability to agree on the details of administration.

is certainly no provision in the Charter which empowers the Council to exercise the function of a head of State."[14] Then abruptly Kelsen came to the conclusion: "The United Nations has not the legal, but it has certainly the actual power to assume for the Security Council the functions conferred upon it by the Peace Treaty with Italy." He referred then to the resolution adopted by the Council by which it did assume such responsibilities. More recently John Halderman, while agreeing substantially with the criticism of Kelsen, has viewed the action as constituting "a development of the Charter through assertion of a power not specified therein."[15]

Whichever way one may view the whole episode—whether as an "actual power" or as a "power by assertion" as distinguished from a "legal power"—it brought to light the latent potentialities of the UN and its powers by implication. The point that deserves due care at this stage is the one made in the Secretariat memo mentioned earlier, i.e. that "the responsibility to maintain peace and security carried with it a power to discharge this responsibility" and that this power "was not unlimited, but subject to the purposes and principles of the United Nations." In other words, the peace-keeping powers of the UN were limited only by the purposes and principles of the Charter. Kelsen, on the other hand, was of the opinion that such a wide deduction could not be drawn from the *travaux preparatoires*. There was ample evidence, however, in the preparatory documents, as well as awareness among statesmen and scholars, to show that the Council was not deemed to be totally limited by the specific Charter provisions.

Now, what is the rationale behind this liberal interpretation of the constitutions of international organizations. The simple truth is that since international organizations are not mere public corporations, and have to have an organic existence to live with the changing patterns of international behaviour and international requirements, they should be treated with a measure of reasonable

---

[14]*Ibid.*, p. 186.

[15]John W. Halderman, "United Nations Territorial Administration and the Development of the Charter," *Duke Law Journal*, 1964, reprinted in *World Rule of Law Booklet Series*, Durham, N.C., No. 25, p. 97.

latitude. This is done through the employment of a legal concept —jural or international personality.[16] The latitude of liberal interpretation, then, depends upon the nature of jural personality an international organization, or, for that matter, any other legal entity, possesses. We will come to that after a brief reference to practice among international organizations.

IMPLIED POWERS AND POST-WAR PRACTICE
AMONG INTERNATIONAL ORGANIZATIONS

The post-war practice of international organizations tends to show that the organizations have not always conformed to their express provisions when performing their functions. The Charter of the Organization of American States for instance does not provide for the power to conclude treaties expressly. Nevertheless it signed a headquarters agreement with the host State on 22 July 1952. In fact, the practice to draw on unexpressed powers for the effective functioning of the organization has a long history. The International Institute of Agriculture, whose constitution provided no such powers, did conclude an agreement with the League of Nations as early as 25 October 1935.[17] Its international personality was recognized by an Italian law on 20 June 1930,[18] and in the judgment in *Profili* v. *International Institute of Agriculture*.[19]

A good many international organizations have since World War II, begun to maintain offices in territories of member States. Most States have accredited permanent delegations or

[16]For a short but comprehensive bibliography on the subject, see Wilfred C. Jenks, "Legal Personality of International Organizations," *British Yearbook of International Law*, Vol. 22, p. 267; see also Quincy Wright, "The Jural Personality of the United Nations," *American Journal of International Law*, Vol. 43, 1949, p. 509; Guenter Weissberg, *The International Status of the United Nations*, London, 1961, and Finn Seyersted, *Objective International Personality of Inter-governmental Organizations: Do their Capacities really depend upon their Constitutions?* Copenhagen, 1963, also published in *Indian Journal of International Law*, Vol. 4, Nos. 1 and 2, 1964.

[17]For the document, see *The Legal and Moral Position and the Diplomatic Prerogatives of the International Institute of Agriculture*, published in French and English by the Institute in Rome, 1943.

[18]*Ibid.*

[19]*Annual Digest*, Case No. 254, 1929-30, pp. 213-5.

missions to inter-governmental organizations. Sometimes members of diplomatic missions are concurrently accredited to organizations which happen to have their headquarters in that particular territory. Both the members of such delegations and the members of the organizations enjoy almost similar privileges and immunities. It would be vain to look into the constitutional documents of these organizations for express powers to send or receive diplomatic representatives.

International organizations have presented and paid international claims, have concluded agreements with member States providing that disputes between them shall be settled by elaborate arbitral procedures, involving, sometimes, an advisory opinion of the International Court of Justice.[20] No specific provisions can be found in the constitutions of these organizations expressly authorizing such powers.

The United Nations

The record bears witness to the fact that at San Francisco the delegates were most anxious to avoid the impression that what they were about to create was the dreaded spectre of a super State.

Article 104 of the Charter, which deals with the question, reads: "The Organization shall enjoy in the territory of each of its members such legal capacity as may be necessary for the exercise of its functions and the fulfilment of its purposes."

A Belgian suggestion made at Dumbarton Oaks that the international status of the United Nations form the subject of a special text was rejected. Its manoeuvre later at San Francisco to move an amendment to the Article to replace the phrase "such legal capacity" with "international status, together with the rights thus involved' was considered superfluous by the Sub-Committee of Committee IV/2.[21] The Committee took the view that "in effect it will be determined implicitly from the provisions of the Charter taken as a whole."[22] The predominant political conside-

---

[20]For this and other examples bearing on the practice of international organizations in this respect, see Seyersted, *op. cit.*, pp. 15-29.
[21]*UNCIO* Docs., Vol. 3, p. 343.
[22]*Ibid.*, Vol. 13, pp. 104, 654-5, 710, 803, 933.

ration as expressed in the United States Delegations' Report to the President, was "to avoid any implication that the United Nations will be in any sense a 'super State'."[23]

The view has been expressed that "what was contemplated within the scope of the legal capacity in Article 104 was left for future determination."[24] Sir Gerald Fitzmaurice expressed the opinion that the Article is "neutral" on the issue.[25] But the better view seems to be that the framers considered it "superfluous" in view of the repeated references to its independent identity in the specific provisions of the Charter.

Paragraph 6 of Article 2 states that the "Organization shall ensure"; Article 58 says that the "Organization shall make recommendations"; Article 60 speaks of "the functions of the Organization"; Article 75 reads "The United Nations shall establish"; Articles 83 and 85 refer to the "functions of the United Nations"; while by virtue of Articles 104 and 105 "The Organization shall enjoy." Again, the following provisions bring out the independent identity of the Organization. Paragraph 5 of Article 2 reads: "All members shall give the United Nations every assistance in any action it takes in accordance with the present Charter, and shall refrain from giving assistance to any State against which the United Nations is taking preventive or enforcement action." The Charter further specifically recognizes the contractual capacity of the United Nations. Under Article 43, the Security Council can conclude military agreements with members. Article 63 empowers the Economic and Social Council to enter into relationship agreements with the agencies specified in Article 57. Paragraph 3 of Article 105 provides that the Assembly may propose conventions to members of the Organization in order to

[23]*Report to the President on the Results of the San Francisco Conference, D.S.P.* 2349, Conference Series 71 (1945), p. 157; "The Charter of the United Nations," *Hearings before the Senate Committee on Foreign Relations,* 79th Congress, 1st Session, 1945, p. 135.

[24]Yuen-Li Liang, "The Legal Status of the United Nations in the United States," *International Law Quarterly,* Vol. 2, 1948, p. 578.

[25]ICJ, *Pleadings, Oral Arguments, Documents Reparation for Injuries Suffered in the Service of the United Nations,* Advisory Opinion, 11 April 1949, p. 118; hereinafter cited as ICJ *Pleadings.* See Weissberg, *op. cit.,* for an exhaustive account of the international personality of the UN.

determine the detailed application of the Organization's privileges and immunities. The convention on the Privileges and Immunities of the United Nations of 1946 was concluded under this Article.

It is sufficient to stress here that the constitutive document contained sufficient indications, express and implied, to show that the UN possessed objective international personality, and the omission of an express provision to that effect is far from fatal.[26] To say, however, that the organization possessed international personality is one thing and to equate it with that of a State, a super State, or a mere corporation is another. Legal personality can be possessed by anybody and anything on earth—from plants to reptiles and from the temple deity to a self-confessed scoundrel.[27] Legal personality is a convenient device of law whereby a clear distinction is created between the rights and duties of the entity to others and the rights and duties of others to the entity.[28] Legal entities are not equal or co-extensive. They differ both in degree and in kind.[29] The extent and implication of the personality concept, especially on the international plane, has had an interesting history. A great deal of credit goes to the International Court of Justice for the development of jurisprudence in the field, towards which attention will be drawn in due course. One such implication of the personality concept is the doctrine of Implied Powers.

INTER-RELATIONSHIP BETWEEN INTERNATIONAL PERSONALITY AND IMPLIED POWERS OF INTERNATIONAL ORGANIZATIONS

Legal scholars are not agreed on the criteria by which one may decide whether an organization possesses international personality, and whether, if it does, it has implied powers. Hans Kelsen, for example, believes that an organization "has only those special capacities" as are "conferred upon it by particular pro-

---

[26]Hugo J. Hahn, "Euratom: The Conception of an International Personality," *Harvard Law Review*, Vol. 71, 1958, p. 1045.

[27]See for an interesting account of the concept, Alexander Nakam, *The Personality Conception of the Legal Entity*, Cambridge, Mass., 1938, pp. 25-6; and Hahn, *op. cit.*, pp. 1042-3.

[28]George W. Paton, *A Textbook of Jurisprudence*, London, 1946, pp. 267-8.

[29]Clyde Eagleton, "International Organization and the Law of Responsibility," *Recueil des Cours*, 1950, p. 327.

visions."[30] Finn Seyersted, at the other extreme, affirms that:

> ... no constitutional provisions are necessary to establish the capacity of an inter-governmental organization to perform those "sovereign" or international acts which States have an inherent capacity to perform. ... Constitutional provisions have only negative significance, inasmuch as they may preclude the exercise of such capacities in certain respects. However, this is true of States, too.[31]

Sir Hersch Lauterpacht, on the other hand, doubts if express conferment of international personality amounts to "unrestricted legal capacity under international law."[32] For Sir Gerald Fitzmaurice, the "personality and capacities of the Organization have their origin in an instrument contractual in form, but once created and established they come to assume an objective, self-existent character, effective for all the world."[33]

These conflicting and somewhat dialectical views show the eternal problem of treaty interpretation. In what manner is a treaty relating to an international organization to be interpreted? On the one hand there is the fundamental principle which demands that obligations imposed upon States ought to be interpreted restrictively—the doctrine of restrictive interpretation. On the other hand there is the hardly less important maxim that the treaty must remain effective rather than ineffective—the doctrine of effectiveness.[34] A substantial part of the jurisprudence of the International Court of Justice, as Sir Hersch Lauterpacht points out, "can be viewed in terms of the effort, which cannot

---

[30]*The Law of the United Nations*, 1950, p. 330.

[31]Seyersted, *op. cit.*, pp. 38-9.

[32]Lauterpacht, UN Doc. A/CN. 4/63, 1952, p. 155.

[33]Fitzmaurice, "The Law and Procedure of the International Court of Justice: International Organizations and Tribunals," *British Yearbook of International Law*, Vol. 29, 1952, p. 21.

[34]H. Lauterpacht, *The Development of International Law by the International Court*, London, 1958, p. 227; "Restrictive Interpretation and the Principle of Effectiveness in the Interpretation of Treaties," *British Yearbook of International Law*, Vol. 26, 1949, p. 48.

easily be put within the framework of any single rule of interpretation, to strike a balance between these potentially conflicting principles."[35] But in cases concerning interpretation of constituent instruments of international organizations the International Court has shown a conspicuously general tendency in favour of an interpretation permitting a wider rather than a more restricted display of activity in order to make effective the general purposes of the organizations. This tendency was clearly discernible in the PCIJ's advisory opinions concerning the activities of the ILO.

CONTRIBUTION BY THE PERMANENT COURT OF INTERNATIONAL JUSTICE

The PCIJ was called upon to pronounce upon the validity of some of the most important regulations of the ILO. In one of its earliest opinions the Court, for instance, was called upon to decide the question whether the ILO possessed competence in regard to the international regulation of the conditions of labour of persons employed in agriculture.[36] The Director of the organization, in an impassioned plea made before the Court, urged the Court to realize that the question was decisive for the character and scope of much of the work of the ILO.[37]

On the other hand, it was contended by those representing certain States (France, for example) that the establishment of the ILO involved an abandonment of rights of national sovereignty and that the competence of the organization should not, therefore, be extended by interpretation. The contention was that the provisions of the Treaty of Versailles relating to the ILO constituted a limitation on the sovereignty of States. It was conceded that the obligations of the Treaty in this respect had been undertaken with due deliberation, and that the resolutions of the Conference of the ILO were in law and in fact merely in the nature of recommendations. However, it was urged that, according to the Constitution of the organization, there was an obligation to submit these recommendations to the national legislatures, and that this was, therefore,

[35]*The Development of International Law by the International Court*, p. 228.
[36]PCIJ, *Series B*, No. 2, 1922.
[37]*Series C*, No. 1, p. 267.

a case of the exercise of an international, as opposed to a purely national initiative. This, it was argued, implied a restriction of national sovereignty with the resulting duty to interpret these provisions strictly and in the narrowest sense.[38]

The Court admitted that there might be some force in the argument, but proceeded to state that "the question in every case must resolve itself into what the terms of the Treaty actually mean."[39] The Court held that the term "industry" constantly occurring in Part XIII of the Treaty of Versailles could not be interpreted in the limited meaning of the word to the exclusion of agriculture and navigation. The Court considered that the failure to regulate conditions of work in agriculture by way of international agreement might frustrate the purpose of the Treaty by acting as a check upon the adoption of more humane conditions of labour and by constituting "a handicap against the nations which had adopted them and in favour of those which had not, in the competition of the markets of the world."[40]

The Court adopted a similar method of approach in its thirteenth advisory opinion when it had to answer the question whether the ILO was competent to regulate the personal work of the employers when this was incidental to the regulation of the work of the employers.[41] The Court's consideration in this case was that the organization would be prevented from drawing up and proposing measures essential to the accomplishment of its purpose for the protection of workers, measures "to the efficacious working of which it was found to be essential to include to some extent work done by employers."[42] Interpreting the prohibition contained in the International Convention of 1906 concerning white phosphorus in the manufacture of matches, the Court stated that in determining the nature and the scope of a measure it "must look to its practical effect rather than to the predominant motive that may be conjectured to have inspired it."[43]

[38]*Ibid.*, p. 174.
[39]Series B, No. 2, 1922, p. 23.
[40]*Ibid.*, p. 25.
[41]Competence of the International Labour Organization to Regulate, incidentally, the Personal Work of the Employers, PCIJ, *Series* B, No. 13, 1926.
[42]*Ibid.*, p. 18.
[43]*Ibid.*, p. 19.

Again, the Court was called upon in 1932 to answer whether the Convention of 1919 concerning the employment of women during the night applied to women who held positions of supervision or management and were not ordinarily engaged in manual work.[44] It was argued before the Court that the amelioration of the lot of the manual worker was the main preoccupation of those who created the ILO and that any extension of its field of activity was unwarranted. The Court, however, was "not disposed to regard the sphere of activity of the International Labour Organization as circumscribed so closely, in respect of the persons with which it was to concern itself, as to raise any presumption that a Labour Convention must be interpreted as being restricted in its operation to manual workers, unless a contrary intention appears."[45]

The three opinions discussed above bear ample testimony to the fact that the PCIJ was not only prepared to grant the ILO incidental and implied powers that effectuated the general purposes of the organization, but willing to subordinate the motives of those who evolved the organization to the "practical effect" of the measures it took. A substantial, though not decisive, support for the contrary opinion of the minority of the Court is to be found in the *travaux préparatoires* of the Conventions at issue.

CONTRIBUTION OF THE COURT OF EUROPEAN COMMUNITIES

The Court of Justice of the European Communities has not a little to contribute to the law of implied powers of international organizations.[46]

In *Federation Charbonniere de Belgique C. Haute Autorite*[47] the Court upheld the intervention of the High Authority in a dispute concerning regulation of the gradual integration of the

[44]Interpretation of the Convention of 1919 concerning Employment of Women during the Night, PCIJ, *Series* A/B, No. 50, 1932.
[45]*Ibid.*, p. 374.
[46]J.F. McMahon, "The Court of the European Communities, Judicial Interpretation and International Organization," *British Yearbook of International Law*, Vol. 37, 1961, pp. 320-50.
[47]*Recueil de la Jurisprudence de la Cour*, Vol. 2, 1955-56, p. 302.

coal and steel of the six countries, though the High Authority had no express power to do so. The Court held that since the object of the Convention in question could not be implemented without the direct intervention of the High Authority, if there was no express power permitting such a course of action, then it must of necessity be implied.

The doctrine of implied powers was further reiterated in two subsequent cases, viz. *Gouvernement de la republique italienne c. Haute Autorite*[48] and *Gouvernement du royaume des Pays—Bas C. Haute Autorite.*[49]

DEVELOPMENT OF LEGAL PERSONALITY AND THE DOCTRINE OF INSTITUTIONAL EFFECTIVENESS

Hardly two years had elapsed since the Charter came into existence when the International Court of Justice was called upon to interpret the provisions of the Charter relative to the law of admission.[50] The question before the Court was whether a member of the UN was legally entitled, when called upon to vote on admission of a new member, to make its consent to the admission dependent on conditions not expressly provided in paragraph 1 of Article 4. In particular, could a member link another new member's admission to its assent?

The Court first catalogued the "conditions" required under paragraph 1 of Article 4 of an applicant for admission: "The requisite conditions are five in number: to be admitted to membership in the United Nations, an applicant must (1) be a State; (2) be peace-loving; (3) accept the obligations of the Charter; (4) be able to carry out these obligations; and (5) be willing to do so."[51]

Then the Court declared in what amounts to a milestone in the development of an independent, objective, international personality of the United Nations: "All these conditions are subject to the *judgment* of the Organization."[52]

[48]*Ibid.*, 1960, p. 688.

[49]*Ibid.*, p. 757.

[50]Conditions of Admission of a State to Membership in the United Nations (Article 4 of the Charter), ICJ *Reports*, 1947-48, p. 57.

[51]*Ibid.*, p. 62.

[52]*Ibid.*, p. 62. (Italics added.)

Though admitting immediately that the judgement of the Organization, in the last analysis is that of the members thereof, the Court made an affirmation that clearly lifted the Organization from the national fiats of member States. It did so by finding, first, that the text of Article 4 was apparently clear about what constituted the conditions of membership; second, that the conditions were exhaustive; lastly, that members were not free to import into the application of this provisions considerations extraneous to the conditions laid down therein. The thesis was that the sovereign and equal members of the UN must subordinate their judgment to that of the Organization and that their discretion in matters of admission was clearly limited to the provisions of Article 4 of the Charter.

In a spirited joint dissent judges Basdevant, Winiarski, Sir Arnold McNair, and John Read held the opposite view.[53] They argued that, unlike the system of accession common to all multilateral treaties which created international unions, whereby a declaration of accession made by a third State involved automatically the acquisition of membership in the union by that State, the United Nations Charter evolved an entirely different system of admission. For them the admission of a new member was preeminently a political act of the greatest importance.[54] Consequently, members of the Organization were legally entitled to base their decisions upon political considerations.[55]

The majority view was that the discretionary "right of appreciation" of member States had to be confined to the clear

[53]*Ibid.*, pp. 82-90.

[54]*Ibid.*, p. 85.

[55]Judge Zoricic, in his individual dissent, even suggested some of the extraneous considerations which might well fall outside the pale of Article 4 and yet might legitimately, in his opinion, be applied: ". . . the admission of a State might create tension with other members or non-members of the Organization, and might give rise to expressions of mistrust, discontent, and injustice; whilst, on the other hand, its admission might be held undesirable from the point of view of harmonious co-operation within the Organization." (*Ibid.*, p. 102.)

Judge Krylov read into the system of admissions a distinction between (1) legal criteria as prescribed in paragraph 1 of Article 4; and (2) political considerations consistent with the purposes and principles of the UN. He attributed, accordingly, to the member States "a right of appreciation" in matters of admission. (*Ibid.*, p. 111.)

text of the law as contained in Article 4, paragraph 1. And so, too, was the case with the "judgment of the Organization."

In the *Second Admissions* case[56] the Court clarified the thesis further. The question here was whether the General Assembly could make a decision to admit a State when the Security Council transmitted no recommendation to it as required under paragraph 2 of Article 4.[57] The Court found that it required two things to effect admission; a "recommendation" of the Security Council and a "decision" of the General Assembly. "Both these acts," said the Court, "are indispensable to form the judgment of the Organization to which the previous paragraph of Article 4 refers."[58]

Simultaneously, there was a strikingly new phenomenon bearing on the direction of the UN's organic development. In 1949 the Court was seized of an issue that was destined to become a landmark in the progressive development of the jural status of the UN and in the jurisprudence of the Court.[59] The question posed by the General Assembly was whether the UN had the capacity to bring an international claim against a State responsible for an injury to an UN official on duty. Finding no express provisions in the Charter conferring such a capacity, the Court proceeded to inquire if such a capacity could be implied from the provisions of the Charter concerning the functions of the Organization.

The Court started with the assumption that the capacity to espouse international claims is a necessary concomitant of international personality. For, in the Court's view, "if the Organization is recognized as having that personality, it is an entity capable of availing itself of obligations incumbent upon its members."[60] The Court found that this capacity certainly

[56]Competence of the General Assembly for the admission of a State to the UN, ICJ *Reports*, 1950, p. 2.

[57]Paragraph 2 of Article 4 reads: "The admission of any such State to membership in the United Nations will be *effected* by a *decision* of the General Assembly upon the *recommendation* of the Security Council." (Italics added.)

[58]ICJ *Reports*, 1950, pp. 7-8.

[59]See Reparation for Injuries Suffered in the Service of the United Nations, ICJ *Reports*, 1949, p. 174.

[60]*Ibid.*, p. 179.

belongs to States. It had only to be seen if the UN too possessed such a personality.

The Charter, said the Court, had not been content to make the Organization created by it merely a centre "for harmonizing the actions of nations" (Paragraph 4 of Article 1). After a brief account of its purposes and principles, functions and powers, the Court pronounced: "The Organization was intended to exercise and enjoy, and is in fact exercising and enjoying, functions and rights which can only be explained on the basis of the possession of a large measure of international personality and the capacity to operate upon an international plane."[61]

The Court, though refusing at first to be drawn into the doctrinal controversy, could not resist the temptation of classification. Declaring that the Organization is an international person, it went on to add: "That is not the same thing as saying that it is a State, which it certainly is not, or that its legal personality and rights and duties are the same as those of a State. Still less is it the same thing as saying that it is 'a super State,' whatever that expression may mean."[62] In a further passage the Court clarified: "Whereas a State possesses the totality of international rights and duties recognized by international law, the rights and duties of an entity such as the Organization must depend upon its purposes and functions as specified *or implied* in its constituent document and developed in practice."[63]

In the opinion of the Court the Organization could engage the services of agents to observe and report from the disturbed parts of the world in furtherance of the Organization's foremost function of maintaining international peace and security. If this was conceded, "fundamental protection" to such agents as expose themselves to unusual dangers was a minimum necessity without which efficient and independent performance of the missions could not be ensured. The Court in this connection declared: "Upon examination of the character of the functions entrusted to the Organization and of the nature of the missions of its agents, it

[61]*Ibid.*
[62]*Ibid.*
[63]*Ibid.*, p. 180. (Italics added.)

becomes clear that the capacity of the Organization to exercise a measure of functional protection of its agents arises by necessary intendment out of the Charter."[64]

On these considerations it was not difficult for the Court to lay down the general rule: "Under international law, the Organization must be deemed to have those powers which, though not expressly provided in the Charter, are conferred upon it by necessary implication as being essential to the performance of its duties."[65]

Thus emerged the theory of implied powers on the international plane. The letter of the law still ruled supreme. Only implied and ancillary powers were derived by necessary intendment out of the Charter. The condition, however, was that these powers must enable the Organization to carry out its functions effectively and efficiently.

Judge Hackworth, on the other hand, preferred a more conservative view. In a powerful dissenting note he pointed out that the Court's theory of implied powers was not "warranted under rules laid down by tribunals for filling lacunae in specified grants of powers."[66] Though conceding that implied powers flow from a grant of express powers and are limited to those that are "necessary" to the exercise of powers expressly granted, he took exception to the way the Court wanted to grant the particular power in question. His stand was that the theory of "functional protection" amounted to a transfer of the most vital attribute of a nation's sovereignty to the Organization. Though the international agent owed unfettered fidelity to the Organization, his allegiance to the state of his nationality could not be undermined. The prerogative (that of taking up the cause of a national by the State) could not be sacrificed at the altar of fidelity to the Organization. Judge Hackworth's contention, therefore, was that unless such an important function of sovereignty was delegated to the Organization expressly in the Charter or in complementary agreements concluded by them, the Organization could not claim it. In the words of Judge Hackworth,

[64]*Ibid.*, p. 184.
[65]*Ibid.*, p. 182.
[66]*Ibid.*, p. 198.

there "could be no gainsaying the fact that the Organization is one of delegated and enumerated powers. It is to be presumed that such powers as the member States desired to confer upon it are stated either in the Charter or in complementary agreements concluded by them. *Powers not expressed cannot freely be implied.*"[67]

The Court, however, took the view that "functional protection" of the employee, in the light of Article 100 of the Charter, was the supreme duty of the Organization and to make the person's allegiance to the State more predominant would render the Organization ineffective.

In striking contrast to Judge Hackworth's opinion was the view advocated by Judge Alvarez. In the *First Admissions* case he recommended a frankly teleological principle. It was his view that an institution, once established, acquires a life of its own independent of the elements which have given birth to it, and it must develop not in accordance with the views of those who created it but in accordance with the requirements of international life.[68]

International law, Judge Alvarez maintained, is progressing speedily from the traditional *juridical* and *individualistic* concept to the politico-economic and socio-psychological character. He named it the "*law of social interdependence.*"[69] This phenomenal change, he argued in the *Second Admissions* case, has necessitated, *inter alia*, an alternative technique of treaty interpretation. Under the new system of interpretation, he propounded, (a) distinction must be made between treaties of different character; (b) the text of the treaties must not be slavishly followed; (c) reference to the *travaux preparatoires* must be avoided, except in exceptional cases; and (d) the interpretation must not be immutable—it will have to be modified if important changes take place in the matter to which it relates.[70] Judge Alvarez made the same approach in the *Reparations* case, too, in claiming for the UN very wide powers, including "functional protection" to its employees.

The Court presumably felt that the course adumbrated by Judge Hackworth would unduly hamper the functioning of inter-

---

[67]*Ibid.* (Italics added.)
[68]ICJ *Reports*, 1947-48, p. 68.   [69]*Ibid.*, p. 69.
[70]ICJ *Reports*, 1950, p. 16.

national organizations and the one championed by Judge Alvarez would make the Organization an Arabian genie let loose. The Court chose a middle course as seen above.[71]

In the *South-West Africa* case[72] the Court had another opportunity to emphasize the objective and independent existence of international organizations and the perpetuating character of obligations assumed under it. The question before the Court, relevant for this discussion, was whether or not the Union of South Africa continued to have international obligations under the Mandate System of the League (especially the obligation to submit to the supervision of its successor, the UN) even after the League's demise. The issue had far-reaching consequences, both legal and political. If the answer was affirmative, international organizations would have unending regimes of law not necessarily limited to their physical existence. The alternative involved the violation of the "sacred trust" of civilized nations assumed under international guarantees. The Court naturally chose the former path. It accordingly declared:

> The necessity for supervision continues to exist despite the disappearance of the supervisory organ under the Mandate System. It cannot be admitted that the obligation to submit to supervision has disappeared merely because the supervisory organ has ceased to exist, when the United Nations has another international organization performing similar though not identical supervisory functions.[73]

In 1954, the divergence in the views held by the Court, Judge Hackworth, and Judge Alvarez on the Organization's implied powers and the scope of interpretation of its organic law was seen again in the *Administrative Tribunal* case.[74] The question posed to the Court was whether the General Assembly had the right to refuse to give effect to an award of compensation made by the Adminis-

---

[71]See Fitzmaurice, *op. cit.*, pp. 5-10, for a short but stimulating account of the subject.

[72]International Status of South-West Africa, ICJ *Reports*, 1950, p. 128.

[73]*Ibid.*, p. 136.

[74]Effect of Awards of Compensation made by the UN Administrative Tribunal, ICJ *Reports*, 1954.

trative Tribunal (created by the General Assembly) in favour of a member of the staff of the UN whose contract of service had been terminated without his consent.

The theory of implied powers was invoked both by those who favoured an affirmative reply and by those who opposed it. The legal power of the General Assembly to establish a tribunal competent to render judgments binding on the UN was challenged. The Court, admitting that there was no express provision for the establishment of judicial bodies or organs and insisting that there was no indication to the contrary, invoked the implied powers rule of the *Injuries* case.[75] It found support for such a course in Articles 7(2), 22, and 101(1), which authorize the UN to create subsidiary organs in general, empower the General Assembly to establish one to perform its functions effectively, and authorize it to make staff regulations. On the basis of these provisions, the Court held:

> The power to establish a tribunal, to do justice as between the Organization and the staff members, was essential to ensure the efficient working of the Secretariat and to give effect to the paramount consideration of securing the highest standards of efficiency, competence, and integrity. *Capacity to do this arises by necessary intendment* out of the Charter.[76]

It was contended that while the implied power of the General Assembly to establish a tribunal might be both necessary and essential, nevertheless, it could not impose limitations upon the General Assembly's express Charter powers. The argument was that the General Assembly was expressly authorized under paragraph 1 of Article 17 "to consider and approve the budget of the Organization." The discretion to "consider and approve" must be deemed to mean the discretion to delete and disapprove particular items in the budget. Any interpretation, therefore, which limited the Organization, to that extent, would abridge the Assembly's approving authority under the said Article.

The Court answered this by saying that "the function of approving the budget does not mean that the General Assembly has an

[75] ICJ *Reports*, 1954, p. 56.
[76] *Ibid.*, p. 57. (Italics added.)

absolute power to approve or disapprove the expenditure proposed to it; for some part of that expenditure arises out of obligations already incurred by the Organization, and to this extent the General Assembly has no alternative but to honour these engagements."[77] The Court added that the Tribunal's awards partake of this obligatory character.

The third contention was that the Tribunal being a subsidiary, subordinate, and secondary organ, its judgments could not bind the General Assembly which established it. To this the Court replied:

> By establishing the Administrative Tribunal, the General Assembly was not delegating the performance of its own functions, it was exercising a power which it had under the Charter to regulate staff relations. In regard to the Secretariat, the General Assembly is given by the Charter a power to make regulations, but not a power to adjudicate upon, or otherwise deal with, particular instances.[78]

Earlier the Court had said that the General Assembly itself, in view of its own composition and functions, could hardly act as a judicial organ: considering the arguments of the parties, appraising the evidence produced by them, establishing the facts, and declaring the law applicable to them.[79]

Judges Alvarez and Hackworth dissented vigorously. For Judge Alvarez, the majority opinion was a retrogressive step. The General Assembly, according to Judge Alvarez, represented a virtual international legislative power: "The Assembly is a real international legislative power, for, apart from *recommendations* made to States, it adopts *resolutions* whose provisions are binding on them all."[80] Judge Alvarez saw in the General Assembly an omnipotence and supremacy which "is bound only by the Charter which established it, or by its own resolutions. There is nothing above the Assembly except moral forces."[81] The logical and

[77]*Ibid.*, p. 59.
[78]*Ibid.*, p. 61.
[79]*Ibid.*, p. 56.
[80]*Ibid.*, p. 71.
[81]*Ibid.*, p. 72.

inevitable deduction from such a view was "that any attempt to limit the power of the General Assembly of the United Nations would run counter to the realities of international life."[82] What is more, Judge Alvarez invoked the same implied powers to prove that what was not expressly delegated (i.e. the power to review and reject the Tribunal's verdict) was retained by the General Assembly.

Judge Hackworth argued that the task before the Court was to ascertain the compatibility of the statute by which the Tribunal was created with the Charter of the UN which gave the Assembly power to create such organs—and to put them in their "proper places":

> The nature of the Tribunal, the method by which it was created and the purpose for which it was created belie any such action (viz. that the General Assembly has no power to review or reject the Tribunal's award). Any and all power not specifically delegated, including the power of review, was, as a matter of law, reserved to the Assembly.[83]

Further, Judge Hackworth contended that Article 22 of the Charter empowered the General Assembly to create "subsidiary organs." The term subsidiary organ had a special and well-recognized meaning, argued Judge Hackworth, "it means an auxiliary or inferior organ; an organ to furnish aid and assistance in a subordinate or secondary capacity."[84] The General Assembly, in his opinion, could create such organs to perform its functions efficiently, but could not "abdicate" or "reassign" any of its functions in such a manner as to relinquish its control over the subject matter, and no subsidiary organ with delegated authority could bind the principal organ possessing plenary powers under the Charter.

The majority, as noted above, took the view that by making the Administrative Tribunal's awards non-appealable in the interest of finality and for the sake of avoiding vexatious proceedings

[82]*Ibid.*
[83]*Ibid..* p. 80.
[84]*Ibid.*, p. 79.

the General Assembly did not abdicate thereby a function but only promoted the highest standards of efficiency, competence, and integrity, so vital for the impartial functioning of the Secretariat; nor did the Court believe that such a course would belittle the august stature of the General Assembly.

The next phase was indeed a leap forward in the jurisprudence of the Court relative to the progressive development of the law of international organizations. The Advisory Opinion related to the legality of expenditure incurred by the UN over the United Nations Emergency Force (UNEF) and the United Nations Operations in the Congo (ONUC).[85] The General Assembly sought the Court's legal guidance to ascertain if the expenditure incurred on the Middle East and Congo operations constituted "expenses of the Organization" under paragraph 2 of Article 17 of the Charter. To answer the question the Court had to find out whether the operations were legal so that the expenses incurred on them could be treated as the "expenses of the Organization."

The Court arrived at an affirmative answer by a simple process. First, it declared a general proposition to the effect that "the 'expenses' of any organization are the amounts paid out to defray the costs of carrying out its purposes."[86] Then it proceeded to examine whether the expenditure related to any such purpose of the Organization and found that it did.

But the main contention put forth by those who favoured a negative reply was that when the maintenance of international peace and security was involved it was only the Security Council which was authorized to decide on, and take any action relative thereto, and that since the General Assembly's power was limited to discussing, considering, studying, and recommending it could not take action nor could it create binding financial obligations, embarking upon projects on the basis of non-binding resolutions. The French Government,[87] particularly, feared that vesting such a discretionary and unlimited budgetary power in the General

---

[85]Certain Expenses of the UN (Article 17, paragraph 2, of Charter), ICJ *Reports,* 1962, p. 151.

[86]*Ibid.,* p. 158.

[87]*Pleadings, Oral Arguments, Documents,* etc., ICJ, 1962, pp. 130-5.

Assembly, which States had not given even to more closely integrated organizations, would lead to the establishment of a world legislative power. Also, it was argued, it would impose on member States the obligation to tax their citizens and induce their parliaments to vote the credits fixed by the Assembly and the taxes needed to pay for them. A number of governments, however, came out strongly in favour of what must appear to be a virtual discretionary power of the General Assembly.[88]

On the first count, viz. the power of the General Assembly to take action in the field of international peace and security, the Court found after a close scrutiny of the provisions in the Charter that the field was not an exclusive domain of the Security Council in view of Articles 10-14 of the Charter; that the General Assembly could and did take decisions under Articles 5, 6, 14, and 18 in spite of its hortatory character; that in fact "there is a close collaboration between the two organs,"[89] and that organizing peace-keeping operations (such as the UNEF) "is a special power"[90] which the General Assembly possessed in the field of international peace and security.

The power, the Court explained, to set up subsidiary organs such as commissions and committees for investigation, observation, and supervision emanated from the broad purpose of the Organization to maintain peace and security.

It is on the second count (viz. the budgetary powers of the General Assembly) that the Court came nearest to the establishment of a world legislative power. After laying down the general proposition that expenses of any organization were the amounts paid out to defray the costs of carrying out its purposes, the Court came out with a statement which is destined to become a land-

---

[88]*Ibid.*, for statements by Italy, p. 126; Denmark, pp. 63-4; the Netherlands, pp. 170, 172, 175; the US, pp. 193-4, 200, 204; Canada, pp. 220-2; Japan, pp. 224-6; the UK, pp. 242-3; and Ireland, p. 249. Typical was the view expressed by the US representative, Abram Chayes, at the oral hearings, "The United Nations can pay for what it is empowered to do" and "what the United Nations can do it can finance under the provisions of Article 17." *Ibid.*, pp. 424-6.

[89]ICJ *Reports*, 1962, p. 163.

[90]*Ibid.*, p. 164.

mark in the jurisprudence of the Court and the evolution of the UN. It declared:

> Save as they entrusted the Organization with the attainment of these common ends, the member States retain their freedom of action. But when the Organization takes action which warrants the assertion that it was appropriate for the fulfilment of one of the stated purposes of the United Nations, the presumption is that such action is not *ultra vires* the Organization.[91]

A more daring proposition followed:

> If it is agreed that the action in question is within the scope of the functions of the Organization but it is alleged that it has been initiated or carried out in a manner not in conformity with the division of functions among the several organs which the Charter prescribes, one moves to the internal plane, to the internal structure of the Organization. If the action was taken by the wrong organ, it was irregular as a matter of internal structure, but this would not necessarily mean that the expense incurred was not an expense of the Organization. Both national and international law contemplate cases in which the body corporate or politic may be bound, as to third parties, by an *ultra vires* act of an agent.[92]

There emerges from the passages quoted above what has been termed the doctrine of "institutional effectiveness."[93] Under this doctrine the stated purposes of the Organization subordinate the functional division of the Organization and thereby the provisions of the Charter in this regard. Action by the wrong organ is only an "internal irregularity." The powers of the Organization are not limited to the express provisions or to the attendant "implied" activities but extend to the sweeping panorama of the purposes of the Organization as contained in Article 1 of the Charter. The opinion, of course, applies only to those activities which fall within the purview of the stated purposes (or expressed functions of the

[91]*Ibid.*, p. 168.
[92]*Ibid.*
[93]See Dissenting Opinion of Judge Bustamante, *Ibid.*, p. 298.

Organization as a whole). Nevertheless the doctrine marks a giant step towards raising the Organization to colossal heights.

The combined effect of the theory of "implied powers" and the doctrine of "institutional effectiveness" might be formulated thus: international organizations, which possess an objective jural personality assume, once created, unrestricted *legal* capacity under international law. Their capacity proceeds not only from the express provisions of their constituent instruments but also from all those implied and ancillary powers. If the end is within the ambit of their stated purposes and objectives all means which are appropriate, which are plainly adapted to that end, and which consist with the letter and spirit of their constituent instruments are constitutional, any minor lapse in the internal competency notwithstanding.

A CRITIQUE AND AN EVALUATION

The doctrine of institutional effectiveness understandably could not go unchallenged. The strongest criticism came from the Soviet Government. The doctrine was characterized by Tunkin at the oral hearings as a step in the direction of the long-discarded principle: the end justifies the means.[94] Similar was the opinion of the dissenting Judge Koretsky.[95] Even the concurring judges made some reservations about the doctrine.[96]

The most elaborate criticism, however, came from Professor Leo Gross, who in a review article published in *International Organization* took the Court to task. Characterizing the doctrine as a total reversal of the *Lotus* dictum (propounded by the Permanent Court of International Justice to the effect that "the rules of law binding upon States . . . emanate from their own free will" and that "restrictions upon the independence of States cannot therefore be presumed"),[97] Professor Gross held that "under international law an organization has no plenitude of powers like sovereign States; on the contrary, being 'an artificial person' it

---

[94]See *Pleadings*, 1962, p. 411.
[95]See Dissenting Opinion, ICJ *Reports*, 1962, p. 262.
[96]See, for example, separate opinion of Judge Fitzmaurice.
[97]PCIJ, *Series* A. No. 10, p. 18.

has only such powers and competences as are conferred upon it by its Constitution. What is not so conferred is retained by the member States."[98]

Needless to point out, Professor Gross's affirmation tallies totally with that of Judge Hackworth mentioned earlier, which was rejected by a majority of the Court. Also Professor Gross seems to think of the UN as "an artificial person" and not as a living organism. The whole jurisprudence of the Court as shown above tends towards the latter view. If one can say so, the ICJ has traversed more towards Judge Alvarez's stand that international organizations are not limited to what is expressed in, or follows by implication from, their constituent instruments but must be regarded as having all such powers as are necessary to enable them to "develop" in accordance with the requirements of international life. The Court was careful, however, to insist that such powers still owe their existence to the consent of States: the express or implied consent as evidenced from the purposes of the Organization, and the acquiescence obtained from the affected parties through a majority vote in the Organization, and the compliance of those parties whom the activities affect.

Therefore, it cannot be said that the Court's latest doctrine is a reversal of the *Lotus* dictum. Consent still constitutes the pivot on which the Organization revolves. The purposes of the UN are as much important if not more, as the provisions of the Charter. They were not inserted in a fit of rhetoric or with the aim of exciting the heart of the reader but were the product of prolonged negotiation, compromise, and debate. All that the Court was saying was that unless the States delegate such power in their plenitude of powers to the Organization, they retain their freedom of action. This is true of every treaty to which two or more States are parties. There can be no loss of sovereignty of member States unless they themselves agree, or already have agreed, to such a course. The States can create such an organization and endow it with such powers. As Professor Schwarzenberger has rightly asserted:

---

[98]Leo Gross, "Expenses of the United Nations for Peace-keeping Operations: The Advisory Opinion of the International Court of Justice," *International Organization*, Vol. 17, 1963, pp. 9-10.

"The existing subjects of international law are free to extend the application of international law to any entity whom they see fit to admit to the realm of the international legal system."[99] The Court sanctioned the concept in the *Injuries* case, too: "Fifty States, representing the vast majority of the members of the international community, had the power, in conformity with international law, to bring into being an entity possessing objective international personality."[100]

The Court, it is true, has projected the objective personality of the UN a little too far into the sensitive domain of State sovereignty by its latest Advisory Opinion, but that is the way it has been created and that is how the founders have, consciously or unconsciously, brought it into being. An Arabian genie it surely is, but subject to the orders of its masters.

The last decision of the Court, as Professor Quincy Wright had suggested in a different context on an earlier occasion,[101] manifested the tendency displayed by Chief Justice Marshall in dealing with the American Constitution and by the Permanent Court of International Justice in dealing with the Constitution of the International Labour Organization.

The tendency, as pointed out by Professor Lauterpacht in relation to the Permanent Court, was in terms of a restrictive interpretation of the claims of State sovereignty and reciprocally, a liberal interpretation of the competence of international bodies although in words the Court usually made "courteous obeisance to the tradition of State sovereignty."[102] In the admirable summation of Professor Wright:

> In a world, shrinking but inadequately regulated, interdependent but imperfectly aware of its condition, it is probably safer to treat the claims of international society liberally, even if such treatment restricting the traditional sovereignty of States involves

[99]Schwarzenberger, *International Law*, London, 1949, p. 71.
[100]ICJ *Reports*, 1949, p. 185.
[101]Quincy Wright, *op. cit.*, p. 515.
[102]H. Lauterpacht, *The Development of International Law by the Permanent Court of International Justice*, London, 1934, p. 89; M.O. Hudson, *The Permanent Court of International Justice*, 1920-42, New York, 1943, p. 660.

some danger of stimulating revolt by the States least aware of the situation.[103]

The criticisms of the dissenting judges and the hesitations of the concurring judges in the *Expenses* case, coupled with Professor Gross's scathing criticism, apparently look justified. But if one goes deeper into the law thus evolved by the International Court one would perceive that the doctrines of implied powers and institutional effectiveness do not provide a *carte blanche* to the Organization. The ICJ dicta have built-in checks and balances, or auto-limitations, both legal and political. Consider for instance the famous *Reparations* dictum: "Under international law, the Organization must be deemed to have those powers which, though not expressly provided in the Charter, are conferred upon it by necessary implication as being essential to the performance of its duties."[104]

The clause, "as being essential to the performance of its duties," is the auto-limitation in the formula. The activity embarked upon must be *essential* to the performance of its duties. The Secretariat is bound to render impartial and objective service. Can it do so by making its employees, who take an oath of loyalty to the Organization's international character, fall back upon their national States for claiming damages for injuries sustained in the service of the Organization? The answer is obvious. Imagine for a moment a drastic step like the severance of citizenship altogether for the purpose of achieving the "international outlook." That undoubtedly would be an extreme step, involving hardships to employees who retire or resign from service. The requirement of essentiality carries within itself the seed of reasonableness.

The formula that the UN's capacity to establish an administrative tribunal "arises by necessary intendment out of the Charter,"[105] too, has the controlling word "necessary." Also, the capacities were subjected to the overall "purposes and functions as specified or implied in the constituent instrument and developed in practice."[106]

[103]Quincy Wright, *op. cit.*, p. 516.
[104]ICJ *Reports*, 1949, p. 182.
[105]ICJ *Reports*, 1954, p. 57.
[106]ICJ *Reports*, 1949, p. 180.

The tests (*i*) that the activity must come within the stated purposes; (*ii*) that it must be "essential" for the performance of its duties; (*iii*) and that it must arise by "necessary intendment" out of the Charter are formidable indeed. Would a UN decision to deport all unkind critics to the moon stand this test? Would it be reasonable and essential to the performance of its duties to declare total inviolability of its premises even for purposes of law and order? Can it employ a million soldiers to enforce its peace-keeping decisions? Can it ban outer-space probe because it could be used for military purposes? Can it for purposes of finance undertake to exploit the oceanic resources wthout proper authorization? The answer obviously would be in the negative. Implied powers necessarily presuppose the effectuation of express authority, stated purposes, and earmarked functions.

Apart from the fact that it would be doctrinally inconsistent, it would be practically impossible. True, the Charter sets forth a few basic principles and is not a prolix code to be strictly construed. But the responsibility of finding suitable means of carrying out those principles devolves upon the successive generations who live under it. Also it will be used in ways commensurate with the genius, and in accordance with the changing needs, of these generations. The United Nations will be what the members that constitute that body will want it to be. Theoretically, it can not only do all the above things but also set up an international court of human rights, an agency with powers of inspection of armaments, etc. Such activities will be perfectly within the broad stated purposes of its Charter. But it has not, and will not be able to undertake such ambitious projects because the present membership and the current stage of international developments do not permit it to do so.

The British Parliament, in theory, can legislate on matters ranging from granting independence to British colonial possessions to prohibiting the docking of dogs' tails in order to facilitate their efficient wagging—as the famous saying goes. It could even decree, it is asserted, that all blue-eyed babies born on a particular day be killed. But it does not. The British Constitution relies on the good sense of the people and the members chosen to represent them.

To claim a cluster of implied powers for the UN is not to suggest that it be accorded extraordinary powers over and beyond the wishes or powers of the members that constitute it. And, since the levers of operation continue to be within the hands of its members there is no danger of its going out of control.

This brings us to the problem of the majority. Often we hear complaints in some Western quarters that the Afro-Asian majority in the General Assembly has been adopting irresponsible resolutions. The latest manifestation of this grievance was heard in the British Parliament recently. The Prime Minister, Harold Wilson, criticizing the resolutions of the United Nations urging Britain to use all means, including the use of force to end the illegal regime in Rhodesia, stated that the UN had been passing "irresponsible resolutions leaving us to do the dirty work."[107] It is quite understandable that the British Prime Minister should feel so. But, if other resolutions of the General Assembly more important to the Afro-Asian majority like the ones dealing with the economic disparities and urging the industrially advanced nations to earmark 1 per cent of their GNP and if the highly retarded advances that the UNCTAD has been making are kept in mind, none can say that the Afro-Asian majority has in fact been running the show. The talk, therefore, that the Organization has been behaving irresponsibly cannot be related directly to its claims of powers beyond those accorded to it expressly, but must be related to its tendency to tread occasionally on the sensitive toes of some of its members.

Viewed in this background, the doctrine of institutional effectiveness propounded by the ICJ becomes only an extension of the doctrine of implied powers. The stated purposes under this doctrine assume priority over the earmarked functions, or as it was called by the ICJ, the "spheres of competence." Once it is established that a particular activity is within the stated purposes of the Organization the question of who undertakes it is only of secondary importance. If a certain organ is not prohibited expressly from doing that particular activity and if it is not within the "exclusive" jurisdiction of another organ then the first organ is entitled to embark upon that particular activity. To give a specific

[107] *The Times*, London, 2 November 1968.

example since the General Assembly was not specifically prohibited from taking action in the nature of ONUC and UNEF—though the former was initiated originally by the Security Council—and since these operations did not fall within the exclusive jurisdiction of the Security Council, as for example, action under Chapter VII of the Charter, the action was held to be consistent with the letter and spirit of the Charter.

The Court, however, went a step further and said that even if the activity which is within the stated purposes is taken by a wrong organ, it will be a matter on the internal plane which would not vitiate the legality of the act; and then the Court proceeded to draw the municipal analogy of an agent binding the principal. The analogy, it cannot be denied, is a bit too far-fetched. The logic behind the municipal rule is the protection of an innocent third party who is affected by the capricious exercise by an agent of the principal's general delegation of a power. The Security Council, of course, acts on behalf of the members (Article 25) as an agent when it takes action in matters concerning peace and security. But has the General Assembly such a delegation of power? Are there any innocent third parties whose interests need protection?

The enhancement of, or emphasis on, the implied powers of international organizations need not cause undue anxiety. It is not the case of national governments claiming implied powers over various modes of social, commercial, and other activities. The need to have a powerful federal authority to keep nations strong financially and militarily at the expense of component States has no comparative significance in the case of international organizations. Foreign affairs, currency, defence, and other important attributes of State sovereignty are not delegated by member States to international organizations. These bodies act only in limited spheres and have only few powers.

The ICJ formula that member States retain their freedom of action "[s]ave as they have entrusted the Organization with the attainment of these common ends" (i.e. purposes of the UN) will lose much of its sting if one remembers that the Court itself affirmed that the purposes are not unlimited, and that it is the majority of the members, including the concurring vote of the permanent members in the case of the Security Council, that decides upon all courses of action, not some strange phantom sitting as the Organization in the glass and steel structure on the East River in New York. The initial fears of the framers of the Organization likewise that insertion of a provision concerning the jural personality of the UN would give an idea of a super State, were misplaced. Jural personality of an international organization connotes an organic entity with rights and duties, capable of adapting at the wishes of its component members to the growing needs in changing times. It has nothing to do with a super State. Well, a super State might have jural personality, so has a man, a woman, a tree, a cobra. It is a legal fiction by which legal rights and duties are attached to a particular person or a thing. The doctrine of institutional effectiveness sounds like a startling proposition. But it is not.

Essentially, the principle of effectiveness is a vehicle of interpretation. It is one of the many principles of interpretation. It aims at rendering the institution effective rather than ineffective. In the process, sometimes, recourse to the preparatory work has been avoided; the primary assumption being that the institutions are meant to perpetuate the purposes set forth by the parties and not as means of avoiding obligations. Even as a vehicle of interpretation it has limitations in application. It cannot, as Lauterpacht pointed out, "be allowed to degenerate into a rule of thumb as distinguished from a flexible, critical, and discriminating guide to interpretation."[108] The ICJ itself had occasion to demarcate the limitation of the rule in the Advisory Opinions on the *Interpretation of Peace Treaties with Bulgaria, Hungary, and Romania (Second Phase)*[109] and the *International Status of South-West Africa.* [10]

In the first Opinion the Court was concerned with the powers of the Secretary-General of the UN, upon whom the Peace Treaties had conferred the power to appoint the third member of a Commission entrusted with the task of settling disputes concerning the interpretation or execution of the Treaties in case the parties failed to agree on his appointment. The question posed to the Court

[108]Lauterpacht, *op. cit.*, p. 283.
[109]ICJ *Reports*, 1950, p. 65.
[110]*Ibid.*, p. 128.

was whether or not the Secretary-General was empowered to do so even in the event of one of the parties refusing to appoint its own commissioner on the ground that, in its view, there was no dispute to be submitted to the Commission.

Here was a case which was not contemplated by the parties. The Court had a good opportunity to invoke the rule of effectiveness. But it could not have done so without doing damage to the entire regime established by the Treaties. In the circumstances before it the approval of the Secretary-General's power to appoint the third member would have resulted in the constitution of a two-member Commission only and thereby the opposition of a member appointed by the only party represented could prevent the Commission so constituted from reaching any decision whatsoever. The Commission would have to act on the unanimity basis whereas the Treaties prescribed, *expressis verbis*, a majority rule. In every respect, as the Court felt, "the result would be contrary to the letter as well as the spirit of the Treaties."[111] Hence the Court held that no such power rested with the Secretary-General "according to the natural and ordinary meaning of the terms it was intended that the appointment of both national Commissioners should precede that of the third member."[112]

Again, in the first South-West Africa Advisory Opinion, after having come to the conclusion that South-West Africa continued to be a territory under the international mandate assumed by South Africa and that the supervisory functions devolved upon the UN after the demise of the League, the Court was confronted with the further question: was South Africa under an obligation to conclude a Trusteeship Agreement with the UN? The Court refused to read such an obligation in the mandate system. This would have involved stretching the principle of effectiveness to a breaking point. The Opinion, as Sir Hersch concludes, shows that the circumstance that the Court has gone a long way towards safeguarding the effectiveness of the texts before it does not mean that it will go all the way in that direction.[113]

[111]ICJ *Reports*, 1950, p. 228.
[112]*Ibid.*, p. 227.
[113]Lauterpacht, *op. cit.*, p. 292.

PART TWO

PRACTICE

CHAPTER 2

IMPLIED POWERS AND PEACE-KEEPING FUNCTIONS OF THE UNITED NATIONS

THE PRESENT CHAPTER is divided into three sections which outwardly look disjointed with each other and collectively far from the central theme of this study. A note of explanation at the beginning bringing out the cementing factors relevant for the present discussion, it was felt, was therefore necessary. Any discussion on implied powers of the UN in matters affecting world peace and international security cannot be done without touching upon its express authority in this all-important field. And this is a subject full of misconceptions and mirages. Much of the present disenchantment with the Organization, for instance, with its inability to solve the questions of divided countries (Germany, Korea, and Indo-China) and to tackle hot problems like Vietnam or Kashmir, originates in the misconceived role with which the Organization is associated. Was the UN ever designed to deal in a big way with all and every crisis affecting world peace? In other words, was it meant to be an effective instrument of collective security? This is a vital question without an unambiguous answer to which any probe into the latent potentialities or powers by implication relative to the Organization's peace-keeping functions would have been an exercise in futility. The first section therefore is devoted to such an examination.

The deduction that the above analysis yields is that the UN machinery, if at all it was meant (and it was not) to be an effective instrument of collective security was conceptually still-born; that though it was best suited to tackle minor fry it nevertheless had embedded in its Charter seeds which could sprout a secondary role which in itself was highly useful in a bloc-ridden world. The development of this role took place in stages, in successive situations, in favourable conditions mainly under the stewardship of

Secretary-General Dag Hammarskjoeld. This role, which the author himself had christened as the role of "preventive diplomacy," forms the subject of the second section of the present chapter, with a brief mention of the problems attendant thereto. And this has been viewed by the present writer as the UN's implied powers in matters of peace and security.

The final section of the chapter has been earmarked for the identification process of the seeds that gave birth to this role, for an examination of the legal bases, the constitutional provisions, in the Charter. Since this has been done, in not a very different context, by the International Court of Justice in the *Expenses* Advisory Opinion, the analysis relies heavily on the Court's authority.

GENERAL

"The dramatic weakness of traditional international law," wrote Philip C. Jessup in 1946, "has been its admission that a State may use force to compel compliance with its will. This weakness has been the inevitable consequence of two factors—one, the concept of absolute sovereignty, and two, the lack of a well-developed international organization with competent powers." And, evidently with the establishment of the UN in view, he declared, both "these factors are losing their old significance."[1] The UN which symbolizes these two trends, proceeds to impinge upon the absolute nature of sovereignty of member States by making them subject to extensive obligations. The members agree to "settle their international disputes by peaceful means,"[2] to "refrain in their international relations from the threat or use of force against the territorial integrity or political independence of any State, or in any other manner inconsistent with the purposes of the United Nations,"[3] to "give the United Nations every assistance in any action it takes,"[4] and to "fulfil in good faith the obligations assumed by them in accordance with the present Charter."[5] Thus is surrendered the most sensitive segment of sovereignty—the right to wage

[1]Philip C. Jessup, "Force under a Modern Law of Nations," *Foreign Affairs*, Vol. 25, 1946-47, p. 91.
[2]Article 2, paragraph 3.
[3]Article 2, paragraph 4.
[4]Article 2, paragraph 5.   [5]Article 2, paragraph 2.

war to compel compliance. The vacuum is filled by a supra-national body, the Security Council, with very wide powers. "In order to ensure prompt and effective action by the United Nations, its members confer on the Security Council primary responsibility for the maintenance of international peace and security, and agree that in carrying out its duties under this responsibility the Security Council acts on their behalf."[6]

Complementary to these principal provisions is the scheme for effective peace-enforcement. "To maintain international peace and security" the UN is "to take effective collective measures."[7] The scheme is fully laid out in Chapter VII. Article 39 empowers the Security Council to determine the existence of any threat to the peace, breach of the peace, or act of aggression and to make recommendations, or decide itself what measures it should take in accordance with Articles 41 and 42. Article 40 provides for "provisional measures" to end hostilities. Article 41 provides for enforcement action, not involving the use of armed force. Article 42 provides for such action involving the use of armed force. Article 48 empowers the Security Council to decide if all or some of the members should take part in such enforcement measures. The armed forces are made available to the Security Council through special agreements under Article 43.

It was fully realized that "between the moment the illegal attack starts and the moment the centralized machinery of collective security is put into action, there is, even in the case of its perfectly prompt functioning, a space of time, an interval, which may be disastrous to the victim."[8] Hence use of private force was permitted as an extraordinary and temporary measure under Article 51. In this way a centralized direction[9] of force was created.

The working of the centralized machinery thus created depends, however, on the unity of the permanent members of the Security

[6]Article 24, paragraph 1. [7]Article 1, paragraph 1.
[8]Hans Kelsen, "Collective Security and Collective Self-Defence under the Charter of the United Nations," *American Journal of International Law,* Vol. 42, 1948, p. 785.
[9]The phrase—as distinguished from "centralized monopoly"—was suggested by Professor Quincy Wright to the writer in a different context. Since it is a better description of the scheme of the Charter it has been adopted in the current discussion.

Council. Paragraph 3 of Article 27 states that the decisions of the Security Council "on all other matters [i.e. substantial] shall be made by an affirmative vote of seven members including the concurring votes of the permanent members provided that, in decisions under Chapter VI, and under paragraph 3 of Article 52, a party to a dispute shall abstain from voting."

All actions under Chapter VII therefore being substantial in nature require the joint approval or acquiescence of the permanent members. The Big Five form a super-directorate designed to ensure peace and security in the world. This fact warrants careful appreciation for an understanding of the role of the Organization in matters relating to peace and security. The requirement of permanent-member-unanimity—in other words, the veto—bars effectively the application of collective action against the Big Five and in all cases where they are interested.

COLLECTIVE SECURITY—RE-EXAMINED

The first and most important misconception which mars any appraisal of the Organization's peace-keeping powers is the popular view of the notion of collective security. It is assumed by the critics of the UN that the Charter creates a system of collective security without which there is no justification for the existence of the Organization. The concept of collective security is worth examining to see if the United Nations creates any such system.

No single document or authoritative pronouncement exists to which the authorship of the idea of collective security can be attributed.[10] Howard Johnson and Gerhart Niemeyer define the

[10]For a modern exposition of this subject, see Kenneth W. Thompson, "Collective Security Re-examined," *American Political Science Review*, Vol. 47, 1953, pp. 753-72; Howard C. Johnson and Gerhart Niemeyer, "Collective Security—The Validity of an Ideal," *International Organization*, Vol. 3, 1954, pp. 19-35; Ernst B. Haas, "Types of Collective Security; An Examination of Operational Concepts," *American Political Science Review*, Vol. 49, 1955, pp. 40-62, Arnold Wolfers, "Collective Security and the War in Korea," *Yale Review*, Vol. 43, 1954; and "Collective Defence versus Collective Security," *Alliance Policy in the Cold War*, ed., Baltimore, 1959; the last two articles reprinted with minor modifications in Arnold Wolfers, *Discord and Collaboration*, Baltimore, 1962, pp. 167-80, 181-204; see also George Liska, *International Equilibrium*, Cambridge, Mass., 1957, pp. 81-118, for a lively presentation of the problem.

concept as "a system based on the universal obligation of all nations to join forces against an aggressor State as soon as the fact of aggression is determined by established procedure."[11] "The rock bottom principle upon which collective security is founded," asserts Kenneth Thompson, "provides that an attack on any one State will be regarded as an attack on all States."[12] And to conclude, in Arnold Wolfers' words, collective security "is directed against any and every country anywhere that commits an act of aggression, allies and friends included."[13]

Three basic tenets emerge from the definitions and views given above. An ideal system of collective security envisages: one, a condemnation of aggression as a crime; two, a procedure to establish the guilt; and, three, the creation of sanctions and an obligation on the part of the members of the system to suppress aggression against any and every country.

The philosophy behind this ideal is that aggression is a universal crime, which, inasmuch as it endangers peace and security of every nation, should be suppressed with the collective might of the combined forces of the rest of the world. Can such a philosophy be read into the Charter of the UN? Or more precisely, does the Charter contain the three elements listed above of an ideal collective security system? The Charter provisions enumerated at the beginning would show that the Charter creates something more and something less than the three requisites of collective security.

As for the first requisite, the Charter not merely condemns resort to force or the threat thereof but also promotes conciliatory process and substitutes a peace-enforcing machinery. As regards the second requisite, namely, the procedures for determining aggression, the Charter provides not only for the determination of act of aggression by the Security Council under Article 39 but also goes further to determine threats to the peace and breaches of peace and proceeds to lay down the modalities of meeting these contingencies by various means in proportion to the gravity of disturbance to the peace.

[11]Johnson and Niemeyer, *op. cit.*, p. 20.
[12]Thompson, *op. cit.*, p. 755.
[13]Wolfers, *Discord and Collaboration*, p. 183.

As regards sanctions, Chapter VII has an elaborate procedure but the obligation of member States to participate in the same is not wholly clear. Article 2, paragraph 5, lays down that members shall give the United Nations every assistance in any action it takes. Under Article 25 the members "agree to accept and carry out the decisions of the Security Council *in accordance with the present Charter*" (italics added). Who is the deciding authority if the decision taken by the Security Council is in accordance with the Charter? If a member feels that a particular decision is *ultra vires* the competence of the Security Council, even an advisory opinion of the ICJ would be of no avail.

Again, Article 48 says that the "action required to carry out the decisions of the Security Council for the maintenance of international peace and security shall be taken by all the members of the United Nations or by some of them as the Security Council may determine." The determination applies only to the number of members who take part in the action and does not extend to the nature and scope of action each member should take. Moreover, the action is taken by the members and not by the Security Council as such.

Article 44 states that the members shall "provide armed forces in fulfilment of the obligations *assumed* under Article 43" (italics added) and Article 43 stipulates that members "undertake to make available to the Security Council on its call *and* in accordance with a special agreement or agreements, armed forces, assistance," etc. (italics added). The members thus are obligated only to the extent of obligations assumed (it might be a token contribution or even merely transit facilities). But there is nothing in the Charter which can compel members to conclude the said agreements.[14] If no agreement exists no obligation exists.

Thus the obligation of member States in the collective security measures are largely tenuous and depend upon the goodwill and good faith of the members.

The Veto

The most vital element, however, which determines the alchemy of the system of collective security created under the Charter

[4]For a suggestion to the same effect, see Hans Kelsen, *The Law of the United Nations*, London, 1950, p. 754.

is the veto. No single provision is as effective as the veto in subordinating the independent identity of the UN to the will of the chosen five. This veto virtually shrinks the whole sphere of UN action. The veto bars effectively the application of collective security against the five permanent members and in all cases in which they are interested.

The post-war developments and the rapid spread of cold war leave little in which the major powers are not interested. And even outside of these sphere zones the application of collective measures should have the tacit acquiescence of the permanent members. The question then arises, was it really meant that way by the creators of the UN. A look into the history of the UN would show that the framers of the Charter were aware of the paralysing effect of the veto which they were incorporating into the otherwise laudable scheme of collective security.

Even in the earliest pronouncements on the proposed United Nations the Western powers and the Soviet Union exhibited a certain cleavage of opinion as to the nature of the security organization they had in mind.[15] The United States, to which a large measure of credit goes for the initiation of the idea of the world organization, favoured a system wherein a general conference and an executive council will have a prominent role. The general conference would be represented by all the members of the Organization and would confine itself to the promotion of economic and social cooperation. And the executive council, which would be manned by great power representatives and a limited number of small power representatives would be responsible for ensuring peace and security in the world.

The Soviet Union, on the other hand, while showing a lukewarm enthusiasm to the idea of a general conference, had strong opinions about the role of the executive organ. It had in view a concert of five great powers which would keep all other States, whether ex-enemy or friendly, whether small or middle-sized, in effective check, and thus would preserve the peace. The Soviet Union was firm

---

[15]For a succinct exposition of the evolutionary process of the role of the Security Council and the General Assembly in this field, see Leland M. Goodrich, "Expanding Role of the General Assembly," *International Conciliation*, 1951, pp. 236-47.

in its stand that no executive action was to be taken without an unanimous decision of the Big Five and hence no action could be taken against them or against States they wished to protect.

At Dumbarton Oaks and thereafter, owing to the mounting pressure of small powers for more representation in the decisions relative to peace and security, the great powers conceded to the General Assembly powers to discuss, deliberate, and recommend. But the primordeal power and responsibility of enforcing peace remained in the hands of the Security Council, and especially in the hands of the permanent members.

The San Francisco records reveal an abundant awareness of the founding fathers of the handicap under which the Organization was to work. Though speaker after speaker rose up to sing the glory of the wonderful system of collective security they were about to create, quite a few voices of reason were heard, too. These delegates admitted that the Organization was not free from imperfection. The Indian delegate, for instance, warned against the delusion "that the proposed Organization could prevent wars between the great nations or even between small nations if the great powers were divided in their sympathies."[16]

The Mexican delegate went so far as to say that they "were engaged in establishing a world order in which the mice could be stamped out but in which the lions would not be restrained."[17] It was generally appreciated that "if a major power became the aggressor the Council had no power to prevent war."[18] To overcome this deficiency the inherent right of nations to have recourse to individual or collective self-defence was recognized. Victims of major power aggression were to seek protection with another great power.

Statements were also made to the effect that the delegates were *acquiescing* and not *agreeing* to the veto with the hope that "if not now then in the future improvements in the voting system may be introduced."[19] The delegate from Canada felt that the veto

[16]*UNCIO Docs.*, Vol. 12, pp. 307-8.
[17]*UNCIO Docs.*, Vol. 11, p. 474.
[18]*Ibid.*, p. 514.
[19]*Ibid.*, *per* Netherlands delegate, p. 330.

"was not too high a price to pay for a world organization which was good in so many other respects."[20] And the four sponsoring governments in a joint statement assured that it "is not to be assumed that the permanent members, any more than the non-permanent members, would use their 'veto' power wilfully to obstruct the operation of the Council."[21]

Thus the framers of the UN Charter evolved a collective security system applicable only as against minor disturbers of peace, provided the great powers were united in the desire to take action or were willing to permit such action being taken by the Organization. This deduction tallies with President Roosevelt's decisive assertion: "We are not thinking of a super State with its own police force and other paraphernalia of coercive power."[22]

Collective security in the ideal sense was considered impracticable by the great powers, and especially by the strongest supporter of the UN, the US. The framers of the Charter provided in the UN an instrument which can be used as an overwhelming force, with authority and power to preserve peace, *if* the great powers so desire; and also an instrument which can be employed as a firebrigade rushing to the troubled spots before they escalate into consuming conflagrations.

For the first role the directorship was placed in the hands of the Big Five; and the second role was to be managed by a majority of minor powers. In a highly inflammable, explosive world the role of a firebrigade is not without value. When as the result of the cold war the Big Five fell apart, the Organization was left with no choice but to develop its secondary role. Secretary-General Dag Hammarskjoeld and the newly emergent Afro-Asian nations played a great part in tapping this source in a few inflammable situations.

DEVELOPMENT OF THE ROLE OF PREVENTIVE DIPLOMACY

The evolution of the role of preventive diplomacy can be viewed in two distinct phases: the period of experiments, and the phase of assertion.

[20]*Ibid.*, p. 459.   [21]*Ibid.*, p. 713.
[22]*Postwar Foreign Policy Preparation,* 1939-1945, Department of State Publication, 3580; *General Foreign Policy Series,* Vol. 15, Washington, 1949, p. 269.

The Period of Experiments

Suez, 1956. The Anglo-French-Israeli armed action in 1956 against Egypt shook the world organization from the morass of helplessness in which it had found itself since the very first meeting of the General Assembly due to great power disunity. The British and French direct involvement in the unhappy affair ruled out any collective action on behalf of or by the Organization. A Soviet suggestion to the US that the two powers join in giving military support to the Assembly's wishes was brushed aside by President Eisenhower as "unthinkable."[23]

Lester B. Pearson of Canada, the then Secretary of State, proposed that the Secretary-General be authorized to begin to make arrangements with member States for the creation of a "truly international peace and police force" large enough to keep the Israeli-Egyptian borders at peace while a political settlement was being worked out.[24] As he later explained the Middle East crisis required not a fighting force but one "to ensure that fighting would not be resumed."[25]

The suggestion caught the imagination of the delegates at the UN. The British and French willingness to withdraw their forces if peace is restored between Egypt and Israel, and the US enthusiasm coupled with the Soviet acquiescence made matters easy.[26]

On 4 November 1956 the General Assembly adopted a resolution unanimously requesting the Secretary-General to submit a plan for creating, with the consent of the nations concerned, an emergency international force for the purpose of securing and supervising the cessation of hostilities in the troubled region.[27] Within a matter of hours a force was assembled by the Secretary-General, who also laid down the broad lines on which UNEF would work.

[23]For the correspondence in this connection between President Eisenhower and Premier Bulganin, see *Documents on American Foreign Relations*, Paul E. Zinner (ed.), New York, 1957, pp. 355-8.

[24]*General Assembly Official Records (GAOR)* F.E.S.S., 562nd Meeting, p. 36.

[25]Lester B. Pearson, "Force for U.N.," *Foreign Affairs*, Vol. 35, 1957, p. 401.

[26]For an exhaustive analysis of the creation and operation of UNEF, see William R. Frye, *A United Nations Peace Force*, New York, 1957; Gabriella Rosner, *The United Nations Emergency Force*, New York, 1963; Guenter Weissberg, *International Status of United Nations*, New York, 1961, pp. 106-40.

[27]General Assembly Resolution 998 (ES-I).

UNEF was to have a direct relationship with the UN. The Commander-in-Chief was to be fully independent of the politics of any one nation,[28] the Force was to be composed of troops supplied by States other than the permanent members of the Security Council. The Secretary-General stated categorically that the force "was not established to undertake enforcement actions. While UNEF has a military organization, it does not use all normal military objectives."[29] The Force was established "to secure the cessation of hostilities, with a withdrawal of forces," and not "with a view to enforcing a withdrawal of force."[30]

The UNEF experience yields three deductions: one, the positive contribution the UN could make even in a negative role of a policeman interposing between two or more combatants; two, the possibility of eliminating big power participation; and three, that such a step is possible only if the permanent members acquiesce in the creation and operation of the force.

Lebanon, 1958. The crisis in Lebanon in 1958 added another dimension to the new role of the UN in the maintenance of peace and security. A civil war had erupted in Lebanon following the refusal of President Chamoun to step down from office. US marines were landed to put down the rebellion. The Lebanese government charged UAR with intervention in the internal affairs of the country by supplying arms and ammunition to the rebels. The Security Council decided to set up an observer group (UNOGIL) to ensure that there was no illegal infiltration of personnel or supply of arms or other material across the Lebanese borders.[31]

A small goup of UN experts, military personnel, and a handful of diplomats prevented the two countries from drifting to a colli-

[28]UN Doc. A/3302, para 4 (a).

[29]UN Doc. A/3694, para 31.

[30]UN Doc. A/3302, para 10.

[31]For a summary of operations, see *UN Review*, Vol. 5, July 1958, pp. 37-9, and January 1959, pp. 22-6; Gerald L. Curtis, "The United Nations Observation Group in Lebanon," *International Organization*, Vol. 18, No. 3, 1964, pp. 738-65; and on the question of the legality of US intervention, see Quincy Wright, "United States Intervention in the Lebanon," *American Journal of International Law*, Vol. 53, 1959, p. 112.

sion. This experience proved that the mere "presence" of UN in the troubled spot might sometimes have a cooling effect on frayed tempers.

The Phase of Assertion

Drawing upon the experiences in Suez and Lebanon the United Nations began to carve out a new function of its own. This phase might be described as that of preventive diplomacy. A word on the origin of this phase may be quite in order.

When the great power rift widened and the Organization was deprived of the "teeth" even to deal with minor breaches of peace Secretary-General Dag Hammarskjoeld set about to find for the UN a modest function of a police-man-cum-fire-brigade. The idea developed in Hammarskjoeld's mind slowly. He began to conceive of the UN as a forum for a diplomacy of conciliation[32] and tried to restore the age-old technique of private diplomacy.[33] Then the trouble in Congo began.

The Congo trouble should be seen, as Hammarskjoeld did, in the broader perspective of the world situation. The ever-freezing cold war, the phenomenal development of nuclear destructive power resulting in a precarious balance of terror had rendered the UN largely ineffective in matters of peace and security. The towering superiority of the Soviet Union and the United States had relegated the other three permanent members to a position of second-rate powers. The British and French failure in Suez to have their own way as opposed to the wishes of the two super powers had substantially reduced their real strength in the Security Council. China was a permanent member only in name. The battle for world power began now to be waged between the US and the Soviet Union. The areas frozen in the cold war blizzard went out of the UN sphere of influence. Only a handful of non-aligned nations exercised for a long time a sober and stabilizing influence in the bloc struggles.

---

[32]See Hammarskjoeld's address to both the Houses of the British Parliament, *UN Reviews*, Vol. 4, May 1958, pp. 6-10.

[33]See Hammarskjoeld's address delivered at Ohio University, *ibid.*, March 1958, pp. 10-3.

Added to the above process was the emancipation of a host of African States by the colonial powers sometimes under the auspices of the UN Trusteeship System, sometimes on their own. With the entrance of these newly independent countries into the UN, the membership rose to more than a hundred and with this the prestige, ambition, and power of the General Assembly.

Simultaneously a struggle ensued between the power blocs for the winning over of these emergent nations. Dag Hammarskjoeld perceived "the first beginning" in Africa "of those conflicts between ideologies and interests which split the world."[34] The attitude of the UN, felt Hammarskjoeld, in this situation should be to support the independence movements "protecting the possibilities of the African peoples to choose their own way without undue influences being exercised and without attempts to abuse the situation."[35] As a universal Organization neutral in the big power struggle over ideology and influence in the world, subordinated to the common will of the member governments and free from any aspirations of its own for power and influence over any group or nations, the United Nations can render service which can be received without suspicion and which can be absorbed without influencing the free choice of the peoples.[36]

Such was the mood and time in which the UN engaged itself in Congo "in the greatest single task which it has had to handle by its own means and on its own conditions."[37] A manifestation of the new role of preventive diplomacy, the Congo operations constituted a landmark in the organic development of the UN, independent of the conceptual wishes of the members or of its founding fathers.

Secretary-General Hammarskjoeld spelt out the new task of the Organization in the same Report. The UN's role in preventive diplomacy consisted in "keeping newly arising conflicts outside the sphere of bloc differences ... through solutions aiming ...

[34]*Introduction to the Annual Report of the Secretary-General on the Work of the Organization,* 16 *June* 1959-15 *June* 1960, *General Assembly Official Records,* 15th Session, Suppl. No. IA, p. 1.

[35]*Ibid.,* p. 2.

[36]*Ibid.*

[37]*Ibid.,* p. 1.

at their strict localization," "so as to forestall developments which might draw the specific conflict ... into the sphere of power bloc differences."[38] The Organization would do so "by introducing itself into the picture sometimes with very modest means" as in Lebanon, "sometimes in strength" as in Gaza and Congo, "so as to eliminate a political, economic, and social, or military vacuum."[39]

In his Introduction to the sixteenth Annual Report Hammarskjoeld listed the instruments employed by the UN in perpetration of this new-found role:

> Subcommittees have been set up for fact-finding or negotiation on the spot. Missions have been placed in areas of conflict for the purpose of observation and local negotiation. Observer groups of a temporary nature have been sent out. And, finally, police forces under the aegis of the United Nations have been organized for the assistance of the governments concerned with a view to upholding the principles of the Charter.[40]

UN practice in this phase of preventive diplomacy has mainly consisted in achieving agreement of the parties in conflict to the cessation of hostilities, either through a cease-fire or a formal assistance. It has assisted in securing the observance of such arrangements through various forms of UN presence, thus providing opportunities for observing reporting, mediating, and exercising a restraining influence.[41] This has been possible because of the agreement, or in the absence of positive disagreement, of the permanent members of the Security Council, to which, among other things attention will now be diverted.

Problems

The Problem of Major Power Acquiescence. The theory which attempts to quarantine trouble spots from major power interference rests upon the assumption that the major powers would

---

[38]*Ibid.*, p. 4.

[39]*Ibid.*

[40]See *UN Review*, Vol. 8, September 1961, p. 16.

[41]See an admirable analysis of this new trend by Leland M. Goodrich, "The Maintenance of International Peace and Security," *International Organization*, Vol. 19, No. 3, Summer 1965, p. 429.

consent actively or passively to such a course of operation by the world organization. Or, as Inis Claude Jr. puts it, "the theory rests upon the assumption that conflict of interest breeds a limited community of interest particularly in the thermonuclear era."[42] The success therefore of preventive diplomacy depends upon the *permission* or *acquiescence* of the power blocs, on the realization that the price involved is too meagre for a mutual confrontation. The blocs have not only a stake in avoiding a military showdown but must *realize* that it is so. If the awareness is not in proportion to the danger there will be chaos and confusion as in the Congo. The Soviet Union and the US for a long time refused to see the significance of the Congo operations (ONUC). Or it might well be that the two blocs suspected that the ONUC was not acting as impartially as it ought to and hence the scramble for back door entry.[43]

The Problem of Consensus. The second problem of preventive diplomacy is the question of consensus.

A heated debate flared up in the General Assembly after the formation of UNEF following the Secretary-General's agreement with the Egyptian government in which the two parties agreed to carry out the operations in good faith and in which the Egyptian government reaffirmed "its willingness to maintain UNEF until its task is completed."[44]

The Indian delegate V. K. Krishna Menon emphatically maintained that "the forces would arrive only with Egypt's consent, and . . . *could not stay or operate* unless Egypt continued to give such consent."[45] As against this stand the Canadian delegate Lester B. Pearson had earlier asserted:

> The control of this Force . . . is in the hands of the United Nations and must remain there. Otherwise it would be not a United Nations Force, but merely a collection of national forces.

[42]Inis Claude Jr., "United Nations' use of Military Force," *Journal of Conflict Resolution*, Vol. 7, No. 2, 1963, pp. 117-29.

[43]See for a fuller analysis of the problem, *ibid.*, pp. 125-9.

[44]UN Doc. A/3375 Annex.

[45]*General Assembly Official Records*, 11th Sess. Plenary Meetings, 596th Mtg., 26 November, 1956, p. 333.

. . . The Secretary-General should certainly consult with the government of the country in which the Force is serving on all matters of any importance that affect it; also, as we understand it, the Force is to remain in the area until its task is completed, and that would surely be for the determination of the United Nations itself.[46]

Since the agreement with Egypt did contain the government's willingness to maintain UNEF until its task was completed the discussion was hypothetical. But the problem could hardly be neglected.

It would appear that since the origin and establishment of a peace force of the UNEF or ONUC type is based upon a non-binding recommendation of the' competent organ of the UN and the consent of the countries in question, it might be that its continued operation must also depend upon the consent of the party concerned.

Dr. Guenter Weissberg, however, forcefully argued[47] that the answer is otherwise. First, the "recommendations" of a UN organ are not completely devoid of any importance, they possess a "legal significance."[48] Second, once a State accepts a particular recommendation "there is a legal obligation to act in good faith in accordance with the principles of the Charter."[49] Third, if a State assumes an obligation a legal nexus is created which amounts to an "international agreement," and the laws of treaties and estoppel apply to the agreement henceforth. Thus Weissberg concluded that Egypt "cannot reach a unilateral determination whereby the Force is requested to withdraw."[50]

This question assumed grave importance in 1967 when President Nasser of UAR asked the UN to withdraw UNEF. The Secretary-General, it is well known, complied with this demand

---

[46]*Ibid.*, 592nd Mtg., 23 November, 1956, p. 268.

[47]Guenter Weissberg, *op. cit.*, pp. 131-40.

[48]The phrase and the argument concerning the binding force of recommendations is borrowed from Judge Lauterpacht's dicta in "South-West Africa—Voting Procedure," Advisory Opinion of 7 June 1955, ICJ *Reports*, 1955, p. 120.

[49]*Ibid.*

[50]Weissberg, *op. cit.*, p. 140.

rightly, according to some, and wrongly according to others.[51] But, if it is remembered that the UNEF was symbolic of not enforcement by force but pacification by pressure, and that it was not an occupation force U Thant's action might well be understood. The legal-constitutional subtleties combined with the military realities of the situation had rendered the continued stationing of the Force untenable.

The Problem of Status Quo Ante. Closely related to the problem of consent is the question of *status quo ante*. Can the UN while interposing between combatants also suggest solutions to the causes of conflict. Secretary-General Hammarskjoeld's theory was that the only job of the UN was to separate the combatants and restore order; hence the political solution of the problem was beyond the competence of the UN.

The theory, indeed, fits well into the role of a firebrigade, yet nothing stops the UN from opening up its venues of conciliations if the parties consent. An experiment was tried in the case of Cyprus. There is one caveat, however. In cases of clear-cut aggression—though the UN might refuse to so determine for reasons of its own—the conciliation process is bound to fail. For, this involves treating the aggressor and the victim on equal level, which the victim may resent. The present author has brought this out in his *Kashmir and the United Nations*.[52]

The Problem of Finances. In spite of the Advisory Opinion of the ICJ the financial problems of the peace-keeping operations of the UN remain unsolved. Member States' reluctance in this respect has been so great that the UN has had to rely upon the parties concerned for financial amelioration. The Yemeni operations were financed by UAR and Saudi Arabia. A new experiment is being tried out in Cyprus where not only the immediately

[51]E.L.M. Burns, "The Withdrawal of UNEF and the Future of Peace-Keeping," *International Journal*, Vol. 13, 1967-68, p. 1; Maxwell Cohen, "The Demise of UNEF," *International Journal*, Vol. 23, 1967-68, p. 18, Yashpal Tandon, "UNEF, the Secretary-General, and International Diplomacy in the Third Arab-Israeli War," *International Organization*, Vol. 22, 1968, p. 529.

[52]Rahmatullah Khan, *Kashmir and the United Nations*, Delhi, 1969.

affected parties are made to bear partial costs but the remaining costs are being raised by voluntary contributions.[53]

The initial difficulties at assembling the forces in Cyprus and member States' hesitation to send no more than token contingents portend a difficult future for the peace-keeping operations of the UN.

The Problem of Military Strategy and Logistics. The recent trend in entrusting executive, technical, and logistic matters to the Secretary-General on the basis of mandates of a general nature, has put the Secretariat, which hitherto had been taken as a UN pantry. The military and technical operations are something for which the round-shouldered, self-effacing officers of the Secretariat had not flexed their muscles. The late Secretary-General Hammarskjoeld had repeatedly requested the General Assembly to provide for him a skeleton staff well-versed in such matters.[54]

In spite of these apparently insuperable problems the record of UN's preventive diplomacy, though not "shining examples" of peace-keeping as Oscar Schachter rightly remarks,[55] gives rise to hope. It now remains to be seen if the Charter provides sufficient legal basis for functions of this kind.

LEGAL BASES FOR PREVENTIVE DIPLOMACY AND IMPLIED PEACE-KEEPING POWERS OF UN

The development of the technique of preventive diplomacy, as was pointed out at the beginning, can be viewed as the development of the Organization's latent potentialities in peace-keeping. It might also be viewed as a display of its implied powers in the field. For, when the scheme of the Charter became unworkable due to

---

[53]The latest manifestation of the financial problem is the Indo-Pak refusal to bear the costs of the truce observation groups stationed on the cease-fire line after the hostilities between the two countries in 1965.

[54]*Introduction of Annual Report*, p. 3; for a varied discussion of the problems, political and strategic, of a UN Peace Force, see *International Organization* Vol. 17, No. 2, 1963.

[55]Oscar Schacter, "The Quasi-Judicial Role of the Security Council and the General Assembly," *American Journal of International Law*, Vol. 58, 1964, p. 961.

external factors some general provisions in the Charter, like Article 10, etc., under which the General Assembly had wide and unspecified powers, were tapped. The General Assembly has acted under these loose powers most conspicuously in Gaza (1956) and in the Congo (1960-1964). These two actions gave rise to an occasion to seek legal guidance from the ICJ.

That the Security Council was designed to be the guardian of peace and consequently was empowered to create and maintain an international force to subdue the law-breaker was never in doubt. But the authority of the UN (especially that of the General Assembly) to create a force to supervise cease-fires and insulate trouble-spots from big power rivalry came to be seriously questioned, particularly by the Soviet bloc countries. Also, they refused to share the costs of such activities. While a few Latin American, African, and Asian member States pleaded poverty, some others (notably France) took the view that since such a force could be established only on the basis of non-binding recommendations, the costs of these operations should be met by voluntary contributions and that no member State should be compelled to pay for the same which either was opposed to the establishment of the force or was unwilling to share the financial burden.

It must be mentioned here, however, that as a result of extensive research in the academic quarters it has been found that the Charter provides sufficient basis for the establishment of an "interposition" force of the nature sketched above.[56] The ICJ lent its *imprimatur* to this view in an advisory opinion, to which attention now will be diverted.

[56] See for the constitutional bases, functions, and potentialities of such a force, *Report of Committee on Study of Legal Problems of the United Nations, Proceedings, American Society of International Law,* Washington, 1957, p. 205; *Report on Problems of a United Nations Force, International Law Association,* 49th Conference Report, Hamburg, 1960, p. 130 and the bibliographical note given therein (Dr. Schwargenber employs the phrase "interposition force" in the Report); Finn Seyersted, "United Nations Forces: Some Legal Problems," *British Yearbook of International Law,* Vol. 37, 1961, pp. 351-475; Louis B. Sohn, "The Authority of the United Nations to Establish and Maintain a Permanent United Nations Force," *American Journal of International Law,* Vol. 52, 1958, p. 229; D.W. Bowett, *United Nations Force: A Legal Study,* New York, 1964.

To determine whether the costs of such activities can be duly classified as the "expenses of the Organization" within the meaning of Article 17, paragraph 2, of the Charter, the Court had to investigate whether the Organization and especially the General Assembly had such peace-keeping powers.[57]

The advocates of a negative answer to the question put to the Court relied mainly on the ground of, what has been called, the "spheres of competence" of the organs of the UN. The argument was that when the maintenance of international peace and security was involved, it was only the Security Council which was authorized to decide on—and take—any action relative thereto, and that since the General Assembly's power was limited to discussing, considering, studying, and recommending, it could not take action of itself, nor could it create binding obligations. The Court was thus faced with the problem of delimiting the respective roles of the Security Council and the General Assembly in matters of peace and security. The Court took up the loose threads and wove them into a delicate fabric.

First, it exploded the myth that the General Assembly is merely a "town meeting of the world" with no effective powers.[58] It found support in Articles 5, 6, 14, and 18[59] for the view that the General

---

[57]Rahmatullah Khan, "Peace-keeping Powers of the UN General Assembly Advisory Opinion of the ICJ," *International Studies*, Vol. 6, No. 3, 1965, pp. 317-32. See Judge Koretsky's remark that the "opinion may be used as an instrument of political struggle." ICJ *Reports*, 1962, p. 254; Judge Sir Percy Spender's postulate in his separate opinion that "the majority has no power to extend, alter or disregard the Charter" and that "when . . . the Court is called upon to pronounce upon a question . . . only legal considerations may be invoked and *de facto* extension of the Charter must be disregarded." *Ibid.*, p. 197.

[58]ICJ *Reports*, 1962, pp. 163-4.

[59]Article 5 reads: "A member of the United Nations against which preventive or enforcement action has been taken by the Security Council may be suspended from the exercise of the rights and privileges of membership by the General Assembly upon the recommendation of the Security Council. The exercises of these rights and privileges may be restored by the Security Council."

Article 6 prescribes: "A member of the United Nations which has persistently violated the principles contained in the present Charter may be expelled from the Organization by the General Assembly upon the recommendation of the Security Council."

Assembly's powers are not merely hortatory. Under Article 14, said the Court, the General Assembly can "recommend measures for the peaceful adjustment of any situation, regardless of origin, which it deems likely to impair the general welfare or friendly relations among nations, including situations resulting from a violation of the provisions of the present Charter setting forth the purposes and principles of the United Nations."

Article 18 deals with "decisions" of the General Assembly "on important questions." These decisions, said the Court, do indeed include certain recommendations, but others have dispositive force and effect. Among these latter decisions, Article 18 includes suspension of rights and privileges of membership and expulsion of membership under Articles 5 and 6. The powers of the General Assembly under Articles 5 and 6 are specially related to preventive or enforcement measures. By Article 17, paragraph 1, the Court continued, the General Assembly is given the power not only to "consider" the budget of the Organization but also to "approve" it, and under paragraph 2 of the same Article the General Assembly is also given the power to apportion the expenses among the members, creating a binding obligation.

Article 14 affirms: "Subject to the provisions of Article 12, the General Assembly may recommend measures for the peaceful adjustment of any situation, regardless of origin, which it deems likely to impair the general welfare or friendly relations among nations, including situations resulting from a violation of the povisions of present Charter setting forth the purposes and principles of the United Nations."

Article 18 lays down: "1. Each member of the General Assembly shall have one vote.

"2. Decisions of the General Assembly on important questions shall be made by a two-thirds majority of the members present and voting. These questions shall include: recommendations with respect to the maintenance of international peace and security, the election of the non-permanent members of the Security Council, the election of the members of the Economic and Social Council, the election of members of the Trusteeship Council in accordance with paragraph 1(c) of Article 86, the admission of new members to the United Nations, the suspension of the rights and privileges of membership, the expulsion of members, questions relating to the operation of the trusteeship system, and budgetary questions.

"3. Decisions on other questions, including the determination of additional categories of questions to be decided by a two-thirds majority, shall be made by a majority of the members present and voting."

Further it found by reciting Article 24[60] of the Charter that the responsiblity conferred on the Security Council was "primary" not exclusive and that the primary responsibility was conferred upon the Security Council "in order to ensure prompt and effective action." To this end, it is the Security Council which is given a power to impose an explicit obligation of compliance if for example it issues an order or command to an aggressor under Chapter VII. It is only the Security Council which can require enforcement by coercive action against an aggressor.[61]

The Court came to the conclusion that "there is a close collaboration between the two organs"[62] and that the field of international peace and security is not a reserved domain of the Security Council alone.

Referring to the argument that in view of the last sentence of Article 11, paragraph 2,[63] the General Assembly is debarred from taking action by itself, the Court said that the action referred to in this article is coercive or enforcement action. The word "action" must mean such action as is solely within the province of the Security Council. The "action" which is solely within the province of the Security Council, according to the Court, is that which is indicated by the title of Chapter VII of the Charter, namely, action "with respect to threats to the peace, breaches of the peace, and acts of aggression." The Court accordingly found that the argument which sought, by reference to Article 11, paragraph 2, to limit the authority of the General Assembly in respect to the maintenance of international peace and security, was unfounded.[64] The Court also said that the power of the General Assembly to organize peace-keeping operations "is a special power which in no way derogates from its general powers under Article 10 or Article 14, except as limited by the last sentence of Article

[60]The article reads: "In order to ensure prompt and effective action by the United Nations, its members confer on the Security Council primary responsibility for the maintenance of international peace and security."

[61]ICJ *Reports*, 1962, p. 163.

[62]*Ibid.*

[63]The paragraph reads in part: "Any such question on which action is necessary shall be referred to the Security Council by the General Assembly either before or after discussion."

[64]ICJ *Reports*, 1962, p. 165.

11, paragraph 2."[65] It can set up committees or commissions for investigation, observation, and supervision, which amount to "organizational activity—action—in connection with the maintenance of international peace and security."[66] It may establish subsidiary organs under the authority of Article 22 of the Charter to carry out its functions effectively.

Another argument put forward before the Court was that Article 43 of the Charter constitutes a particular rule, a *lex specialis*, and in the absence of special agreements envisaged thereunder the Security Council could not take enforcement action. The Court ruled that "the operations known as UNEF and ONUC were not *enforcement* actions within the compass of Chapter VII of the Charter and that therefore Article 43 could not have any applicability to the cases with which the Court is here concerned. However, even if Article 43 were applicable, the Court could not accept this interpretation,"[67] for the reason that the argument "would seem to exclude the possibility that the Security Council might act under some other Article of the Charter."[68] Refusing to accept such a limited view of the powers of the Security Council, the Court declared:

> It cannot be said that the Charter has left the Security Council impotent in the face of an emergency situation when agreements under Article 43 have not been concluded.
>
> Articles of Chapter VII of the Charter speak of "situations" as well as disputes, and it must lie within the power of the Security Council to police a situation even though it does not resort to enforcement action against a State.[69]

Examining specifically the relevant resolutions under which the two operations were established, the Court found full support for its thesis. In the case of UNEF the Court relied on the following. The General Assembly in its resolution[70] of 4 November

[65] *Ibid.*, pp. 164-5.
[66] *Ibid.*, p. 165.
[67] *Ibid.*, p. 166.
[68] *Ibid.*, p. 167.
[69] *Ibid.*
[70] General Assembly Resolution No. 998 (ES-I), 1956.

1956 requested the Secretary-General to submit a plan "for the setting up, with the *consent* of nations concerned, of an emergency international United Nations Force to *secure* and supervise the cessation of hostilities in accordance with all the terms of" the General Assembly's previous resolution of 2 November 1956.[71] The Court said that the verb "secure" as applied to such matters as halting the movement of military forces and arms into the area and the conclusion of a cease-fire, might suggest measures of enforcement, were it not that the Force was to be set up with the consent of the nations concerned.[72]

The Court, further, drew inspiration from the second and final report of the Secretary-General on the plan for the Force of 6 November 1956, paragraphs 9, 10, and 12, of which read partly:

(9) While the General Assembly is enabled to establish the Force with the consent of those parties which contribute units to the Force, it could not request the Force to be *stationed* or operate on the territory of a given country without the consent of the government of that country. This does not exclude the possibility that the Security Council could use such a Force within the wide margins provided under Chapter VII of the United Nations Charter. . . .

(10) . . . There is an obvious difference between establishing the Force in order to secure the cessation of hostilities, with a withdrawal of forces, and establishing such a Force with a view to enforcing a withdrawal of forces.

(12) . . . The Force obviously should have no rights other than those necessary for the execution of its functions, in cooperation with local authorities. It would be more than an observers' corps, but in no way a military force temporarily controlling the territory in which it is stationed; nor, moreover, should the Force have military functions exceeding those necessary to secure peaceful conditions on the assumption that the parties to the conflict take all necessary steps for compliance with the recommendations of the General Assembly.[73]

[71]*Ibid.*, No. 997 (ES-I), 1956.   (Italics added.)
[72]ICJ *Reports*, 1962, p. 170.
[73]As cited by the Court, *ibid.*, pp. 170-1.

The Court concluded that from the description of the functions of UNEF, as outlined by the Secretary-General and concurred in by the General Assembly without a dissenting vote, and from the subsequent operations of the Force, no evidence could be found that the Force was designed or used for purposes of enforcement. It also found that Article 14 constituted a sufficient legal basis for the establishment of the Force.[74] In the case of the ONUC the Court felt that

> it is not necessary for the Court to express an opinion as to which article or articles of the Charter were the basis for the resolutions of the Security Council, but it can be said that the operations of ONUC did not include a use of armed force against a State which the Security Council, under Article 39, determined to have committed an act of aggression or to have breached the peace. The armed forces which were utilized in the Congo were not authorized to take military action against any State. The operation did not involve "preventive or enforcement measures" against any State under Chapter VII and therefore did not constitute "action" as that term is used in Article 11.[75]

Objection was taken to the Court's lumping together such diverse operations as the UNEF and ONUC both in nature and scope. Professor Leo Gross characterizing the question put to the Court as "a double-barrelled one" said that the Court in its anxiety to emphasize the similarities left out completely the inherent differences between the two.[76] G.I.A.D. Draper demonstrated convincingly the dissimilarities between the two operations in "their respective constitutional bases, their essential nature, and the task they were called upon to perform."[77]

The Court emphasized the similarities between the two actions by reducing them to a common denominator, namely, "peace-keeping

[74]*Ibid.*, pp. 171-2.

[75]*Ibid.*, p. 177.

[76]Leo Gross, "Expenses of the United Nations for Peace-Keeping Operations: The Advisory Opinion of the International Court of Justice," *International Organization*, Vol. 17, 1963, p. 30.

[7] G.I.A.D. Draper, "The Legal Limitations upon the Employment of Weapons by the United Nations Force in the Congo," *International and Comparative Law Quarterly*, Vol. 12, Part 2, 1963, pp. 391-2.

operations"; it considered that neither was enforcement action, that neither was obligatory, since both actions depended upon the consent of the concerned governments, Egypt and Congo, respectively, that therefore both were within the recommendatory powers of the General Assembly and the Security Council respectively and therefore in conformity with the Charter.

There cannot be much difficulty in construing the Middle East operations as peaceful in conception and operation. Attention here might be drawn, however, to the possibility envisioned by Judge Monreno Quintana in his dissenting opinion. "And what would be the position," he queried, "if tomorrow Israeli armed forces, renewing the aggression unleashed in 1956 against Egypt, attacked Gaza strip and obliged the United Nations forces to repel them? Would this be enforcement action or would it not?"[78] It might be pointed out in answer that in such an event the force could be transformed into an enforcement one by the Security Council, as was envisaged by the Secretary-General in paragraph 9 of his final report of 6 November 1956, as stated above. But essentially the UNEF was designed and operated as an "interposition"[79] force and evidently lacked authority to enforce law and order or go beyond the exigency of strict self-defence.

The case of ONUC is different. ONUC was established and deployed under the Security Council mandate. Though there might have been some errors in the course of its operations, the allegation that the Secretary-General had usurped the Security Council powers was rightly refuted by the Court. But the graver charge was that the functions entrusted to the instrumentality in question (i.e. ONUC) was of a compulsive nature. The allegation, when brought into contact with the actual course of events, appears irrefutable. Judges Quintana and Koretsky levelled a bitter attack on the Court's generalization that ONUC, too, was not a "preventive or coercive measure." Judge Quintana was content with a sweeping categorization: "Any use of armed forces intended for whatever purposes implies by definition enforcement action";[80] while Judge

[78]ICJ *Reports*, 1962, pp. 246-7.
[79]See for literature on the interposition force note 56.
[80]ICJ *Reports*, 1962, p. 246 (dissenting opinion).

Koretsky declared: "Ergo, they were forces of compulsion, whether they were only 'stationed' there, i.e. 'supervised,' or were acting, i.e. undertook 'actions'."[81]

The final stages of the Congo operation do provide ample evidence for the view that the UN forces in Congo were indeed "forces of compulsion." It is common knowledge that ONUC did employ bomber aircraft, fighter aircraft, mortars, anti-tank and anti-aircraft weapons, machine-guns, and small arms. There were dead and wounded, pitched battles were fought, cease-fires were negotiated, Belgian mercenaries were arrested or expelled, radio stations and aerodromes were closed; in short, the ONUC did perform belligerent acts.[82] It did so, no doubt, under a mandate of the Security Council. In its resolution[83] of 21 February 1961 the Security Council had authorized "all appropriate measures to prevent the occurrence of civil war in the Congo, including arrangements for cease-fires, the halting of all military operations, the prevention of clashes and *the use of force, if necessary, in the last resort*." Not in self-defence, be it noted. The final "omnibus" resolution[84] of the Security Council of 24 November 1961, recapitulating the aims in earlier resolutions, authorized the Secretary-General to take vigorous measures, including the use of force, to safeguard the territorial integrity of the Congo, restore law and order, prevent civil war and apprehend the Belgian mercenaries. It might be said that the Security Council did so with the consent of the Government of Congo. But this does not alter the position. The fact was that force was used, first, against Belgian mercenaries, second, against secessionist Katanga. UN military assistance was invited by the Government of Congo to meet the Belgian paratroops—the cables sent by the President and PM of the Congo specifically mention that the Belgian action amounted to an act of aggression.[85] The force was created and designed to vacate Belgian aggression. It is another matter that Belgium withdrew voluntarily.

[81]*Ibid.*, p. 259 (dissenting opinion).
[82]See Draper, *op. cit.*, p. 407.
[83]UN Doc. S/4741.
[84]UN Doc. S/5002.
[85]UN Doc. S/4382.

Also, it must be remembered, the ONUC was *authorized* to end secessionist activities of the province of Katanga. And not until the policy of non-intervention was abandoned and military compulsion used against Katanga could the ONUC fulfil its task.[86] The Court's stand that no determination of aggression was made by the Security Council and the forces were not employed against any State is not tenable on two grounds: one, that the Security Council abstained from branding Belgium an aggressor for diplomatic reasons;[87] two, it is difficult to deny secessionst Katanga a belligerent status.[88] It is hard to maintain in the face of facts, that the Congo operation was not of a compulsive character. Harder still is it to refute the charge that "the United Nations Force was sent there, not to persuade or to parade, but to carry out military operations" and that "they did so."[89]

The charge, in the present submission, could have been avoided if the Court had drawn a distinction between the interpository character of the UNEF and the compulsive (or policing) nature of the ONUC. The General Assembly could—as it did—create the former and only the Security Council could—as it happened —establish the latter. An interposition force could be transformed into a policing force or an enforcement action by the Security Council in the event of a contingency dramatically posed by Judge Quintana.

The Congo operations could have been construed as "provisional measures," not amounting to enforcement action, under Article 40 to "prevent aggravation" of a situation threatening international peace and security. Only then could the employment of force and the neutralist intervention in the internal affairs of the Congo be

[86]See Stanley Hoffmann, "In Search of a Thread: The United Nations in the Congo Labyrinth," *International Organization*, Vol. 16, 1962, pp. 331-61.

[87]See in this connection the statement of the representative of Tunisia who spoke in support of the draft resolution submitted by Ceylon and Tunisia: "We have refrained ... from using the word 'aggression' or even the term 'aggressive acts' in resolutions, since we are anxious not to exacerbate the feelings of the Belgian people." Cited by Judge Korestsky in his dissenting opinion, ICJ *Reports*, 1962, p. 276.

[88]See Dissenting opinion of Judge Monreno Quintana, *ibid.*, p. 246.

[9]See Dissenting opinion of Judge Koretsky, *ibid.*, p. 276.

justified.[90] By persistent reiterations that the Congo operations were not "enforcement action" *stricto sensu* the Court, probably, had in mind the task of facilitating the General Assembly, if the latter chose to embark upon such activity in the future by itself.

A word must be said here with regard to the connection of the Court's opinion with the "Uniting for Peace" resolution. It has been suggested that the Court has indirectly affirmed the validity of the "Uniting for Peace" resolution.[91] In the present submission however, the Court was not seized of the question of the validity of this resolution directly or indirectly and any such deduction would be longwinding and remote.[92] It might be recalled that the "Uniting for Peace" resolution[93] not only was designed to transfer a deadlocked issue from the Security Council to the General Assembly but also envisioned the creation of an international force to be kept at the disposal of the General Assembly.

[90]See for similar suggestions that Article 40 constitutes the legal basis for Congo operations, E.M. Miller, "Legal Aspects of the United Nations Action in the Congo," *American Journal of Interntional Law*, Vol. 55, 1961, p. 1; Quincy Wright, "Legal Aspects of the Congo Situation," *International Studies*, Vol. 4, No. 1, 1962, p. 22; see also Introduction to Secretary-General's Annual Report, 17 August 1961, *United Nations Review*, September 1961, p. 12.

[91]Leo Gross, *op. cit.*, p. 26.

[92]Not once did the Court mention the "Uniting for Peace" resolution or the legality of the same. The case, however, of those who favoured a negative answer was based mainly on the alleged illegality of the resolution.

[93]Abundant literature is available on the validity of the "Uniting for Peace" resolution. See, in particular, Juraj Andrassy, "Uniting for Peace," *American Journal of International Law*, Vol. 50, 1956, pp. 526-82; Leland M. Goodrich and Anne P. Simons, *The United Nations and the Maintenance of International Peace and Security*, Washington, D.C., 1955, pp. 406-8; Hans Kelsen, "Is the Acheson Plan constitutional," *Western Political Quarterly*, Vol. 3, 1950, pp. 512-27; also *Recent Trends in the Law of the United Nations*, 1951, pp. 953-90; Josef L. Kunz, "Legality of the Security Council Resolutions of June 25 and 27, 1950," *American Journal of International Law*, Vol. 45, 1951, pp. 137-42; Myres S. McDougal and Richard N. Gardner, "The Veto and the Charter: An Interpretation for Survival," *Yale Law Journal*, 1951, pp. 258-92; F. Blaine Sloan, "The Binding Force of a 'Recommendations' of the General Assembly of the United Nations," *British Yearbook of International Law*, Vol. 25, 1948, pp. 1-33; F.A. Vellat, "The General Assembly and the Security Council of the United Naions," *ibid.*, Vol. 29, 1952, pp. 63-104; P.F. Walters, "The Authority of the United Nations General Assembly," *International Relations*, 1957, pp. 349-61; L.H. Woolsey, "The Uniting for Peace Resolution of the United Nations," *American Journal of International Law*, Vol. 45, 1951, pp. 129-37.

Most important of all, the resolution purported to empower the General Assembly with powers in the one special field where the Security Council alone is entitled to act, i.e. action in relation to "threats to the peace, breaches of the peace or acts of aggression."[94] In other words, the resolution attempted to replace the Security Council with the General Assembly in the field of enforcement under Chapter VII of the Charter. The only difference was that while the Security Council acted itself by means of *authoritative or comminatory decisions*, the General Assembly under this procedure acted through member States by means of *non-binding, hortatory recomendations*. The end result was the same though the means were different.

An examination of the Advisory Opinion would reveal that the Court asserted more than once that the Security Council alone was entitled to act under Chapter VII, i.e. take enforcement action. The passages quoted below bring out fully the Court's mind in this regard.

Referring to Article 24, the Court pronounced: "It is the Security Council which is given a power to impose an explicit obligation of compliance if for example it issues an order or commend to an aggressor under Chapter VII. It is only the Security Council which can require enforcement by coercive action against an aggressor."[95]

Again, referring specifically to the nature of Middle East and Congo operations, the Court declared that "the operations known as UNEF and ONUC were not *enforcement* actions within the compass of Chapter VII of the Charter."[96] With particular reference to the ONUC the Court repeated: "The operation did not involve 'preventive or enforcement measures' against any State under Chapter VII."[97]

The Court, in fact, went out of the way to insist that the word "action" in Article 11, paragraph 2, referred to action "with respect

[94]The preamble of the resolution reads: "*Conscious* that failure of the Security Council to discharge its responsibilities on behalf of all the member States . . . does not relieve member States of their obligations or the UN of its responsibility under the Charter to maintain international peace and security."

[95]ICJ *Reports*, 1962, p. 163.

[96]*Ibid.*, p. 166.   [97]*Ibid.*, p. 177.

to threats to the peace, breaches of the peace and acts of aggression" which is dealt under Chapter VII and that such action is *solely* within the province of the Security Council.[98]

What, then, were the UNEF and ONUC? The operations, as has been pointed out in the beginning were the tools of "preventive diplomacy." As the Court said in relation to the UNEF "this power of the General Assembly is a special power"[99] which in no way derogates from the powers of the Security Council. The power consists, to repeat, in embarking upon organizational activity, such as, setting up committees and commissions, establishing subsidiary organs under the authority of Article 22 of the Charter for purposes of investigation, observation, supervision, etc.[100] Patrolling a cease-fire line (UNEF) is obviously an offshoot of such organizational activity. So is the Security Council empowered to establish and maintain subsidiary organs under Article 29 to create conditions conducive to peace, or take "provisional measures" to "prevent aggravation" of a situation threatening international peace and security under Article 40. The Security Council in such cases, is not bound to take these organizational activity through the "special agreements" envisaged under Article 43. That was the crux of the opinion.

However, there are certain passages in the Advisory Opinion which do cast a damper on the challengers of the validity of the "Uniting for Peace" resolution:

> But when the Organization takes action which warrants the assertion that it was appropriate for the fulfilment of one of the stated purposes of the United Nations, the presumption is that such action is not *ultra vires* the Organization.

> If it is agreed that the action in question is within the scope of the functions of the Organization but it is alleged that it has been initiated or carried out in a manner not in conformity with the division of functions among the several organs which the Charter prescribes, one moves to the internal plane, to the

[98]*Ibid.*, p. 165.
[99]*Ibid.*, p. 164.
[100]*Ibid.*, p. 165.

internal structure of the Organization. If the action was taken by the wrong organ, it was irregular as a matter of that internal structure, but this would not necessarily mean that the expense incurred was not an expense of the Organization. Both national and international law contemplate cases in which the body corporate or politic may be bound, as to third parties, by an *ultra vires* act of an agent.[101]

The above passages indicate that if the validity of the "Uniting for Peace" resolution had been before the Court for active consideration the Court, probably, would have treated it as a matter of the internal structure of the Organization, and in keeping with the doctrine of "institutional effectiveness," would have approved the action initiated under this procedure in so far as the financial credit of the Organization was involved in the particular activity. It probably would have said that the activity in question was irregular internally, but as the expenses involved were costs of carrying out one of the primary purposes of the Organization, the members could not escape financial liability. But that is not legalizing the action or approving the procedure under which such action was taken.

SUMMATION

The schematic conception, the organizational practice, and the development of the role of preventive diplomacy provide ample and conclusive proof to the theory that the UN was intended to have, and has, abundant unexpressed powers in matters relating to world peace. These could be drawn by necessary implication from the primary objective of maintenance of international peace and security, which is stated as the first of the purposes under Article 1 of the Charter. Unless liberal interpretation is given to the provisions in this regard and a large measure of implied powers are deduced from its purposes and functions, facilitating the establishment of interpository forces, observer groups, truce commissions, etc., for which no specific authority exists in the Charter but which can be subsumed under the Organization's

[101]*Ibid.*, p. 168.

peace-keeping powers by implication, the UN can hardly perform its essential duties and can never adapt itself to the immense strides the nations are making in technology and weaponary. This was the spirit in which the ICJ accorded its *imprimatur* to the Gaza and Congo operations. It is true the UN powers by implication in the field of world peace and security are beset with problems of a grave nature, as was cursorily shown in the body of the present chapter, but the constitutionality, or "charterability," of such activities are beyond doubt, especially after the advisory opinion of the ICJ in the *Expenses* case. This does not mean that all acts of the UN are inherently legal. There might be instances where the UN went clearly beyond its powers. What happens in such cases? This forms the subject of our enquiry in the penultimate chapter of this work.

CHAPTER 3

IMPLIED TREATY-MAKING POWERS OF INTERNATIONAL ORGANIZATIONS

THE EXTENSION by implication of the powers of international organization has the most beneficial result in the treaty-making field. In consonance with the thesis presented in Part I it is intended to prove in the present chapter that the absence of an express authorization in the constituent instrument of an international organization to employ the treaty-technique is not a real hindrance, provided the treaty so adopted serves the goal of effective functioning of the organization and promotes its purposes and principles. This is not the same as saying that an international organization has unlimited treaty-making capacity as the sovereign State. Much of the controversy among legal scholars can be attributed to the misplaced identification of the source of this power. In the present submission the power springs from the purposes and functions of the organization, whether or not there is an express provision granting such authority in the constituent documents.

Article 1 of the *Draft Articles on the Law of Treaties*[1] prepared by the International Law Commission states categorically that the "present articles relate to treaties concluded between States." Nevertheless, international organizations figure in a number of places in the ILC *Draft*. Pragraph 1(*i*) of Article 2 states : " 'International organization' means an inter-governmental organization." Paragraph 2(*c*) of Article 6 exempts representatives accredited by States to an international organization from producing full powers. Under Article 17, which deals with acceptance of and objection to reservations, reservation to a treaty which is a constituent instrument of an international organization, requires the acceptance of the competent organ of that organization. An international organization under Article 71 can be a depositary of

[1] A/CN. 4/190 of 22 July 1966; cited hereafter simply as the ILC *Draft*.

treaties; and paragraph 2 of Article 72 lays down that in the event of any difference appearing between a State and the depositary as to the performance of the latter's functions, the depositary shall bring the question to the attention of the other States entitled to become parties to the treaty, or, where appropriate, of the competent organ of the organization concerned.

In addition to the above the United Nations and its Charter provisions are referred to at various places. The validity of treaties is subjected specifically to Article 103 of the Charter (Article 26). Under Article 62, which deals with the procedure to be followed in cases of invalidity, termination, etc., the parties are enjoined to seek a solution through the means indicated in Article 33 of the Charter. Article 70 states that the *Draft* "articles are without prejudice to any obligation in relation to a treaty which may arise for an aggressor State in consequence of measures taken in conformity with the Charter of the United Nations with reference to that State's aggression." As regards correction of errors in texts, paragraph 4(*b*) of Article 74 states that the correction of the text of a treaty that has been registered shall be notified to the Secretariat of the United Nations. Article 75, finally, lays down that treaties entered into by parties to the *Draft* articles shall as soon as possible be registered with the Secretariat of the United Nations; and that their registration and publication shall be governed by the regulations adopted by the General Assembly of the United Nations.

The above provisions warrant no special comment except, perhaps, Article 75. The phrase therein that "treaties entered into by parties to the present articles" would exclude non-signatories to the *Draft* from the obligations of registration. The corresponding provision in paragraph 2 of Article 102 of the UN Charter, however, makes the disabilities arising therefrom clear: "No party to any such treaty or international agreement which has not been registered . . . may invoke that treaty or agreement before any organ of the United Nations."

There are provisions in the *Draft* which, by implication, effect the status and law of international organizations. Article 30, for instance, proclaims that a "treaty does not create either obligations or rights for a third State without its consent." As a corollary

Article 34 states that this does not preclude a rule set forth in a treaty from becoming binding upon a third State as a customary rule of international law. Article 38 significantly lays down that a treaty "may be modified by subsequent practice in the application of the treaty establishing the agreement of the parties to modify its provisions."

Juxtaposed with paragraph 6 of Article 2 of the UN Charter, which empowers the Organization to "ensure that States which are not members of the United Nations act in accordance with these principles so far as may be necessary for the maintenance of international peace and security," Article 30 of the *Draft* appears a contravention. But this provision might be treated as a *lex specialis* peculiar to the UN, which could be accommodated under the corollary of Article 34 of the *Draft*. It is here that Article 3 and 4 of the *Draft* assume great significance. Article 3 provides, partly:

The fact that the present articles do not relate:

(*a*) to international agreements concluded between States and other subjects of international law or between such other subjects of international law. ...

... shall not affect the legal force of such agreements or the application to them of any of the rules set forth in the present articles to which they would be subject independently of these articles.

Again, Article 4 of the *Draft* clearly states: "The application of the present articles to treaties which are constituent instruments of an international organization or are adopted within an international organization shall be subject to any relevant rules of the organization."

The last cited provision defuses the contradiction of Article 30 of the *Draft* with paragraph 6 of Article 2 of the UN Charter. It had to be so. The Charter provision is in the nature of a *lex specialis* in a regime of order created by the UN. Moreover, it is a *power* rather than a *right* or *duty* given to the Organization in the field, and limited only to that sphere, of maintenance of international peace and security. As against this *power* the question of rights and duties of third parties (non-members) is not strictly relevant.

For a correct appraisal of Articles 3 and 4 of the *Draft* it is necessary to go into the drafting history of the International Law Commission with respect to the treaty-making power of international organization, preceded by a brief resume of scholarly opinion.

DOCTRINAL POSITION

Opinion among scholars has ranged from complete denial of any treaty-making power for international organizations to unlimited authority of the kind, a few conceding qualified competence. The Harvard Draft on the Law of Treaties, for instance, omitted any mention of international organizations in its definition of a treaty. Article 1 of the Draft defined:

> (*a*) A "treaty" is a formal instrument of agreement by which two or more States establish or seek to establish a relation under international law between themselves. ...
>
> (*b*) The term "treaty" does not include an instrument to which a person other than a State is or may be a party.[2]

The comment in the Harvard Draft explained that international organizations were excluded from the definition "because of their abnormal character and the difficulty of formulating general rules which would be applicable to a class of instruments which are distinctly *sui generis*."[3] The attitude was typical of the feeling that existed in the academic circles up to World War II. But for a few stray cases,[4] legal authorities generally held that treaty-making was a feature peculiar to sovereign States.

On the other hand, Shabtai Rosenne, an authority on the subject, says, that "treaty-making power is an incident of their (i.e. inter-

---

[2]For this and other standard definitions of treaty, see J.L. Brierly, *Report on the Law of Treaties*, UN Doc. A/CN. 4/23 of 14 April 1950.

[3]*Ibid.*, 14 (Comment, 692).

[4]See, for example, Fior (*International Law Codified*, 5th ed., 1915, Article 748), who held that the capacity to conclude treaties may be "possessed by associations to which international personality has been attributed." Cited in Professor Lauterpacht's Report.

national organizations) objective international personality."[5] In other words, if an international organization possesses objective international personality it automatically has treaty-making powers. Objective international personality, consequently, becomes the source of the treaty-making power.

Clive Parry, an equally eminent authority on the subject, however, makes a qualification: "treaty-making power is to be deduced, if at all, not from the mere fact of its 'personality,' but from evidence pointing to its having that sort of personality which involves capacity to make treaties."[6] Aron Broches, discussing the international legal aspects of the World Bank at the Hague Academy, laid down three criteria by which the treaty-making attribute of an international organization could be ascertained: (*i*) international personality carries with it inherent treaty-making capacity; (*ii*) the treaty-making power of international organizations possessing international personality is not unlimited; (*iii*) the scope of the treaty-making power of such organizations is determined by their constitutional purposes and functions.[7]

The deliberations on the subject of the law of treaties in the International Law Commission would reveal that a complete denial of treaty-making capacity to international organizations is no more considered the current reflection of the doctrinal position. The opinions in this body by its rapporteurs and the debators tally with those of Parry and Rosenne, with the consensus emerging in

[5]Shabtai Rosenne, "United Nations Treaty Practice," *Recueil des Cours*, 1954-II, p. 408; *Yearbook of International Law Commission*, Vol. 1, 1962, p. 62, where he comments: "International personality had many facets and consequences, of which the treaty-making power was only one." The leading monograph on the subject of treaty-making capacity of international organizations is J.W. Schneider, *Treaty-Making Power of International Organizations*, Geneva, 1969. See also Guenter Weissberg, *The International Status of the United Nations*, New York, 1961, pp. 33-77.

[6]Clive Parry, "The Treaty-Making Power of the United Nations," *British Yearbook of International Law*, Vol. 26, 1949, p. 110. Schneider (*op. cit.*, pp. 129, 135) goes a step further when he asserts that "the treaty-making power is not based on international personality" at all and thinks that the "power is conferred upon organizations by customary international law."

[7]"International Legal Aspects of the Operations of the World Bank," *Recueil des Cours*, 1959-III, p. 338.

favour of the Broches formula. Attention, now, will be diverted to the ILC efforts of codifying the law of treaties.

Discussion in the International Law Commission on the Treaty-Making Powers of International Organizations

When the International Law Commission appointed Professor J.L. Brierly, as Rapporteur on the Law of Treaties he included specifically international organizations in his draft definition of a treaty: "A 'treaty' is an agreement recorded in writing between two or more States or international organizations which establishes a relation under international law between the parties thereto."[8] Commenting on the failure of the Harvard Draft to include international organizations in its definition of treaty, Professor Brierly pointed out that it was impossible to ignore this class of agreements or to regard their existence as an abnormal feature of international relations.[9] And he felt that the "difficulty of finding rules common to the treaties of States and to those of international organizations is morever, not insuperable."[10]

The Report was discussed by the International Law Commission during its sessions in 1950 and 1951. At its second session in 1950 the ILC made the following observation:

A majority of the Commission were also in favour of including in its study agreements to which international organizations are parties. There was general agreement that, while the treaty-making power of certain organizations is clear, the determination of the other organizations which possess capacity for making treaties would further need consideration.[11]

But in 1951 the Commission modified its stand. It adopted the suggestion put forward the previous year by Hudson, and supported by other members of the Commission, that it should leave aside, for the moment, the question of the capacity of inter-

---

[8]Brierly, *op. cit.*, p. 1.
[9]*Ibid.*, pp. 14-5.
[10]*Ibid.* p. 15.
[11]*Yearbook of ILC*, 1950, Vol. II, para 162.

national organizations to make treaties, that it should draft the articles with reference to States only.[12]

Professor Lauterpacht who succeeded Professor Brierly to the task of codifying the law of treaties, defined treaties in the following terms: "Article 1. Treaties are agreements between States, including organization of States, intended to create legal rights and obligations of the parties."[13]

In an obvious attempt to alleviate the fears that time was not yet ripe for the inclusion of international organizations within the jurisdiction of the Commission, Professor Lauterpacht adopted the formula, "including organization of States." He explained that the definition does not offend the traditional notions of subjects of international law. The formula, he maintained, would reaffirm that "States only — acting either individually or in association— are the normal subjects of international intercourse and of international law."[14] Referring to the treaty-making practice of the League, Professor Lauterpacht saw "no reason why ... the rules otherwise applicable to treaties should not apply to those concluded by or between international organizations created by and composed of States."[15] He expressed the wish that it would be "desirable to direct political and juristic effort to making available, in the interest of the progressive integration of international society on a functional basis, the experience of the law of treaties to the collective activities of States in their manifold manifestations."[16] Professor Lauterpacht appealed for the revision of the view adopted provisionally by the Commission during its discussions in 1950-51 that agreements by or between organizations of States did not fall within the province of the law of treaties formulated by the Commission.[17]

---

[12]*Ibid.*, 1951, Vol. I, p. 136. The position was reiterated in 1959. See *ibid.*, 1959, Vol. II, pp. 89 and 96.

[13]Hersch Lauterpacht, *First Report on the Law of Treaties*, UN Doc. A/CN. 4/63 of 24 March 1953, p. 4.

[14]*Ibid.*, p. 16.

[15]*Ibid.*, p. 22.

[16]*Ibid.*, pp. 22-3.

[17]*Ibid.*, p. 29.

In view of the fact that a bulk of treaties concluded in the post-war days are those by or between international organizations, and inasmuch as the format, the clauses concerning settlement of disputes, entry into force, approval by competent constitutional authorities, modification and denunciation of the agreement and the like, read like the ones concluded by the States the omission of such treaties would, in the opinion of Professor Lauterpacht, "render incomplete and deficient any codification of the law of treaties."[18] Moreover, these agreements do conform to the test laid down by Judge Read in his Opinion in the case concerning the status of South-West Africa, namely "a meeting of minds; and an intention to constitute a legal obligation."[19] Therefore, argued Professor Lauterpacht, "there seems to be no reason why, in the sphere of treaty-making power, States acting collectively should not be in the position to do what they can do individually."[20] The ILC did not discuss Professor Lauterpacht's report due to other preoccupations.

Sir Gerald Fitzmaurice attempted altogether to do away with the distinction between States and international organizations as far as treaty-making power is concerned. In his Report to the ILC he defined a treaty as:

an international agreement embodied in a single formal instrument (whatever its name, title or designation) made between entities both or all of which are subjects of international law possessed of international personality and treaty-making capacity, and intended to create rights and obligations, or to establish relationships, governed by international law.[21]

Fitzmaurice's definition of international organization, likewise, places emphasis on the personality concept of international organization. He defines international organization in the following manner: "The term 'international organization' means a

[18]*Ibid.*
[19]ICJ *Reports*, 1950, p. 170.
[20]Lauterpacht, *First Report, op. cit.*, p. 32.
[21]G.G. Fitzmaurice, *Report on the Law of Treaties*, UN Doc. A/CN. 4/101, p. 14.

collectivity of States established by treaty, with a constitution and common organs having a personality distinct from that of its member States and being a subject of international law with treaty-making capacity."[22]

The definition of treaty as well as the definition of an international organization itself reveal that Sir Gerald favoured firstly, international personality as the criterion for granting treaty-making power for any entity, whether a State or an international organization. Secondly, he was equally clear that the power should not be granted indiscriminately to all entities which possess such personality. They must, in addition, have treaty-making power, too. In other words, though international personality was a *sine qua non* for treaty-making power, the latter power did not necessarily flow from the broader concept. While Sir Gerald Fitzmaurice insisted on both international personality and treaty-making capacity,[23] Professor Hersch Lauterpacht suggested that the capacity to conclude treaties was both a corollary of international personality and a condition of the effective fulfilment of their functions on the part of international organizations.[24]

The Commission, nevertheless, felt that it would be fruitful to confine itself to treaties concluded by or between States and discussion on the treaty-making capacity of international organizations was again postponed.[25]

The ILC at its thirteenth session appointed Sir Humphery Waldock to succeed Sir Gerald, who retired from the Commission on his election as judge of the ICJ. Waldock in his first Report on the law of treaties[26] defined in Article 1:

(*a*) "International agreement" means an agreement intended

---

[22]*Ibid.*, p. 16.

[23]*Ibid.*, p. 14.

[24]Lauterpacht, *op. cit.*

[25]See *Yearbook of the International Law Commission*, 1956, Eighth Sess. 368th-37th Mtgs., also in 1959 the same course was adopted, see UN Doc. A/4169, 1959, p. 10.

[26]UN Doc. A/CN. 4/144 of 26 March 1962, *Yearbook of ILC*, 1962, Vol. 2, pp. 27-83. The definitions of "international agreement" and "party" were deleted by the Drafting Committee as being inappropriate in the context of Article 1, See *ibid.*, pp. 214, 239-40.

to be governed by international law and concluded between two or more States or other subjects of international law possessing international personality and having capacity to enter into treaties under the rules set out in article 3 below. . . .

(*c*) "Party" means a State or other subject of international law, possessing international personality and having capacity to enter into treaties under the rules set out in Article 3 below, which has executed acts by which it has definitely given its consent to be bound by a treaty in force; "presumptive party" means a State or other subject of international law which has qualified itself to be a "party" to a treaty which has not yet entered into force.

In his commentary on the article Sir Humphery, while affirming his belief that inclusion of international organizations in the scope of the Commission's work was "essential," proceeded to state: "But it is not enough that the party to the agreement should be a 'State' or that it should be a subject of international law; it must also possess 'international personality' and have 'capacity to enter into treaties'."[27]

The above qualifications excluded States, like for instance units in a federation, that did not possess treaty-making power and commercial and other agreements made by subjects of international law with private individuals or firms. Sir Humphery Waldock believed that treaty-making power was not necessarily a concomitant of international personality and that international organizations must have also the ability to conclude treaties. This distinction was more clearly brought out in Article 3 which dealt with the question of capacity.

(1) Capacity in international law (hereafter referred to as international capacity) to become a party to treaties is possessed by every independent State, whether a unitary State, a federation or other form of union of States, and by other subjects of international law invested with such capacity by treaty or by international custom. . . .

[27]*Yearbook of the ILC*, 1962, Vol. 2, p. 32.

(4) International capacity to become a party to treaties is also possessed by international organizations and agencies which have a separate legal personality under international law if, and to the extent that, such treaty-making capacity is expressly created, or necessarily implied in the instrument or instruments prescribing the constitution and functions of the organization or agency in question.[28]

Explaining the position under Article 1 Sir Humphery maintained that the phrase "other subjects of international law" was designed (*a*) to leave no doubt as to the right of entities such as the Holy See to be considered parties to international agreements, and (*b*) to admit the possibility of international organizations being parties to international agreements. The obvious case, stated Waldock, was the United Nations, whose capacity to be a party to treaties was expressly recognized in the Regulations adopted on 14 December 1946 by the General Assembly, concerning the Registration and Publication of Treaties and International Agreements and whose international personality and treaty-making capacity was affirmed by the International Court of Justce in the case of *Reparations for Injuries Suffered in the Service of the United Nations.*[29] He further affirmed that the number of international agreements concluded by international organizations in their own names, both with States and with each other, and registered as such with the Secretariat of the United Nations, was now very large, so that their inclusion in the general definition of "international agreements" for the purposes of the present articles was essential.[30]

Explaining the inclusion of international organizations in the report in the face of the Commission's earlier stand Professor Waldock said that one course, no doubt, might be to leave aside altogether the question of the treaties of international organizations until the whole of the Commission's work on the law of treaties, as it affected States, was complete and then to consider just how much

---

[28]*Ibid.,* pp. 35-6. (Italics added.)
[29]ICJ, *Report,* 1949, p. 179.
[30]A/CN. 4/144, pp. 16-7.

of it was applicable to organizations. But the conclusion, entry into force and registration of treaties, with which the present articles were concerned, was to a large extent a self-contained branch of the law of treaties and, unless it was unavoidable, it seemed better not to postpone all consideration of treaty-making by international organizations until some comparatively distant date, by which time the Commission would have dealt with many other matters not very closely related to this part of the law of treaties. The solution suggested was similar to that adopted by the Commission for the case of honorary consuls in its draft articles on consular intercourse and immunities, namely, a separate chapter specifying the extent to which the provisions of the draft articles apply to the treaties of organizations and formulating any particular rules peculiar to these treaties.[31]

Commenting on para 4 in Article 3 Professor Waldock said that it sought to state the general rule in regard to the treaty-making capacity of international organizations and agencies. The appropriate method of dealing with treaty-making by international organizations was to deal with it in a separate chapter, but it would be logical to regard treaty-making capacity as a general matter distinct from the procedure of treaty-making, and to include it in Chapter I. If that arrangement was accepted, then the appropriate place for the general rule concerning the treaty-making capacity of organizations was in the present article. As to the rule proposed in paragraph 4, Professor Waldock said, it was based upon principles analogous to those laid down by the ICJ in its *Reparations case*.[32]

The Drafting Committee on suggestions of members during the course of the 14th session redrafted paragraph 1 of Article 3 of Professor Waldock's *Report* in the following way: "Capacity to conclude treaties under international law is possessed by States and by other subjects of international law." This version was adopted by the Commission at its 666th meeting on 22 June 1962. Paragraph 4 was changed and adopted at the same meeting to read: "In the case of international organizations capacity to conclude

[31]A/CN. 4/144, pp. 11-2.
[32]Waldock, A/CN, 4/144, p. 32.

treaties depends on the constitution of the organization concerned.[33]

At the seventeenth session, again, the ILC debated the draft articles prepared by the Secretariat[34] on the basis of the deliberations in the previous sessions. Article I, 1(*a*), of this draft defined treaty as an "international agreement in written form . . . concluded between two or more States or other subjects of international law and governed by international law." Article 3, again, mentioned "other subjects of international law" in paragraph 1; and paragraph 3 laid down that "in the case of international organizations, capacity to conclude treaties depends on the constitution of the organization concerned."

The above formulae were adopted after a controversial session in the Commission in 1962. In the 673rd meeting De Luna had taken strong objection to the earlier wording of the article. The expression "subjects of international law possessing international personality" in Article 1, paragraph (*a*), was unacceptable to him because all subjects of international law possessed international personality. The two concepts were synonymous: personality expressed a relationship between an individual or collective entity and a given legal system. But, whereas every subject of international law possessed, by definition, legal capacity, every subject of international law did not possess capacity to act through organs of its own or, at any rate, not to an unlimited extent. *Jus contrahendi* was a sub-species of capacity to act. Rebels recognized as belligerents possessed a limited *jus contrahendi*; and Trust Territories, for example, did not possess capacity to conclude treaties. De Luna accordingly proposed the deletion of the words "possessing international personality and."[35]

El-Erian (UAR), on the other hand, was not sure that a subject of international law necessarily possessed international personality.

The position of the individual in international law, for example, had been changed by the inclusion of the provisions on fundamental human rights in the United Nations Charter and by the

[33]*Ibid.*, pp. 240-3.
[34]A/CN. 4/L. 107, 7 January 1965.
[35]*Yearbook of the ILC*, 1962, Vol. 1, p. 49.

Convention on Genocide. The individual might be recognized as a subject of international law, but he did not possess international personality, for all purposes, as appeared from the International Court of Justices' exposition of the concept of limited international personality in the case of Reparation for Injuries suffered in the Service of the United Nations.[36]

Briggs proposed in the 666th Meeting (22 June 1962) that paragraphs 2, 3 and 4 of Article 3 be deleted. On para 4 his objection was that the term "international organization" was unduly vague.[37] Tunkin supported the idea of deletion on the ground that the statement that treaty-making capacity of an international organization depended solely on the constitution of an organization, was inaccurate.[38] Rosenne suggested the deletion of the whole article.[39] Sir Humphery, on the other hand, thought that paragraph 4 had its usefulness because it dealt with the limitations imposed upon the treaty-making capacity of an international organization by its constitution. "The treaty-making capacity of an organization," he pointed out, "was nearly always limited to its object and purpose; the organization was not entitled to enter into any kind of treaty.[40] Liang, Secretary to the Commission, "was doubtful whether the capacity of international organization to make treaties could be based on international custom instead of on express provisions in the constitutions of those organizations, which were international treaties in themselves, or on implied powers granted in those constitutions."[41] The Chariman, thereupon put the proposal for deletion of para 4 to vote, which was rejected by 8 votes to 8, with 2 abstentions. It was retained on separate voting by 9 votes to 8 with 2 abstentions.[42]

Jimenez de Arechaga (Uruguay) said that the discussion had shown conclusively that the law concerning international legal persons was not ripe for codification.[43] The draft articles drawn up during the 14th and 15th session also attracted extensive criticism

---

[36]*Ibid.*, p. 53.
[37]*Ibid.*, p. 241. [38]*Ibid.*, p. 243.
[39]*Ibid.* [40]*Ibid.*, p. 242. [41]*Ibid.*, p. 63. [42]*Ibid.*, p. 243.
[43]*Ibid.*, p. 65.

from member governments when they were sent for comments.[44] Austria while agreeing to the inclusion of the phrase "other subjects of international law" as being "fully in accord with the existing international law" went on to point out that para 3 of this article, however, contained a restriction with respect to international organizations; namely, "in the case of international organizations, capacity to conclude treaties depends on the constitution of the organization concerned." In the view of Austria, that restriction did not appear absolutely necessary. Rather, the starting point might well be that capacity to conclude treaties must be an inherent right of any international organization, if it was at the same time a subject of international law. "Indeed, capacity to conclude treaties even appears to be the essential criterion of the status of a subject of international law. An international organization lacking the capacity to conclude treaties would not be a subject of international law."[45]

Austria pointed out further by reference to practice, that absence of specific authority in constituent instruments has not inhibited the organizations from concluding treaties and that specific provisions have only stipulated the limit or the *extent of freedom* to conclude treaties: "Constitutional restrictions do not, however, affect in principle the capacity to conclude treaties as such."[46]

Japan suggested the deletion of paras 2 and 3 of Article 3 since they do not refer to the other element of international capacity to conclude international agreements—the requirement of recognition of such constitutional capacity by the other contracting party or parties.[47]

Finland stated that since the present articles deal only with States the phrase "or other subjects" could be deleted from sub-para (*a*) of Article 1. It suggested that it might be mentioned in the commentaries on certain articles that these articles should *ex analogia* be applied to, for example, the Holy See and certain inter-

---

[44]See the compilation of comments by governments in A/CN. 4/175, 22 February, 1969.

[45]*Yearbook of ILC*, 1962, Vol. 1, p. 17.

[46]*Ibid.*

[47]*Ibid.*

national organizations, and that a new draft agreement regarding this question could be worked out later.[48]

According to the USA the reference in paragraph 1 of Article 3 to other subjects of international law was so general that it might be of little value. On the other hand, to limit its scope to international organizations, the Holy See, and cases such as an insurgent community was too limiting: "Colonies and similar entities given some measures of authority in foreign relations, especially when approaching statehood, should not have to be in a state of insurgency to conclude a valid international agreement."[49]

As for paragraph 3 of Article 3, in view of the Commissions commentary and the ICJ dicta that the treaty-making capacity of an international organization did not depend exclusively on the terms of the constituent instrument but also on the decisions and rules of its competent organs, etc., the US Government suggested the word "authority" in the place of "constitution." It further pointed out that it would be desirable to be more specific as to what "international organizations" were being referred to.[50]

Similarly, in the Sixth Committee the delegate of Ecuador maintained that it would be desirable to define what entities, besides States, were regarded as subjects of international law.[51]

The delegate of Colombia expressed concern about the scope of the words "other subjects of international law" in paragraph 1 (*a*) of Article 1. He said that the attribution of *jus contrahendi* to insurgents might lead to serious conflicts. There was no comment on international organizations.[52] The Brazilian delegate, likewise, averred to the "copious controversy" about the established limitations of the *jus contrahendi* and the repercussions of problems of constitutional law relating, for example, to the capacity of belligerents.[53]

The decision, therefore, was taken at the 18th session that any reference to the capacity of international organizations would involve

[48]*Ibid.*, pp. 41-2.
[49]*Ibid.*, pp. 158-9.
[50]*Ibid.*, pp. 159-60.
[51]*Ibid.*, p. 201.
[52]*Ibid.*, pp. 196-7.
[53]*Ibid.*, p. 200.

deeper probings of the complex problems peculiar to international organizations.   It was decided to defer the issue for a future date.

During the entire discussion in the International Law Commission, however, the treaty-making power of international organizations was questioned only once, on the ground that they cannot be parties in disputes before the ICJ. It was pointed out in reply that agreements to which international organizations are parties frequently provide for arbitration; and also that means had been found to overcome the inability of international organizations to appear before the Court.   Reference was made by way of example to Section 30 of the General Convention on Privileges and Immunities of the UN.   This section provides that if a difference arises between the United Nations and a member, a request shall be made to the ICJ for an advisory opinion, and that the parties shall accept the Opinion as decisive.[54]

All the ILC Rapporteurs and the debators were agreed on the necessity of conceding treaty-making power to an international organization if it was necessary for the fulfilment of its functions and for the accomplishment of its purposes. Therefore, the assertion that unlimited powers of treaty-making could not be granted to an organization simply because it possessed juridical personality was not in conflict with the stand that objective international personality of necessity accorded treaty-making power to an international organization. Because, though juridical personality of an international organization was not coterminous, in kind and extent, with that of States it was difficult to visualize an intergovernmental organization possessing objective international personality having no need to utilize the instrument of treaty.

The treaty-making power of an international organization therefore is a corollary of its objects and purposes. If the effectuation of its objects and functions dictates a recourse to this technique, it should be deemed to have that capacity. Parry's dictum, that the "treaty-making power is to be deduced ... not from the mere fact of its 'personality,' but from evidence pointing to its having that sort of personality which involves capacity to make treaties,"[55]

[54]UN Doc. A/CN. 4/SR. 50, pp. 11, 22.
[55]Parry, *op. cit.*, p. 110.

looses much of its bite if it is remembered that objective personality itself, even as the treaty-making capacity, is an instrumentality for the effective fulfilment of its purposes and objects. If the objectives demand the utilization of this technique, even if no specific provision exists granting such power, the organization must be deemed to have the treaty-making capacity.

Having arrived at this conclusion about the doctrinal position of treaty-making power of international organizations in the absence of express authority in their constituent documents, it will now be examined how international organizations have used this technique in the course of practice.

TREATY-MAKING PRACTICE OF INTERNATIONAL ORGANIZATIONS

One of the most silent spectacles in the development of the law of international organization is the way these organizations have been asserting and exercising their treaty-making authority even in the absence of express powers to do so—an authority which hitherto had been considered the reserved domain of sovereign States. It needs no marshalling of statistics to prove the statement. A glance at the *UN Treaty Series* would show that international organizations have been having recourse to treaty-making for various kinds of international contracts. If anything, one is only impressed by the prolixity of treaties entered into by one or more international organizations with one or more States or international organizations.[56] They have entered into a plethora of national and inter-

---

[56]Shabtai Rosenne (*op. cit.*, pp. 299-300) classifies these treaties into 9 groups: (1) agreements between the UN, or the UN with one or more of the Specialized Agencies, and an individual State; (2) the relationship agreements between the UN and a Specialized Agency; (3) agreements between the UN and an inter-government organization other than a Specialized Agency; (4) agreements between one or more Specialized Agency and an individual State; (5) agreements between two Specialized Agencies; (6) agreements between a Specialized Agncy and an inter-governmental organization which is not a Specialized Agency; (7) conventions concluded, under the auspices of the UN, by two or more individual States; (8) agreements between a subsidiary organ of the UN and an individual State; and (9) agreements between a subsidiary organ of the UN and a Specialized Agency. The documents coming within 2, 3, 5, 6, and 9 are termed "inter-organizational" agreements.

national, public and private, bilateral and multilateral contracts—ranging from contracts placed with firms of printers to agreements with states to provide contingents to its police forces as in Suez, the Congo, and Cyprus.

Pre-World War Practice

Though the League was not empowered *expressis verbis* to conclude treaties, it did so a number of times. In 1922, for example, a "League loan" was transacted with Austria wherein the League accepted "the duties and liabilities which these Protocols involved."[57] On 4 August 1924 the Reparations Commission concluded a comprehensive agreement with Germany.[58] Again on 28 June 1932 an agreeement, registered with League of Nations, was concluded between Yugoslavia, Romania, and the International Commission of the Danube concerning the setting up of special services at the Iron Gates.[59]

The League of Nations treaty record during 1919 to 1946 shows over 700 multipartite instruments of which the preponderant majority were entered into by a varying number of States. During approximately the same period 54,834 international instruments were registered with the League and were published in 205 volumes.[60] The Conventions concluded under the auspices of the League cover wide field of subjects ranging from international law to arbitration, from security to economic and financial matters, from bones, hides skins to whaling and narcotics.[61] The International Labour Organization during the same period (1919-1946) adopted eighty international labour conventions and the same number of recommendations.[62]

[57]Sir John Fischer Williams, "The Status of the League of Nations in International Law," *International Law Association*, 34th Report, 1926, pp. 675, 688; reprinted in *Chapters on Current International Law and the League of Nations*, London, 1929, p. 477. This and subsequent citations refer to the *Report*.
[58]League of Nations, *Treaty Series*, Vol. 41, p. 432.
[59]*Ibid.*, Vol. 140, p. 191.
[60]See "Historical Survey of Development of International Law and its Codification by International Conferences," a UN Secretariat Memorandum, UN Doc. A/AC. 10/5, p. 2.
[61]*Ibid.*, pp. 32-40.
[62]*Ibid.*, p. 45.

The practice was so common that legal authorities who discussed the juridical personality of the League mentioned the organization's treaty-making practice as proof of its independent personality and none controverted this power.[63] Nevertheless in the post-World War II period provisions began to be specifically inserted in the constituent instruments of international organizations granting express powers to contract.

Post-World War Practice

Many of the international organizations that were established in the post-World War period have a standard provision to the following effect, with suitable variations to fit the special character and purpose of the organization: "The organization shall possess full juridical personality, and, in particular, the capacity (*i*) to contract; (*ii*) to acquire and dispose of immovable and movable property; (*iii*) to institute legal proceedings."[64] Some organizations have a provision which accords "in the territory of each member such legal capacity, privileges and immunities as are necessary for the exercise of its functions and the accomplishment of its purposes."[65] Quite a few Specialized Agencies like the United Nations Educational, Scientific, and Cultural Organization (UNESCO) link their legal status to that of the UN. And a few organizations, though Specialized Agencies, do not contain any special provision as to their legal status or treaty-making capacities.[66] But the Convention on Privileges and Immunities for the Specialized Agencies, which has

[63]See for a discussion of the international personality of the League of Nations, Part I of the present study.

[64]See for example Article 7, paragraph 2 of Articles of Agreement of International Bank for Reconstruction and Development; Article 9, Section 2, of the Articles of Agreement of International Monetary Fund; Article 39 of the Consitution of ILO.

[65]Articles 16, 51, 47, 66, 27(*a*), and 103 of the constitutional documents of the Food and Agriculture Organization, International Maritime Consultative Organization, International Civil Aviation Organization, World Health Organization, World Meteorological Organization, and the Organization of American States, respectively.

[66]For example, the Bank for International Settlements, the International Telecommunication Union, and the Universal Postal Union.

an express provision regarding juridical personality, might be said to fill this lacuna.

Defence organizations like the North Atlantic Treaty Organization (NATO), South East Asia Treaty Organization (SEATO), and the Warsaw Pact are silent on the matter. The League of Arab States though providing for privileges and immunities and for the inviolability of the premises of the organization is also silent on the question of juridical personality and on the issue of treaty-making capacity.

No generalizations region-wise or function-wise can be made from the pattern of provisions concerning the juridical personality or the treaty-making capacity of the above organizations. But one can affirm that all the above-named organizations have important rights and duties to perform and hence must be deemed to possess juridical personality.

It must have been noticed in the case of those provisions which grant full juridical personality that the capacity to contract is mentioned only by way of example. The phrase "in the territory of each member" in the second category and the word "contract" in the first have been considered to refer to the municipal legal capacity of the organization concerned. In the present submission, however, such a limiting construction cannot be placed on the provision because even if the particular capacities listed out refer only to the municipal legal capacity the concept of juridical personality cannot be shrunk so as to accommodate only those powers which are enumerated by way of example.

The difficulty will not hold any spectres in the case of those constitutional documents which grant such legal capacity as might be necessary for the exercise of its functions and the accomplishment of its purposes. Because, in this case the treaty-making capacity must be conceded if it is necessary for the exercise of the organization's functions and if it helps in the accomplishment of its purposes.

The conclusion that can be drawn from the above survey of practice among international organizations (other than the UN) is that they have not felt inhibited by the absence of constitutional authority in entering into treaties before the World War where the use of treaty technique had facilitated their effective functioning. In the post-World War period though organizations have generally inserted into their constituent documents provisions recognizing expressly their juridical personality and in particular their capacity to enter into contracts (which cannot be given a restrictive interpretation of being municipal contracts alone) absence of a specific provision authorizing such capacity is not necessarily an unknown practice. But even such organizations whose constitutional documents do not contain express authority have used the treaty-making power very freely. The shining example, of course, is the the United Nations, an examination of whose practice will be the purpose of the ensuing pages.

THE UNITED NATIONS TREATY-MAKING PRACTICE

The Charter of the UN does not provide in so many words that the Organization shall have treaty-making capacity. But that power can be deduced from a number of express provisions and implied powers and functions of the Charter.

Express Provisions

Lex Specialis of Article 43. The UN or one of its principal organs is empowered directly or indirectly to conclude agreements of an international character. Thus Article 43 of the Charter provides:

(1) All members of the United Nations, in order to contribute to the maintenance of international peace and security, undertake to make available to the Security Council, on its call and in accordance with a special agreement or agreements, armed forces, assistance and facilities, including rights of passage, necessary for the purpose of maintaining international peace and security.

(2) Such agreement or agreements shall govern the numbers and types of forces, their degree of readiness and general location, and the nature of the facilities and assistance to be provided.

(3) The agreement or agreements shall be negotiated as soon as possible on the initiative of the Security Council. They shall be concluded between the Security Council and members or between the Security Council and groups of members and

shall be subject to ratification by the signatory States in accordance with their respective constitutional processes.

It is true no such special agreements have been concluded. It is even suggested that no such agreements were ever intended to be concluded.[67] Sometimes it has also been suggested that member States are under no obligation to enter into these agreements, even as no member which has not concluded such agreement is under an obligation to take military action.[68] It has even been denied that the Security Council enters into these agreements on authority delegated by the Organization, but that it acts on behalf of the member States themselves.[69]

All this is beside the point in the present context. For, it is one thing to say that the Organization has no *power* to compel contributions to its armed strength, or that the members have no *obligation* to do so, and it is another thing to deny the capacity of the Organization to conclude such treaties *qua* organization.

Whatever the intention of the framers of the Charter the letter of the law clearly authorizes the Security Council to *call on* members to contribute to the maintenance of international peace and security, and in pursuance thereof to conclude agreements governing "the number and type of forces, their degree of readiness and general location," etc. The language, to wit, *shall*, used repeatedly in paragraph 3 of the article indicates strongly that the Organization imposes a definite duty on members to negotiate "as soon as possible" the said agreements "on the initiative of the Security Council."

Interrelationship Agreements. The next provisions in the Charter pointing to the treaty-making capacity of the UN are under Articles 57 and 63. Paragraph 1 of Article 63 of the Charter provides: "The Economic and Social Council may enter into agreements with any of the agencies referred to in Article 57," i.e. the various Specialized Agencies established by intergovernmental agreement, and having wide responsibilities, as defined in their basic instru-

---

[67]Robert W. Tucker, "The Interpretation of War under Present International Law," *International Law Quarterly*, Vol. 4, 1951, p. 27.

[68]Parry, *op. cit.*, pp. 119-21.

[69]*Ibid.*, p. 119.

ments, in economic, social, cultural, educational, health and related fields "defining the terms on which the agency concerned shall be brought into relationship with the United Nations. Such agreements shall be subject to approval by the General Assembly."

The Committee that framed the article was explicit that the Economic and Social Council was free to bring any intergovernmental agency besides Specialized Agencies, into relationship with the United Nations. The phrase "bringing into relationship" accords no unlimited authority to the Economic and Social Council, as paragraph 1 of Article 63 stipulates in the last sentence that all such agreements shall be subject to the approval of the General Assembly.

No sooner was the UN installed than a Committee on Negotiations with Intergovernmental Agencies was established which at once started negotiations with the Food and Agriculture Organization (FAO), the International Labour Organization (ILO), the International Monetary Fund (IMF), the International Bank for Reconstruction and Development (IBRD), and the United Nations Educational, Scientific, and Cultural Organization (UNESCO). The Committee successfully negotiated agreements, in consultation with the Secretariat, with ILO, UNESCO, and FAO, and submitted the draft agreements for approval of the General Assembly during the second session.[70]

Meanwhile the Secretary-General on the initiative of the Economic and Social Council[71] proceeded to contact the ITU and UPU for the purpose of bringing them into relationship with the UN. The Economic and Social Council also asked the Secretary-General to move the WHO in this connection.[72] This way the Negotiating Committee and the Secretary-General wove a web of interrelationship agreements with every intergovernmental organization of importance by the end of 1950.

Broadly, the agreements contain standard clauses with a few variations to suit the special stature and needs of the organizations concerned. The agreements provide that the UN acknowledges

[70]Economic and Social Council Resolution 2/4.
[71]*Ibid.*, Resolution 2/7.
[72]*Ibid.*, Resolution 14 (III).

its treaty partner as possessing the status and competence of a Specialized Agency. They invariably provide for reciprocal representation of the official cadre and emphasize the desirability of a "single unified international civil service." Provision is also made for concluding arrangements for the registration and deposit of official documents. The IMF, the IBRD, the Universal Postal Union, and the International Telecommunication Union have all varied and simpler formulae in tune with their technical nature.

The treaties are subject to revision by mutual agreement. But, as Sir Ramaswami Mudaliar pointed out in the Economic and Social Council on 21 June 1946, "no unilateral decision on the part of either the Council or the General Assembly or on the part of the Organizations concerned" may alter them.[73]

Wilfred Jenks describes these treaties as "essentially treaties of amity and goodwill"[74] inasmuch as they provide for closer co-operation and consultation in matters of common concern. Parry casts doubt on the legal nature of these agreements, though he admits that they "establish a regime."[75] Weissberg has effectively challenged Parry's attitude about the legal nature of interrelationship agreements.[76] Professor Lauterpacht deals with this delicate question in his *Report on the Law of Treaties* and suggests that the provision for closer co-operation "does not deprive them of the character of treaties."[77] The agreements might justly be treated, in Rosenne's phrase, as "patterns of international agreement" which the UN employs.[78]

The Trusteeship Agreements. Chapter XII of the UN Charter relating to the trusteeship system is a further proof indicative of the Organization's capacity to enter into treaties with sovereign States. Article 77, paragraph 1, of the Charter provides that the trusteeship system comprises of three categories of territories, namely,

---

[73]Economic and Social Council, Official Records, First Year, Second Session, 14th Mtg., p. 113.

[74]Wilfred C. Jenks, "Some Constitutional Problems of International Organizations," *British Yearbook of International Law*, Vol. 22, 1945, p. 68.

[75]Parry, *op. cit.*, p. 139.

[76]Weissberg, *op. cit.*, pp. 49–50.

[77]Lauterpacht, *op.*, *cit.*, p. 30.

[78]Rosenne, *op. cit.*, p. 299.

mandated territories, territories to be detached from enemy States and territories voluntarily placed under the system. Article 79 stipulates that the terms of trusteeship for each territory to be placed under the system "shall be agreed upon by the States directly concerned."

Again, by virtue of paragraph 1 of Article 80, the rights existing in the trust territories are upheld, except "as may be agreed upon in individual trusteeship agreements." Article 81 provides for the selection of the administering authority which "may be one or more States *or the Organization itself.*"[79]

Article 83, paragraph 1, empowers the Security Council to exercise all "functions of the United Nations relating to the strategic areas, including the approval of the terms of the trusteeship agreements and of their alteration and amendment." Article 85, paragraph 1, empowers the General Assembly with similar powers in relation to non-strategic areas.

It is interesting to speculate if the UN is a party at all to the trusteeship agreements; for, by proving so its treaty-making power can be vindicated. Except for an undefined formula embodied in Article 79 (namely, "States directly concerned") none of these provisions indicate as to what the nature of these agreements is or as between whom these treaties are to be concluded.

The *travaux preparatoires* throw little light on the matter. First, the Committee concerned had no basic draft at its disposal and therefore had to commence its work with a number of individual proposals submitted by national delegations. Second, the delegates came out with altogether unrelated concepts of the system envisaged. The US, French, and Chinese proposals viewed the system where the Council represented by the administering States among others, will have supervisory functions. The UK visualized a system which would create the relation of principal and agent between the UN and the individual "advanced nation," which was to be responsible for the "tutelage" of the dependent peoples "on behalf of the United Nations."[80] The USSR wanted an arrangement under

---

[79]Italics added.
[80]*UNCIO* Docs. Vol. 3, pp. 604-8, 615-9.

which "every member of the United Nations would be responsible for the system to be established."[81]

In the midst of competing claims of various degrees of control none seemed to have brooked over the desirability to clarify as to who should be the parties and what the nature of agreement was to be.

A vague and imprecise guideline to this enquiry could be discerned in the exchange of views between the American and Chinese representatives. The Chinese delegate enquired "whether it was contemplated that the trusteeship arrangements provided for in paragraph 4 ... would be made between the States concerned and the Organization, or merely between the States concerned." In answer, it was stated by the American delegate: "The State or States concerned would reach an agreement among themselves and would present this agreement to the Organization. If the Organization would not approve such an arrangement with respect to a particular territory, then there would be no trusteeship regime over that territory."[82] Again, the query as to whether both the States and the UN would be parties to the agreement was met with the reply that "finally this would be so."[83]

Publicists like Professor Kelsen, however, confidently assert that the trusteeship agreements are treaties which are "concluded by the United Nations on the one hand, and the States competent to dispose of these territories on the other hand."[84] Chariman Toussaint believes that "there are two agreements one between the 'States' directly concerned and the other between the United Nations and, presumably, the future administering authority." She holds that the former undertakes to conclude an agreement, and this agreement forms the contents of a second agreement between the administering authority and the General Assembly (or Security Council).[85]

---

[81]*Ibid.*, p. 448.

[82]UN Doc. A/C. 4/36, 1946, pp. 5-6.

[83]*Ibid.*, p. 6.

[84]Hans Kelsen, *The Law of the United Nations*, London, 1950, p. 332.

[85]Chariman Toussaint, *The Trusteeship System of the United Nations*, New York, 1956, p. 78.

Oscar Schachter has challenged this view as a "questionable interpretation."[86] He maintains that the UN is not a party to the trusteeship agreements.[87] Clive Party[88] and Brierly[89] have deplored the obscurity of the question as to who the parties are. On the basis of latest research on the UN practice it has, however, been conclusively established by Guenter Weissberg that whether or not it was intended to be so the UN in practice has been functioning as a party to the agreements.[90]

The Institutional Treaties. It needs no assertion that the new subjects of international law enjoy extensive prerogatives in the field of privileges and immunities comparable only to that of States. It is intended here to show that the organizations have a capacity to conclude treaties relating to such prerogatives. The investigation therefore will mainly be focussed on the question whether or not the organization, which concludes such convention, is a party to that convention.

Most of the international organizations have a provision in their constituent instrument similar to that of Article 105 of the UN Charter, which lays down that the Organization and its officials shall enjoy in the territory of member States privileges and immunities akin to those applicable to diplomatic envoys. The Preparatory Commission which drew up a draft convention, envisaged in paragraph 3 of Article 105, was emphatic that the article is self-executory and that member States are obliged to accord the required prerogatives even in the asbence of treaties and conventions.[91]

However, it was thought advisable to spell out the privileges and immunities in detail in a General Convention. Accordingly, a General Convention was adopted by the General Assembly on 13 February 1946 which apart from containing detailed provisions in

[86]Oscar Schachter, "The Development of International Law through the Legal Opinions of the United Nations Secretariat," *British Yearbook of International Law*, Vol. 25, 1948, p. 130.

[87]*Ibid.*, p. 131.

[88]Clive Parry, "The Legal Nature of the Trusteeship Agreements," *British Yearbook of International Law*, Vol. 27, 1950, p. 164.

[89]Brierly, *op. cit.*, p. 11.

[90]Weissberg, *The International Status of the United Nations*, New York, 1961, pp. 53-6.

[91]Preparatory Commission, *Report*, p. 60.

this regard also dealt with the legal capacity of the Organization. Member States were invited to accede to this Convention by depositing an instrument of accession with the Secretary-General.[92]

Likewise, the General Assembly adopted a second Convention on the Privileges and Immunities of the Specialized Agencies on 21 November 1947, and the relevant Resolution stated that the Convention was "submitted to the specialized agencies for acceptance and to every member of the United Nations and to every other State member of one or more of the specialized agencies for accession."[93]

The above Conventions provide for accession, ratification by the constitutional authorities, entry into force, modification and denunciation of the agreement, registration and settlement of disputes — in fine, all the features peculiar to the treaties. There cannot be any question as to their legal nature and form as treaties.

The only question is, can the UN and the Specialized Agencies be considered as parties to those Conventions? For, if it can be shown that they are, it automatically follows that the organizations have the capacity to enter into treaties of this type.

Opinion among legal authorities varies on this point. Rosenne, for instance, regards the General Convention "both as a treaty concluded under the auspices of the United Nations, and as one to which the United Nations is party," while the one on Specialized Agencies in his view "is to be regarded solely as a treaty concluded under the auspices of the United Nations."[94] For Parry, however, the General Convention is an instrument exhibiting some marked peculiarities, "for, not only is it assigned but it contains discrepancies between the general text and the final article and also it reaches beyond the confines of Article 105 when it deals with the 'juridical personality' of the Organization."[95]

Nonetheless, it has been held by the ICJ that the UN is a party to the Convention. The Court declared that the instrument "creates rights and duties between each of the signatories and the Organi-

---

[92]UN General Assembly, Resolution 22A (I) sec. 32.
[93]*Ibid.*, Resolution 179 (II).
[94]Rosenne, *op. cit.*, p. 322.
[95]Parry, *op. cit.*, p. 143.

zation," and found it "difficult to see how such a Convention could operate except upon the international plane and as between parties possessing international personality."[96]

The rationale applies with greater force to headquarters agreements concluded between international organizations and the host States.

Other Treaties. There are several other express provisions in the Charter which can be construed as enabling the UN to initiate and adopt conventions of international character either under its auspices or as a party to the same. Thus Article 62, paragraph 3, empowers the Economic and Social Council to prepare draft conventions for submission to the General Assembly with respect to matters falling within its competence. The General Assembly can initiate studies and make recommendations for the purpose of promoting progressive development of international law, and its codification [Article 13, paragraph 1(a)]. Under Article 59 again, the UN is empowered to "initiate negotiations among the States concerned for the creation of any new specialized agencies required" for the accomplishment of the broad social and economic aims of Chapter IX of the Charter.

THE GROWTH OF IMPLIED TREATY-MAKING POWERS
OF THE UN IN PRACTICE

As regards the implied powers to conclude treaties the UN has developed its authority by a bold display of imagination in circumstances of necessity. The succession treaties and other technical assistance agreements fall in this category.

The Succession Treaties

Legally the UN is not a successor to the League of Nations although it was designed to perform similar functions. However, the question of the transfer of assets and of functions between the two organizations could not be avoided.

The League of Nations, issued in 1944 and in 1945 three valuable publications as to its functions and activities with a view to their

[96] ICJ, *Reports*, 1949, p. 179. See also Carroz and Probst, *Personalite Juridiques Internationale et capacite de Conclure des Traites de l' O.N.U. et des Institution Specialisees*, Paris, 1953, pp. 72-3; Weissberg, *op. cit.*, p. 63.

transfer to a successor organization.[97] They posed the problem of succession in three aspects: succession to its tangible assets; continuance of its technical services; and succession to such of its functions as derived from treaties.

The League of Nations Committee of the Executive Committee of the Preparatory Commission which was seized of the matter proceeded with extreme caution. It drew a distinction between the political and other functions and assets of the League. The Committee recommended the General Assembly to reject the former and accept the latter subject to the "exceptions and qualifications" proposed in the Report.[98] And when the Soviet Union repudiated the Report on the ground that it involved "en bloc" transfer, and that it made the UN appear as the legal successor to the League, a deadlock arose.

A fresh beginning was, however, made by the Preparatory Commission. This time a common plan was drawn up with the help of the Economic and Social Council and the League of Nations Supervisory Commission. The common plan did envisage the transfer of both the assets and services and non-political functions. But, to assuage Soviet fears, the UN succession was termed a "taking up or assuming" of the functions of the League instead of a "taking over" of these activities.[99]

For the purpose of the present study the list of functions thus taken up or assumed from the League by the UN is not so much important as the form in which the transfer was affected.

The General Assembly, while approving the common plan and the Preparatory Commission Report, authorized the Secretary-General, with the help of a small negotiating committee, to carry out the succession effectively. A chain of treaties ensued as a result of

[97] *Powers and Duties attributed to the League of Nations by International Treaties* (c. 3, M. 3, 1944, III); *List of Conventions with Indications of the Relevant Articles conferring Powers on the Organs of the League* (c. 1100, M. 100, 1945, VI); and *The Committees of the League of Nations: Classified Lists and Essential Facts* (c. 99, M. 99, 1945, II 2).

[98] Preparatory Commission, *Report*, pp. 108-14.

[99] McKinnon Wood, "The Dissolution of the League of Nations," *British Yearbook of International Law*, Vol. 23, 1946, p. 319.

negotiations between representatives of the Secretary-General of the UN and those of the League.

The first such treaty signed on 19 July 1946 purported to determine the details of the transfer of assets.[100] On 1 August 1946 a second protocol was signed transferring certain services to the UN.[101] Four more protocols were signed in 1947 involving the transfer of custody of the International Press House Fund, the transfer of the Library Endowment Fund, the transfer of administration of the Leon Bernard Fund and that of the Darling Foundation.[102]

As regards non-political functions of the League succession took place through amendment, by agreement between all or most of the contracting parties thereto, of the various instruments by which they were originally created. Important of these were the protocols on various international agreements on narcotics; the Convention for the suppression of traffic in women and children; on obscene publications; and the international convention relating to economic statistics. These protocols replaced the UN in the place of the League.

Other Treaties of a Technical and Humanitarian Character

A number of treaties dealing with technical and humanitarian character concluded by the UN and the United Nations International Childrens' Emergency Fund (UNICEF), are another group of agreements for which no specific approval is to be found in the provisions of the Charter or the UNICEF constitution.

Following the General Assembly's approval during the third session a programme of technical assistance for economic development was instituted. In pursuance of this programme a number of multilateral and bilateral agreements have been concluded. Of the multilateral type the one concluded by the UK as the Administering Power of the Territories of Cyrenecica and Tripolitania, on the one hand, and the UN, FAO, ICAO, ILO, UNESCO, and WHO,

---

[100] *UN Treaty Series*, Vol. 1, p. 109.
[101] *Ibid.*, p. 135.
[102] *Ibid.*, Vol. 4, pp. 443, 449; Vol. 5, pp. 389, 395.

on the other, may be mentioned. The document provides for a host of technical assistance facilities.[103]

In the bilateral category fall, for instance, the agreement between the UN and Thailand.[104] UNICEF, likewise has been extensively utilizing the international agreement for various patterns of technical and humanitarian assistance.

The above agreements apart from providing for the degree and quantum of technical assistace, also contain a number of general clauses, stipulating the time and manner in which they come into force, the modes of modification, termination and inter-pretation, and some authorize the Secretary-General to register the documents.

The question then arises as to whether these can be considered as treaties at all and, if so, whether the organizations were em-powered to conclude such treaties, without express authority? Though essentially administrative in nature and though they with reason contain some "unorthodox provisions," the legal *imprimatur* cannot be denied to them.[105]

REPOSITORY OF THE TREATY-MAKING POWER
IN AN INTERNATIONAL ORGANIZATION

Since no organ or individual represents any position comparable to that of a Head of the State in an international organization, the question assumes added importance. Practice is no certain guide since instruments have sometimes been signed by the Secretary-General, sometimes by officials of lower rank and quite often signature has altogether been discarded.[106]

The question has received no scanty attention among legal autho-rities but no two writers agree as to who wields this power. Professor Brierly, for example, laid down in his *Report* to the ILC: "In the absence of provision in its constitution to the contrary, the

---

[103]*Ibid.*, Vol. 76, p. 120.

[104]*Ibid.*, Vol. 90, p. 45.

[105]Lauterpacht, *Second Report on the Law of Treaties*, UN Doc. A/CN. 4/87 of 8 July 1954, Rosenne. *op. cit.*, p. 296; Weissberg, *op. cit.*, p. 61.

[106]See Rosenne, *op. cit.*, pp. 411-3, for the deduction, after an extensive survey of the treaty-making practice of the UN, that signatures have in some cases been omitted.

capacity of an international organization to make treaties is deemed to reside in its *plenary organ*."[107]

In his comment on the provision Professor Brierly pointed out that since an international organization has no personal Head in the same sense that a State may have, and since no organ within the organization has a marked supremacy over the other[108] a general rule might be laid down to the effect that "if its constitution neither expressly nor impliedly provides for the case, the capacity of an organization to make treaties resides in its plenary organ, wherein are represented the totality of States whoses overeignty is the original source of all power of the organization.[109]

Professor Lauterpacht did not deal with this issue in his two Reports. Fitzmaurice, on the other hand, wanted to entrust the power to negotiate and conclude treaties, in the absence of express provision in the constituent instrument, to the Secretary-General of the Organization.[110] The reason is expressed as follows: "Treaty-making and all other acts connected with treaties are, *on the international plane*, executive acts, and the function of the executive authority."[111]

Rosenne finds no organ or individual who is in a position equivalent to that of the Head of State, and dismisses the issue by the following statement: "The authority of any organ or official of an international organization is prescribed by the constituent texts and the general principles of international law operative in regard to the interpretation of those texts."[112]

But the difficulty arises precisely because no specific provision exists in the constituent texts and there are no general principles in international law covering the matter.

---

[107]Brierly, *Report, op. cit.,* p. 1. (Italics added.)

[108]The power of the Council and the Assembly in the League was co-ordinate and in the case of the UN, though the General Assembly has some ascendency over the Economic and Social Council (Article 63) and the Trusteeship Council in all cases, the General Assembly and the Security Council "are two distinct 'sovereign' organs." Brierly, *op. cit.,* p. 24.

[109]*Ibid.*

[110]Fitzmaurice, *op. cit.,* Article 9, para 2(*b*), p. 18.

[111]*Ibid.*

[112]Rosenne, *op. cit.,* pp. 408-9.

In the present submission the difficulty will be minimized if it is remembered that if a particular treaty involves a policy decision it will certainly be receiving the attention of the competent organ of the Organization, and once the policy is decided under a general mandate the Secretary-General might be deemed to have the power to put into effect, as an administrative officer, that decision, if no specific provision exists in the general mandate authorizing some one else to do the job. And if the treaty relates to minor administrative matters, the Secretary-General again in the capacity of the administrative officer of the Organization, might be deemed to have the power to conclude treaties within his competence.

Practice of International Organizations[113]

Sometimes, a particular organ or official is authorized to negotiate agreements, as for example the General Assembly authorized ECOSOC to make arrangements for the negotiation of agreements bringing the Specialized Agencies into relationship with the UN as foreseen by the Charter in Article 63.[114] A Committee on Negotiation was promptly established by ECOSOC which conducted negotiations and final approval of these arrangements was given by the General Assembly.[115]

The authorization sometimes is given not only to negotiate but also to conclude the agreements. Such, for example, was the Resolution adopted by the Second World Health Assembly on 30 June 1949 delegating to the Executive Board and the Director-General full powers for the selection of a site and a construction of a building thereon. The Director-General accordingly, and on further authorization by the Executive Board, negotiated with the UN an arrangement for the use of *Palais de Nations* for headquarters of the WHO in Geneva. The UN Secretary-General likewise obtained an

---

[113]The writer has had the benefit of Dr. T.I.H. Detter's research done in an article entitled "The Organs of International Organizations exercising their treaty-making power," *British Yearbook of International Law*, Vol. 38, 1962, p. 42, in addition to his own interviews with the concerned officials of the ILO, WHO, GATT, UPU, ITU, and the UN.

[114]See recommendations in *Report of the Preparatory Commission of the UN*, PC/20, 23 December 1945, paras 6-11.

[115]*Repertory of Practice of the UN Organs*, Vol. 1, p. 688.

authorization to conclude such an agreement from the General Assembly.[116]

Again, on occasions a blanket permission is given to a particular organ to negotiate and conclude a series of agreements. Such, for example, was the case with General Assembly Resolution 48 (I) in which the Secretary-General was directed to consider ways and means of collecting and utilizing contributions from persons, organizations, and peoples all over the world equivalent to the earnings of one day's work, for the purpose of helping to meet relief needs during 1947. The Secretary-General in pursuance of this authorization has concluded numerous agreements with different countries.[117]

When once such authorization has been obtained neither the Secretary-General nor the governments observed strict formalities. Subordinate officials of the Secretariat negotiated and concluded agreements with or without express authorization letters. On occasions letters of authorization were sent by telegrams where time was of the essence of the matter.[118] On occasions express provisions were included in the authorization itself that the final terms were subject to the ultimate approval of the plenary body. Such, for instance, were the agreements, signed by the Managing Director of the Special Fund of the UN and the Director General of UNESCO on 29 September and 6 October 1959, which provided that the Agreement would enter into effect upon approval by the UN and UNESCO.[119] It is also the practice at times to reserve the agreement for final approval by superior officials, as when the Assistant Secretary-General of the UN, Ivan Kerno, and the Assistant Director General of the ILO, C.W. Jenks, did concerning

---

[116]See WHO, *Official Records*, 1949, No. 21, 37, No. 22, 9 and UN Doc. A/1251, 28 December 1949 and *UN Treaty Series*, Vol. 46, pp. 329-31 for the relevant documents.

[117]See, for instance, *UN Treaty Series*, Vol. 47, pp. 167, 185, 203, 223, 251, 269, 287, 305, 319, 337 relating to agreements with Canada, Czechoslovakia, France, Greece, Iceland, Pakistan, Thailand, UK, Finland, and San Marino, respectively.

[118]For a detailed analysis, see Detter, *op. cit.*, pp. 434-5.

[119]*UN Treaty Series*, Vol. 363, 378. The approval was given by the Executive Board of UNESCO on 5 December 1959. *Ibid.*, p. 368.

the procedure to be followed for the deposit and registration with the UN of Conventions and other agreements.[120]

It is not necessary, however, that the Secretary-General himself should sign the agreements. The provisional arrangement with Lebanon for a UNEF leave centre in that country was concluded by Major-General Burns, signing as Commander of United Nations Emergency Force (UNEF).[121] The agreement between the UN and Chile for headquarters for the Economic Commission for Latin America (ECLA) was signed by Raul Prebisch, the Executive Secretary of ECLA.[122] The agreement between the UN and Ethiopia for headquarters for Economic Commission for Asia (ECA) was signed by M. de Seynes, on behalf of the UN, who is the Under-Secretary-General for Economic and Social Affairs.[123] Again, the agreement concluded between the World Health Organization and Brazil was signed by Dr. F.L. Soper, Director for the Regional Office for the Americas (Pan-American Bureau).[124] In all these cases the agreements were negotiated and a prior authorization was given by the competent organ of the Organization.

The World Bank, however, has a set practice. It is the Bank's practice to submit drafts of proposed loan and guarantee agreements to the Executive Directors for approval before the agreements are signed. The approval of the Executive Directors is expressed in a resolution authorizing execution of the agreement in question. At the subsequent signing ceremony a copy of that resolution, certified by the Secretary of the Bank, is delivered to the other party or parties. Under a general authority conferred by the Executive Directors, agreements, authorized to be entered into by the Bank may be signed by the President or by any one of its three Vice-Presidents. These officials may designate other persons

---

[120]WHO, *Official Records,* 1953, Vol. 26, p. 328.

[121]R. Higgins, *The Development of International Law through the Political Organs of the United Nations,* London, 1963, p. 253.

[12] *UN Treaty Series,* Vol. 314, p. 49.

[123]*UN Treaty Series,* Vol. 317, p. 101.

[124]See Detter, *op. cit.,* p. 435, for other examples where the status of the officials is not even mentioned.

to sign, but in practice loan and guarantee agreements are as a rule signed by the President or in his absence, by the Vice-President.[125]

The practice, in fine, has varied with the nature of the agreements and the constitutional competence of the delegating body. Surveying the practice of international organizations, Detter concluded:

> The treaty-making power is in principle vested in the "supreme organ" of the Organization. This supreme organ is usually, although not always, identical with the plenary organ of the Organization, that the supreme organ and the plenary organ are the same, is indeed, the main rule. Therefore, unless some other organ is indicated either by the constituent instrument, or by the practice of the Organization, the treaty-making power is vested — as a rule — in the plenary organ. As, however, the plenary organ is not normally a suitable body to negotiate and draw up treaties these tasks are inevitably delegated to sub- sidiary organs, or officials; a problem of "domestic control" of the treaty-making power then arises in a way somewhat similar to that in the case of States. The alternatives are either to control the scope of the powers delegated to subsidiary organs or officials or to retain a subsequent right to approve of the treaty when it is drawn up.[126]

International organizations have adopted a judicious mixture of both the techniques with commendable results.

SUMMATION

It might be said in summation that international organizations have in practice used the treaty-making power very liberally, absence of express provisions and doctrinal divergencies notwith- standing. In the process some of the rules of traditional inter- national law have been occasionally neglected in tune with the special and *sui generis* character of their position.

The question as to whether these organizations have had express or implied authority to do so, and also the issue whether the

---

[125]For a masterly exposition, See Aron Broches, *op. cit.*, p. 385.
[126]Detter, *op. cit.*, p. 444.

organizations have unlimited treaty-making power (a question on which there has been acute difference of opinion), as well as the question of the inter-relationship of treaty-making power and the concept of international personality — all these issues can be resolved by a straight and simple reference to the purposes and functions of the organization concerned. The ICJ dictum that the rights and duties of an international organization such as the United Nations, "must depend upon its purposes and functions as specified or implied in its constituent documents and developed in practice,"[127] applies with particular force to the implied treaty-making power of international organizations. The test, as it has been shown in the preceding pages, is whether or not the utilization of the treaty technique is necessary for carrying out a particular function, and whether or not it serves the purposes of the organization. If it does, it is believed to be authorized.

If the UN and other international organizations had felt hesitant to conclude treaties of humanitarian and technical nature with all kinds of agencies because of lack of express authority to do so, the history of international organizations today would have been different.

In view of the extensive practice and the more or less settled rules pertaining to treaties concluded by international organization,[128] the omission of "other subjects of international law" in the ILC *Draft* is far from fatal in the case of international organizations. It is hoped that the ILC directs its special Rapporteur before long to proceed with a report on this aspect, too.

---

[127]ICJ *Reports*, 1949, p. 180.
[128]See n. 5.

CHAPTER 4

IMPLIED POWERS, SUSPENSION, EXPULSION, FORCED WITHDRAWAL AND PARTIAL EXCLUSION

IT HAS BEEN the theme of the preceding chapters that whether or not the constituent instruments of international organizations contain specific provisions authorizing particular activities a *prima facie* presmuption of legality exists in relation to such activities if they are necessary for the fulfilment of their purposes and functions. A logical extension of the same theme has been that, in the asbence of express prohibition, all operations that are likely to promote the purposes and principles and enhance the institutional effectiveness must be regarded legal, any internal irregularity notwithstanding. The rationale of these doctrines, i.e. the doctrine of implied powers and the doctrine of institutional effectiveness— is that any interpretation of the powers and functions of international organizations must tend towards making them effective rather than ineffective. The legal nexus here is with the objective.

In certain situations, however, the written word, the express authority, might itself stand in the way of the effective functioning of the Organization. In such cases the doctrines of implied power and institutional effectiveness have to be drawn upon in a quite different way. Usually powers by implication are invoked to enhance the scope of the Organizations. But here these powers are utilized to reduce the rigour of its express authority. This is a case of underutilization of express powers. Such is the field of powers of suspension and expulsion of international organizations.

THEORETICAL POSITION

In no other sphere do the complexities of implied powers project so prominently as in the power of international organizations to suspend or expel member States (which for the sake of brevity, is termed, punitive power) for recalcitrant behaviour. The manoeuvrability of organizations is limited *prima facie* in this field by the express provisions in their constituent instruments. Yet, some ingenuous inroads have been made by a few organizations to under-utilize these powers—as, for example, in the unique practice of forced withdrawal and partial exclusion.

"Law is, by its very nature, a coercive order," says Hans Kelsen. "A coercive order," he goes on to explain, "is a system of rules prescribing certain patterns of behaviour by providing coercive measures, as sanctions, to be taken in case of contrary behaviour, or, what amounts to the same, in case of violation of the law."[1] Sanctions, as an antidote for delictual responsibility, are effected under municipal law by a centralized organ of State by a forcible deprivation of certain possessions, such as life and liberty—personal or economic. On the international plane, traditional international law, as a coercive order, too, has specific sanctions against violations of law in the nature of reprisals and war. The dispensing agency, however, in this field, in the absence of a centralized organ of force, has been the State itself.

Wars, having proved extremely costly and a scourge on humanity, efforts have been made to outlaw this mode of punitive action by the League Covenant partially, by the Kellogg-Briang Pact totally —though not entirely satisfactorily—and by the Charter of the UN almost completely. Centralization of the system of sanctions has been sought to be achieved under the League and the UN. This being a special characteristic of these two organizations, a full chapter (II) has been devoted to the subject. The object of enquiry, however, in this chapter is the limited nature of sanctions that international organizations employ against a recalcitrant member State as an internal discipline.[2] The enquiry might be commenced with the League of Nations.

---

[1] Hans Kelsen, *The Law of the United Nations*, London, 1950, p. 706.

[2] Literature on this subject is scarce; but a commendable work by Nagendra Singh fills the lacuna. See *Termination of Membership of International Organizations*, London, 1958. The writer has drawn freely from this source for the

THE LEAGUE OF NATIONS

Suspension. The Covenant of the League of Nations contained no provision for the suspension of the rights and privileges of members.

Expulsion. Paragraph 4 of Article 16 of the Covenant read: "Any member of the League which has violated any covenant of the League may be declared to be no longer a member of the League by a vote of the Council concurred in by the Representatives of all the other members of the League represented thereon."

There was no provision for expulsion in any of the earlier drafts of the Covenant. General Smuts had, however, suggested in his famous pamphlet, *The League of Nations: A Practical Suggestion,*[3] that the Covenant-breaking State be subjected to a perpetual disarmament and also to a general system of control over its foreign policy. President Wilson included this suggestion in all of his three Paris drafts of the Covenant, but not in the final draft submitted to the League of Nations Commission.[4] A similar suggestion came at one stage from British quarters.[5] But these plans fizzled out before the League of Nations Commission. None of the drafts submitted to the Commission, except the one submitted by Italy, contained any proposals for the expulsion of a rebel State. The Italian proposal enumerated exclusion of the "recalcitrant State from the Society of Nations," as one of the thirteen steps of sanctions.[6]

---

present chapter, with grateful acknowledgement. Mention must also be made in this connection to the following: Hans Kelsen, *op. cit.,* pp. 706-65; L.M. Goodrich and E. Hambro, *Charter of the United Nations,* London, 1949, pp. 138 41; Wilfred C. Jenks, "Expulsion from the League of Nations," *British Yearbook of International Law,* Vol. 16, 1935, pp. 155-7; and Louis B. Sohn, "Expulsion or Forced Withdrawal from an International Organization," *Harvard Law Review,* Vol. 77, 1964, pp. 1381-1425.

[3]For the relevant excerpt, see James T. Watkins and J. Williams Robinson, *General International Organization, A Source Book,* New York, 1956, p. 65.

[4]David Hunter Miller, *The Drafting of the Covenant,* New York, 1928, Vol. 2, pp. 80, 101, 149.

[5]*Ibid.,* p. 113.

[6]Florence Wilson, *The Origins of the League Covenant, Documentary History of its Drafting,* London, 1928, p. 208.

The Anglo-American thinking during discussions before the League of Nations Commission was inclined in the direction of exceptional international control rather than expulsion which would release the rebellious State of all international obligations. And since this was considered a very ambitious plan the suggestion was coldshouldered by many.

The appearance, nevertheless, of the provision in the draft covenant was never explained until Hunter Miller published in his monumental work a note circulated to the members of the League of Nations Commission by the British delegation at that time, which read: "A new final paragraph has been inserted to meet the case of a State which after breaking its covenant still claims to vote in the Council or in the Assembly."[7]

The note makes it clear that the clause was introduced into Article 16 not because it was thought that the appropriate method of dealing with a covenant-breaking State was to expel it from the Organization, thereby confessing the complete inability of the League to restrain illegal conduct, but because it was thought that a State in breach of the covenant might attempt to block systematically all League business by voting against every proposal under consideration.[8]

POSITION UNDER THE UNITED NATIONS

The United Nations employs three different types of punitive measures of varying gravity in tune with the seriousness of the violation of its norms. Article 19, for example, empowers the Organization to place a member in default of payment of its arrears under temporary suspension of its voting rights.[9]   Article 5

---

[7] D.H. Miller, *op. cit.*, Vol. 1, p. 417.

[8] Wilfred C. Jenks, *op. cit.*, p. 156.

[9] The text of the Article is as follows: "A member of the United Nations which is in arrears in the payment of its financial contributions to the Organization shall have no vote in the General Assembly if the amount of its arrears equals or exceeds the amount of the contributions due from it for the preceding two full years. The General Assembly may, nevertheless, permit such a member to vote if it is satisfied that the failure to pay is due to conditions beyond the control of the member."

again empowers the Organization to employ the same measure in the case of a member against which preventive enforcement action has been taken by the Security Council.[10] Article 6 can be utilized by the Organization in the still graver situation where a member has "persistently violated the principles" of the Charter.[11]

If we look back upon the *travaux preparatoires*, the Dumbarton Oaks Proposals contained no equivalent provision to Article 19. Taking a lesson from the League's experience—which had some difficulty in having no powers to punish defaulters—the technical committee thought it desirable to deprive States, in arrears of their contributions, of their voting privileges and rights. However, the General Assembly was empowered to waive the penalty if it was satisfied that the reasons for delay in payment were beyond the control of the State in question.[12]

As regards Articles 5 and 6, the San Francisco documents present a useful study of the respective views of the USA, the UK, the Soviet Union, and other participants.[13] There was a general agreement that suspension should be provided for in conjunction with other measures that might be undertaken by the Security Council to maintain peace and security. As for the more drastic sanction of expulsion, the Anglo-American viewpoint was that in view of the security obligations of the Organization in relation even to States which were not members, expulsion was not an essential

[10]The text of the Article runs thus: "A member of the United Nations against which preventive or enforcement action has been taken by the Security Council may be suspended from the exercise of the rights and privileges of membership by the General Assembly upon the recommendation of the Security Council. The exercise of these rights and privileges may be restored by the Security Council."

[11]The text of the Article is as follows: "A member of the United Nations which has persistently violated the principles contained in the present Charter may be expelled from the Organization by the General Assembly upon the recommendation of the Security Council."

[12]*UNCIO* Docs. Vol. 8, p. 419.

[13]For an analysis of the evolution of Articles 5 and 6 through the various stages of study, discussion, and negotiation that led to their final adoption at San Francisco, see Ruth B. Russel and Jeannete E. Muther, *A History of the United Nations Charter*, Washington, D.C., 1958, pp. 352, 355, 363, 397-8, 433, 437-9, 852-4.

or satisfactory remedy. The Chinese also shared the Anglo-American doubts if suspension alone would be a sufficient sanction for the purposes of the Organization. However, the Soviet Union, which was the one member to have tasted the bitter fruit in the League days, curiously, insisted that the step would be essential as a disciplinary measure. After a prolonged debate, the US and the UK decided to accede to the Soviet desire to provide for expulsion in the Dumbarton Oaks proposals.

A Belgian amendment at San Francisco created considerable controversy. The Belgian contention was that, since suspension could be applied indefinitely without releasing a member from its obligations under the Charter, and since expulsion would automatically bring to an end all such obligations, suspension would be a more effective measure than expulsion. Accordingly, it proposed to amend the paragraph to provide for only suspension.[14] The Soviet Union objected to the amendment vehemently and not until the technical committee reconsidered the issue could the Belgian amendment be overruled.

The Soviet contention was that a member engaged in persistently violating the principles of the Charter would be like a cancerous growth which would be better removed than retained. Moreover, since the basic requirements of membership—namely, the peace-loving character and the willingness to accept the obligations of the Charter—would have been flouted by the wrongdoer it would become legally incompatible to retain such member in the Organization.

POSITION UNDER OTHER INTERNATIONAL ORGANIZATIONS

Suspension. A study of the constituent instruments of some of the major international organizations (other than the League and the UN) would reveal that recourse to this form of punishment or sanction is envisaged broadly in two cases: one, failure of the members to meet financial obligations to the Organization; two, other exceptional circumstances.

[14]*UNCIO* Docs., Vol. 7, pp. 100-1.

Majority of the international organizations authorize recourse to this drastic action on both the counts. Thus, for instance, Article 62 of the Constitution of the International Civil Aviation Organization empowers the Assembly to suspend the voting rights of the member States both in the Assembly and in the Council if it fails to discharge within a reasonable time its financial obligation to the Organization. Again, Article 82 stipulates suspension in the event of default under the provisions of Chapter XVIII relating to the settlement of disputes. The World Health Organization postulates, likewise, suspension under Article 7 of voting rights in both the instances. The International Bank of Reconstruction and Development has an omnibus clause which empowers the Organization to suspend a member on failure to "fulfil any of its obligations" [Article VI (2)]. Section 2 of Article XV of the International Monetary Fund Agreement has an all-embracing provision: resources of the Fund are denied to a member if it "fails to fulfil any obligations under the Agreement." Similarly, Article 31 of the World Meteorological Organization provides for suspension of a member State which fails "to meet its financial obligations to the Organization or otherwise fails in its obligations under the present Convention."

A few organizations, like the International Labour Organization (Article 13), envisage suspension only in case of default of financial obligations. Quite a few Specialized Agencies, the United Nations Scientific, Educational and Cultural Organization (Article II, paragraph 4), for instance, link their suspension process with that of the UN itself.

This, however, does not mean that a suspension clause is an essential provision of every constituent instrument. For example, the Food and Agriculture Organization has no provision for the suspension or expulsion of a member of the Organization. So also the International Telecommunication Union, which permits its member States to denounce the Convention, is not expressly empowered to suspend a member for any kind of default.

A further examination of the constituent instruments of the major international organizations would show that the suspension process differs on (*i*) the nature of suspension, (*ii*) the method of suspension, and (*iii*) the extent and effect of suspension.[15]   The point of interest for the present discussion is whether the employment of this power serves the purposes of the organizations and whether or not they have implied powers of lesser punishment. The question will be taken up in conjunction with expulsion powers.

Expulsion. To ensure, as it were, organizational discipline, improve the good conduct of the member States and promote a healthy observation of the code of conduct that every organization sets before itself, international organzations are endowed with an extraordinary power of punishment, expulsion. Designed only as a last resort, expulsion is a drastic step which is supposed to be invoked with the utmost caution and reluctance.   The relative freeplay which the older organizations had in this matter, to be sure, were viewed with alacrity in modern times, with the result that the weapon of expulsion was held in the constitutional order of international organizations more as a threat than with the puropose of actual utilization.

The League of Nations, to illustrate, was empowered to terminate the membership of a member State which had violated "any convenant of the League" [Article 15 (4)].   But, the relative provisions of the United Nations empower the Organization to expel a member only on persistent violations of the principles of the Charter (Article 6).   The Specialized Agencies have also followed a similar cautious path.   The constitution of the International Refugee Organization empowers the General Council to expel a member—with the approval of the UN General Assembly—for a "persistent violation of the principles" contained in the constitution [Article 4 (8)].   The International Bank for Reconstruction and Development and the International Monetary Fund follow a similar course.   The UNESCO has tagged its punitive power of expulsion to that of the UN.

Special mention must be made of the Council of Europe which employs this weapon against any member which has seriously

[15]For a detailed examination of the issue, see Nagendra Singh, *op. cit.*

violated Article 3. The emphasis here is shifted from "persistent" to "serious" violation. It has been suggested that the UN formula is better because it is easily ascertainable and hence more definite as against the vague phrase "serious violation."[16] In the present submission the question depends upon the particular principle or principles which have been violated. A persistent violation of a minor principle, for example, the non-registration of treaties under Article 103, is less serious a matter than a single violation of the principle, for example, failure to carry out a decision of the Security Council taken under Chapter VII of the Charter.

Again, if persistent violation of principles means the violation of the principles as embodied in Article 2 of the Charter even then the formula would be unsatisfactory, for the Article enumerates such undefined principles as "sovereign equality" and "domestic jurisdiction."

The "persistent violation" formula emphasizes the quantitative violation while ignoring the importance of the principle violated, whereas the other formula places emphasis on the nature of the obligation. It might be argued that obligations are obligations, serious or less serious. But it must be remembered that the gravity of punishment demands that the violation should also be grave. That is precisely the reason why expulsion is not prescribed for financial default. If, however, the protection of the sovereign stature of member States is the consideration then the Council of Europe formula is better in that it places maximum discretion in the hands of the Organization rather than tying its hands with precise formulations, so that if violations are persistent the Organization would be left with no other alternative than to employ the crude and flimsy weapon. It is true that the word "may" also makes matters discretionary. But even discretionary powers have legal limitations. The word "persistent" with its ascertainable content places such a limitation, whereas the word "serious" enhances the discretionary power.

[16]*Ibid.*, p. 59.

In this connexion it is interesting to note the remarkable provision in the International Wheat Agreement which, through selective sanctions, reduces the rights and privileges of the member concerned in proportion to its offence—perhaps the best course of action innovated so far.

The European Economic Community comes closer to the League formula. Article 26 of the Convention provides for expulsion if a member ceases to fulfil its obligations under the present Convention. This, like the League formula, would cover any default irrespective of the importance of the obligation.

Again, mention must be made of the unique provision in this regard in the IMF Agreement. In addition to expulsion for persistent failure to fulfil the obligations under the Agreement, it also provides for compulsory withdrawal in the event of uncompromising difference between a member and the Fund, under Article IV, section 6. This, however, does not mean that all organizations have the power to expel. Functional organizations like the International Civil Aviation Organization, the International Labour Organization, the International Telecommunication Union, and the Universal Postal Union do not possess the right to expel.

General international organizations, apart from the UN, like the Organization of American States and the Western European Union have no powers either to suspend or expel. The League of Arab States, however, provides for expulsion if the Council of the League considers that any State "is not fulfilling the obligations resulting from this Pact" [Article 18 (2)].

The more closely integrated organizations, which have a powerful judiciary, provide for expulsion but this power is entrusted to the judicial organ. For instance, the European Coal and Steel Community stipulates under Article 12 for the expulsion of members of the High Authority by the Court for "non-fulfilment of the conditions necessary to the exercise of their functions," or commission of a "gross fault." The European Economic Community, likewise, provides for expulsion, under Article 160, of the member of the Community who "no longer fulfils the conditions required for the performance of his duties or if he commits a serious offence." Here, too, the Court of Justice wields the power, acting on a petition of the Council or of the Commission. The Courts in both the cases possess a right to compel obedience to their judgments vis-a-vis member States.[17]

The case is different with military pacts. The North Atlantic Treaty Organization does not provide for either suspension or for expulsion. Even the right of withdrawal is allowed only after 20 years of the existence of the treaty, with one-year notice. The South-East Asian Treaty Organization, likewise, provides for neither suspension nor expulsion. The members are allowed to denounce the treaty with a year's notice. The duration of the treaty is indefinite. The Warsaw Pact, too, does not provide for suspension or expulsion. An opportunity under Article 11 is given to withdraw at the end of 20 years, with a year's notice.

A broad generalization of the pattern of expulsion powers of international organizations can be laid down thus. Functional organizations meant to look after only the specified non-sovereign functions generally have no powers of expulsion. General international organizations like the League, the UN, and the Arab League, where a certain measure of pooling of sovereignty by members is required, have such authority, the OAS and the Council of Europe being exceptions to the rule. Where functional purposes are combined with a closer integration and an independent judiciary, the judicial organ of the Organization is empowered to rectify the wrong. The European Coal and Steel Community and the European Economic Community are the cases in reference. And lastly, organizations created for defensive purpose with a "one for all and all for one" principle completely do away with expulsion. The pooling of sovereignty is even greater here. Ultimately, it is a question of sovereignty; the more it is delegated to the Organization the less the need for expulsion, the exceptions being functional international organizations.

It remains to be seen if, in theory, international organizations, in the absence of express authority, can take punitive action against recalcitrant member States.

[17]See Chapter IV and Section 4 of the Treaties respectively.

IMPLIED POWERS TO TAKE PUNITIVE ACTION

The question whether international organizations, in the absence of express provisions in their constituent instruments, have punitive power has provoked strong views from Nagendra Singh, the leading authority on the subject. Singh, invoking the well-established principle of international law to the effect that nothing binds a member State which is not expressly stated in a constitutional treaty, denies categorically any such power in favour of the Organization.[18]

However, Nagendra Singh singles out an exception, where an organization might have recourse to this drastic remedy if a member State refuses to ratify an amendment to the constituent instrument duly adopted in accordance with its laws. In the present submission the exception might also be extended, theoretically, to a case where an incorrigible member indulges in grave and persistent violation of the basic principles of the instrument, and refuses to withdraw voluntarily with a view to bringing the normal machinery of the Organization to a standstill and subverting the aims and objectives, purposes and principles of the Organization in question. This, of course, is an extreme situation.

If the Organization, as was shown in Chapter I, has an implied power to embark upon uncharted seas if such voyages will help effectuate its purposes and ensure maximum "institutional effectiveness" of the Organization, it can equally forcibly be maintained that if expulsion or suspension is inevitable for the institutional effectiveness of the Organization, the Organization might well be said to have such an implied power. The real difficulty however, will be to find out if suspension or expulsion will in fact promote the purposes and principles, and, consequently, the institutional effectiveness of the Organization. As the discussion on the legal effect in the ensuing section will bear out, it will not.

EFFECT OF EXPULSION

Expulsion often has strange and perplexing results. In contrast with suspension, which merely puts into abeyance certain or all

[18]Nagendra Singh, *op. cit.*, pp. 79-80.

of the privileges of member States, expulsion severs all connections
with the Organization. The result is that the member which has
been expelled ceases to owe any obligations to the other member
States, which form the Organization. As Kelsen points out,
it might be conjectured that where no voluntary withdrawal is
possible, a member that wishes to leave the burden of membership
to the other members of the Organization might be induced to reach
this goal by creating a situation which may lead to its expulsion.[19]
Thus, as Nagendra Singh suggests, any outstanding obligations,
particularly relating to payment of arrears of subscription of membership, would not be enforceable against a member State after
expulsion.[20]

Jenks, therefore, takes the viewpoint that since the effect
of expulsion is to release a State from its obligations towards other
States members of the Organization it affords "no real remedy for
breaches of international law or of international public morality."[21]
He warns further that it merely provides "an alibi for the failure
of other States to devise effective means of enforcing the provisions
which have been flouted."[22] So Jenks advocates that it should
be adequate to empower the Organization to suspend defaulting
members from all or any of their rights and privileges of membership, without thereby releasing them from any of their obligations
towards the Organization.

The confusion is worse confounded if the curious anomalies,
as pointed out by Kelsen,[23] of the UN are taken into consideration.
The UN Charter creates rights and obligations not only for members
but also for non-members (*vide*, paragraph 6 of Article 2). One
such right is freedom from the Organization's intervention in the
domestic jurisdiction of "any State" (paragraph 7 of Article 2).
Also, non-members, which are parties to a dispute, are entitled to
be represented in the Security Council under Article 32. These

---

[19]Kelsen, *op. cit.*, pp. 714-5.
[20]Nagendra Singh, *op. cit.*, p. 67.
[21]Jenks, "Some Constitutional Problems of International Organizations,"
British Yearbook of International Law, Vol. 22, 1945, p. 25.
[22]*Ibid.*
[23]Kelsen, *op. cit.*, p. 715.

rights are available to non-members, consequently, also to members which are expelled, but not to members under suspension. Hence suspension in certain cases is more effective than expulsion.

As a matter of fact, there was a strong move at San Francisco for the omission of any reference to expulsion in the Charter. It was argued by those who favoured such a course that expulsion would be incompatible with the concept of universality; that it would entail more drawbacks for the Organization itself than for the State concerned; that it would set up a centre in opposition to the Organization around which other discontented States would rally;[24] that it would force member States to break off all relations, diplomatic and otherwise, with the State which is expelled; and that it would prevent reconciliation between the Organization and the State expelled.

The members in favour of expulsion explained that the primary purposes of the Organization were peace and security, not universality. Expulsion, this group felt, would apply only to member States which were admittedly incorrigible and which violated the principles contained in the Charter in a grave and persistent manner. So far as such States were concerned, the argument ran, the attitude which would be adopted towards them by the Organization would have to be stated quite plainly.

Referring to the undesirability of total extinction of obligations between the Organization and the expelled members, those who favoured the inclusion in the Charter of a provision for expulsion contended that insofar as even non-members also were subjected to the discipline of the UN such objections were unfounded. Also, it was made clear that though expulsion was conclusive in character nothing would prevent readmission of the expelled member if its subsequent conduct was proper and dignified.[25] The intention

[24]Indonesia's voluntary withdrawal from the UN and its attempt to form a rival organization (which failed to attract any Asian-African States except China and Cambodia) over Malaysia's election in the Security Council, certainly on a lesser provocation than expulsion, confirms the fears of the framers of the Charter.

[25]*UNCIO* Doc. 1160, 1/2/76(1), p. 7.

behind the inclusion of the provision for expulsion appears to be rather preventive in character, though in effect it assumes the character of a punitive action, i.e. threatening dire consequence to avert indiscipline.

Practice among international organizations shows that though the weapon of expulsion has been used as a guillotine quite often recent tendency is to have it as a sword of Damocles and use lesser forms of punishment as forced withdrawal and partial exclusion, of which the latter seems to be a better remedy.

PRACTICE AMONG INTERNATIONAL ORGANIZATIONS

International organizations confronted with the unpleasant choice between violations of their covenants and the use of the crude and clumsy weapon of expulsion have reacted in numerous ways. They have employed a wide variety of compulsive measures against recalcitrant States. Sometimes the violators have been excluded from some, but not all, activities of an organization; sometimes members are invited to withdraw; and some other time constitutions of organizations have been amended to expel a member outright where no express provision to do so was available in the constitution. A few examples will reveal the variety of compulsive measures employed by the organizations. But before that it must be seen whether there is any precedent for the assertion made earlier that international organizations do have punitive power in the absence of express authority in their constituent instruments. The one case that comes to mind is that of Cuba vis-a-vis the Organization of American States.

The Charter of the OAS does not contain an express provision for expulsion. Article 25 which lists out a number of sanctions that can be taken against a member which threatens hemispheric peace makes no mention, however, of expulsion. Pursuant to a barrage of charges and counter-charges by and against the Castro-government, the Organ of Consultation adopted on 31 January 1962 a resolution excluding the Castro government from the OAS. The reason was that that government was incompatible with the principles and objectives of the inter-American system because of its identification with Marxist-Leninist ideology and its political, economic, and military ties with the Communist countries.[26]

The Cuban Government challenged the legal validity of this decision and even requested the Security Council of the UN to ask the ICJ to give an advisory opinion on the question whether the OAS Charter, in the asbence of express provision, permits expulsion of a member State.[27] The resolution was rejected by the Security Council,[28] and the discussion which preceded in the Council clearly tends to favour the action taken by the OAS.

The Ecuador representative raised the stock plea in the Security Council that nothing could be done by the OAS that was not expressly permitted by its Charter.[29] On the other hand it was argued by others that (*i*) it was for the OAS to interpret its own Charter; (*ii*) that the OAS Charter should be interpreted to give effect to its central purposes; and (*iii*) that no regional organization could be made to accept the presence of a State which the Organization concluded was violating the terms of its Charter.[30] It was also argued that it was an inherent right of any regional organization to determine which countries should participate in that organization.[31] Another argument was also rejected that it would amount to "enforcement action" which the OAS could not take without the prior approval of the Security Council under Article 53 of the UN Charter.[32]

The above incident clearly establishes a precedent that an organization can expel, *a fortiori* suspend, a recalcitrant member even in the absence of express provision in its constituent document.

[26]Pan American Union, Eighth Meeting of Consultation, Final Act, 1962, pp. 1214-46; *Department of State Bulletin*, 1962, p. 281.

[27]*Security Council Official Records*, 17th year, 998 Meeting, 1962, p. 28; see also C.G. Fenwick, *The Organization of Americ an States: The Inter-American Regional System*, Washington, D.C., 1963, p. 85.

[28]*Ibid.*

[29]*Security Council Official Records*, 17th year, 992 Meeting, 1962, p. 19.

[30]*Ibid.*, 993 Meeting, pp. 20-1; see Fenwick, "The Issue at Punta del Este: Non-Intervention v. Collective Security," *American Journal of International Law*, Vol. 56, 1962, pp. 469, 474.

[31]*Security Council Official Records*, 17th year, 998 Meeting, 1962, p. 14, (United States).

[32]*Ibid.*, 993 Meeting, 1962, p. 20 (United States).

The records of other international organizations can now be surveyed to see how they have dealt with defaulting member States in the course of practice. In general the techniques employed can be divided into forced withdrawal and partial exclusion. The enquiry might well be commenced with the League experience in this regard.

Practice of the League of Nations

It might be recalled that the League Covenant did contain a provision (paragraph 4 of Article 16) by which the Organization was empowered to expel any member which broke "any covenant of the League." This, as it has been seen in the theoretical section of this chapter, was designed to meet the case of a State which after breaking its covenant still claimed to vote in the Council or in the Assembly.[33] Keeping in view the intentions of the drafters of the Covenant, Jenks at that time had expressed the hope that "it may well become one of the constitutional traditions of the League never to have recourse to this weapon which was at best clumsy and incapable of achieving the desired results."[34]

As prophesied by Jenks it almost became a constitutional tradition of the League never to use this "clumsy weapon" of expulsion. Its possible application, nevertheless, was discussed on various occasions. It was mooted as a sanction in 1921 in the case of States which failed to pay the contributions due from them under paragraph 5 of Article 6 of the Covenant.[35]

The Secretary-General pointed out that although the Covenant contained no provision imposing a special sanction for failure to pay the contributions due from a member, a "sanction in the shape of expulsion from the League is ... provided for violation of any covenant of the League ... by the last paragraph of Article 16." He considered that it "does not appear reasonably open to doubt that the financial obligation assumed by a member of the League under Article 6 is one of the covenants of the League ... and that

[33] See n. 7.
[34] Jenks, *op. cit.*, p. 157.
[35] "Legal Position of States which do not pay their Contributions to the League," Report by the Secretary-General submitted to the Council on 9 March 1927, Doc. C. 36, 1927 V, League of Nations, *Official Journal*, 1927, p. 505.

the last paragraph of Article 16 applies formally to violation of this covenant no less than to violation of the more fundamental obligations of the Covenant." The Secretary-General concluded that apart from this theoretical possibility of the application of Article 16 there was really no other way of dealing with a recalcitrant member. Nevertheless, no definite action was taken against any of the defaulting member.[36]

On another occasion, 18 May 1934, the UK Government moved in the Council of the League for the expulsion of Liberia, alleging that the latter had been meting out barbarous treatment to the Kru tribes within its boundaries and that the League "would be quite entitled to consider her expulsion under paragraph 4 of Article 16."[37] On the Liberian Government's assurance, however, the Council limited itself to withdrawing a plan of assistance, which was given to it for improving social conditions in that country, leaving the question of expulsion open.[38]

Again, on the commencement of Italian occupation of Ethiopia, ironically, Italy demanded expulsion of Ethiopia on the ground that a country "which has no Government capable of exercising its authority throughout its territory, whose frontiers are not delimited, which not merely fails to meet out equitable treatment to conquered peoples, but exploits them, subjects them to slavery and destroys them," has no business to be in the League.[39] The demand went unheeded. Instead, the League established a committee to co-ordinate the economic measures to be taken against Italy by the members of the League.[40]

A tragic deviation from this tradition, however, occurred in 1939 when the League Assembly, on a Finnish appeal, adopted a resolution which purported to expel the Soviet Union from the Organization. The Resolution condemned Soviet aggression against Finland and its failure to observe Articles 12 and 15 of the Covenant and other agreements with Finland. The same afternoon the League

[36]*Ibid.*, pp. 505-7.
[37]League of Nations, *Official Journal*, 15 Sess., 1934, p. 511.
[38]*Ibid.*, pp. 509, 513.
[39]*Ibid.*, 15th Assembly, Special Suppl. No. 138, 1935, p. 104.
[40]*Ibid.*, pp. 113-4.

Council adopted a resolution which declared that, by its act, the USSR had "placed itself outside the League of Nations. It follows that the Union of Soviet Socialist Republics is no longer a member of the League."[41]

FORCED WITHDRAWAL

Spain vs. *the International Civil Aviation Organization*. At the time of negotiating a relationship agreement with ICAO, the UN raised an issue that the Spanish participation in the former organization would contravene certain resolutions of the UN. The General Assembly, in view of Franco's collaboration with Axis Powers, had passed a resolution in 1946 recommending that the "Franco Government of Spain be debarred from membership in international agencies established by or brought into relationship with the United Nations."[42] The question of according the ICAO Specialized Agency status was therefore made contingent upon compliance with the General Assembly resolution. ICAO thus proceeded to amend the Convention so as to provide that a State which the General Assembly "has recommended be debarred from membership in international agencies" or "which has been expelled from membership in the United Nations" should "automatically cease to be a member" of the ICAO.[43] Though this amendment was never ratified by the requisite majority of the members Spain withdrew from the Organization in 1946, only to be readmitted in 1950 in a different political atmosphere. The UN adopted similar steps to ensure that other international organizations also keep out the Franco government before entering into relationship agreements with these organizations.[44]

Czechoslovakia vs. *the International Monetary Fund and the International Bank for Reconstruction and Development*. As was

[41]League of Nations, *Official Journal*, 1939, p. 506; Leo Gross has severely criticized the League action and has even challenged the legality of the resolution in an article entitled, "Was the Soviet Union Expelled from the League of Nations," *American Journal of International Law*, Vol. 39, 1945, p. 35.

[42]*General Assembly Official Records*, 1st Sess. 2nd pt., Res. 63-64 (A/64/Add.1) 1964.

[43]ICAO, *Assembly Proceedings*, 1st Sess., 1952, p. 237.

[44]See Annual Report of the Secretary-General, *General Assembly Official Records*, 2nd Sess. Supp. No. 1, 1947, pp. 3-4.

noted earlier the Articles of Agreement of the IMF do not envisage an outright expulsion. Section 2(a) of Article 15 empowers the Fund to declare a member ineligible to use the Fund's resources if the member "fails to fulfil any of its obligations under this Agreement." Under clause (b) of the same section the Board of Governors, by an absolute majority, can require such a member to withdraw for persistent failure.[45]

These provisions were invoked by the US when Czechoslovakia failed to provide information concerning its national income and balance of payments which the Fund was authorized to request.[46] Rejecting the Czechoslovak plea of national security the Board of Directors, after due deliberation and providing ample opportunity to that country to rectify its wrong, decided upon settling all accounts between the country and the Fund.[47]

The IBRD, which too was having similar difficulties with Czechoslovakia, proceeded to suspend it in January 1954; one year later Czechoslovakia ceased to be a member of the Bank.[48] This procedure was adopted in spite of a provision in the Articles of Agreement of the Bank under which any member expelled from the Fund "automatically ceases after three months to be a member of the Bank unless the Bank by three-fourths of the total voting power . . . agreed to allow it to remain a member." Apparently the lengthy process was chosen to give the member State an opportunity to avoid the ignominious exit.

It might be added that the IMF started in 1964 similar proceedings against Cuba, but Cuba withdrew before any action was taken.[49]

South Africa vs. *the International Labour Organization.* The South African case presents a classic study of a member which, violating all norms of an international organizational instrument, still refuses to be submitted to its punitive sanctions. On 29 June 1961 the ILO adopted, on the initiative of Nigeria, a resolution

[45]*UN Treaty Series*, Vol. 2, 1947, p. 94.
[46]IMF, *Summary Proceedings*, Annual Meeting, 1954, pp. 137, 53.
[47]IMF, *Annual Report*, 1955, p. 115.
[48]IBRD, *Annual Report*, Vol. 9, 1953-54, pp. 44-5; *ibid.*, Vol. 10, 1945-44, p. 26.
[49]IMF, *Press Release*, No. 480, 1964.

which condemned the racial policy of the Republic of South Africa and requested that it should withdraw from membership of the ILO, until such time as it abandoned its policy of apartheid.[50] South Africa announced in advance that it had no intention of acceding to any such request.[51]

The Governing Body, at its 1963 session, faced with persistent pressure from the African and Arab States, adopted a proposal to amend its constitution so as to enable the Organization to take such action "as might be necessary in order to achieve the objectives of the 1961 resolution on the apartheid policy of the Republic of South Africa. ... "[52] Again in February 1964 the Governing Body adopted drafts of two amendments to the ILO constitution relating, respectively to the suspension or expulsion of a member State when similar action has been taken against the State by the United Nations and to the exclusion from participation of a member State found by the United Nations "to be flagrantly and persistently pursuing by its legislation, a declared policy of racial discrimination such as apartheid."[53] Finally, South Africa announced its withdrawal from the ILO on 11 March 1964.[54]

Partial Exclusion

In addition to the above technique of forcible withdrawal international organizations have employed a new weapon of partial exclusion from some of their organs.

In 1963 the Economic and Social Council acquiesced to the African demand to exclude Portugal and South Africa from the Economic Commission for Africa, a subsidiary organ of the Council.[55] The ILO, too, decided in the same year to exclude South Africa from those meetings of the ILO at which membership is determined by the Governing Body.[56] As these bodies are masters of their own

[50]International Labour Conference, *Record of Proceedings,* 1961, p. 891.
[51]*Ibid.,* p. 692.
[52]ILO, *Official Bulletin,* Vol. 46, 1963, p. 334.
[53]*New York Times,* 16 February 1964, S 1, p. 20, cols. 5-6.
[54]ILO Doc. No. G.B. 159/24/5, 1964, pp. 3-4.
[55]Resolution 074 D (IV2), 30 July 1963, *ESCOR,* Supp. No. 1, Vol. 36, 1963, p. 4; Res. 974 D III 3(b), 24 July 1963, *ibid.,* p. 3.
[56]ILO, *Official Bulletin,* Vol. 46, 1963, p. 333.

committees they were acting *intra vires* of their competence. That, however, does not prevent the members so excluded from attending the other bodies of these organizations.

In this way measures of partial exclusion have added to the loaded arsenal of punitive powers of international action. It might be hoped that the innovations have not been exhausted. As Louis Sohn suggests the UN and other organizations may well tailor the scope of their punitive power to the particular violations.[57] Members which violate human rights can be excluded from the Third Committee of the UN or the relevant committees of the other organizations dealing with the subject, and so on. Also, another novel solution is exclusion through a challenge of credentials.

SUMMATION

The practice of international organizations shows that the alternative to the crude weapon of expulsion is not inaction, but a wide range of equally effective and less drastic remedies that are available for the thinking statesmen. This is a field where implied powers are employed to water down the harsh treatment the Organizations are entitled, under express authority, to impose upon a wrong-doer. This has been necessitated by the need for moderation in the realization of a goal which is not pre-eminent. Universality of membership is a desirable goal, not a principal purpose. The purposes of the organizations being what they are the organizations have concerned themselves mainly with the objective of achieving the same by trying out some disciplinary methods against member States which make it a business to retard the realization of the primary objectives. The measures, in other words, have had to be commensurate with the heirarchy of objectives of international organizations.

To spell out the theory into concrete detail, the ILO's main objective was to promote good labour conditions; it would have been a mockery of its purposes to allow South Africa to continue as a member with its outrageous practice of *apartheid*. It is not the same with the WHO and the FAO. Both the victims of *apartheid*

---

[57]Louis B. Sohn, *op. cit.*, 1422.

as well as its perpetrators need help from these sources. That is one of the strongest grounds of those who oppose economic sanctions by the UN; because it is the people who suffer, not the government. Likewise the predominance of the concern for peace over human dignity has been weighing heavily in the minds of those men. It is a tragic irony that one objective has to be subordinated to the other, but that is how the international community created these organizations.

Reverting to the implied powers of international organizations to take disciplinary action against recalcitrant members, the recent tendency to tailor the punishment to the degree of offences—and the consequent underutilization of the implied powers—is a welcome innovation.

CHAPTER 5

ADMISSIONS AND IMPLIED POWERS OF INTERNATIONAL ORGANIZATIONS

GENERAL INTERNATIONAL ORGANIZATIONS perform a unique function in the process of admission of new members. It is a common occurrence that the newspapers which carry the announcement of independence of one of the Afro-Asian dependencies, also carry in the same column the news that the new-born State has sought admission in the UN. An examination of the provisions and practice of the League of Nations and the United Nations would show that the rules relating to admission to international organizations have been clearing out some of the cobwebs in the traditional international law and striking at the very base of age-old concepts of "sovereignty" and "recognition." A section of the present chapter purports, therefore, to examine how admissions to international organizations affect the traditional concepts of recognition and sovereignty. The main purpose of the present study, however, is to see how far these organizations are bound by their constitutional provisions in the process of admittance of States, new or old, and if any extra-constitutional or implied powers can be claimed for the international organizations in this regard. This is one field where the invocation of the doctrines of implied powers and institutional effectiveness is inhibited by severe limitations. The probe will then be commenced with the provisions concerning admission in the League Covenant.

THE LEAGUE OF NATIONS

Paragraph 2 of Article 1 of the League of Nations Covenant provided:

Any fully self-governing State, Dominion or Colony ... may become a member of the League if its admission is agreed to by two-thirds of the Assembly, provided that it shall give effective guarantees of its sincere intention to observe its international obligations, and shall accept such regulations as may be prescribed by the League in regard to its military, naval and air forces, and armaments.[1]

The first thing to be noted is that the Covenant, unlike other open multilateral treaties to which any State could accede by mere notification of intention, had a system of its own for admission to the League. A two-thirds majority of the Assembly was required for a State to get admitted into the League. The process of admission was not automatic. A proposal, in fact, was made by the Argentine delegation in 1920 to universalize membership of the League.[2] The proposal was that "all sovereign States, recognized by the Community of Nations be admitted to join the League of Nations in such a manner that if they do not become members of the League, this can only be the result of a voluntary decision on their part."

The First Committee of the Second Assembly which was seized of the issue felt that the notion of the "sovereign States" does not express a well-defined idea and that "recognition by the Community of Nations" cannot be expressed in precise legal terms. The proposal therefore was rejected.[3]

The non-automatic system thus established by the League Covenant required of an entrant the following qualifications: (a) it must be a fully self-governing State, Dominion, or Colony; (b) its admission should be approved by a two-thirds majority of the Assembly; (c) it should give effective guarantees of its sincere intention to observe its international obligations ; and (d) it should accept such regulations as may be prescribed by the League in regard to its military, naval and air forces, and armaments.

[1] On admissions to the League, see mainly Manley O. Hudson, "Membership in the League of Nations," *American Journal of International Law*, Vol. 18, 1924, p. 436; Lilian M. Friedlander, "The Admission of States to the League of Nations," *British Yearbook of International Law*, 1928, p. 84; Malbone W. Graham, *The League of Nations and the Recognition of States*, Berkeley, 1933.

[2] League of Nations, *Records of the First Assembly*, Plenary Meetings, pp. 261, 279.

[3] League of Nations, Report of Committee No. 1 to the Assembly on the Argentine Proposal, *Records of the Second Assembly*, Meetings of the Committees, Vol. 1, pp. 5-11, 13-17, 135-6.

It needs no assertion that the first requirement obviously was an advancement over the traditional international law which considered only sovereign States as members of international community with minor concessions to sub-normal subjects like protected States, vassal States, etc. In the League system a dominion or colony had the same status as full sovereign State. The result was dominions and colonies like India, Canada, Australia, and South Africa acquired a definite international status by virtue of being members of the League though not all of them were fully self-governing (India, for instance). The criteria of "fully self-governing State, Dominion or Colony" would apparently preclude any amount of discretion to the Organization. But as the question of "dimunitive States" that cropped up in the course of practice would show the Organization did enjoy some discretionary power in this field too.

The second requirement, i.e. approval by two-thirds majority of the Assembly was probably the first significant break from the traditional rule of unanimity which hitherto was the cornerstone of customary international law.

It was the joint requirement of the third and fourth criteria, i.e. "effective guarantees" to observe international obligations and the need to accept League regulations in regard to military, naval and air forces and armaments—that both in theory and in actual practice affected most the traditional concept of sovereignty. It was here that the Organization enjoyed very wide discretionary powers. What constitute "effective" guarantees and how far an entrant is capable of carrying out, and is willing to carry out League's arms regulations was for the Organization to judge. The express provisions, in short, were broad enough to admit all kinds of political and legal considerations.

Theoretically, the process of admissions in the United Nations is not very much dissimilar, as far as discretionary powers of the Organization are concerned, to that of the League of Nations.[4]

---

[4]On membership in the UN, see Hans Kelsen, *The Law of the United Nations*, London, 1950, pp. 47-16; Leland M. Goodrich and Edvard Hambro, *Charter of the United Nations*, London, 1949, pp. 125-45; L.C. Green, "Membership in the United Nations," *Current Legal Problems*, Vol. 2, 1949, pp. 2588-2; Hans Aufricht, "Principles and Practices of Recognition by International Organi-

THE UNITED NATIONS

Paragraph 1 of Article 4 of the Charter of the United Nations provides: "Membership in the United Nations is open to all other peace-loving States which accept the obligations contained in the present Charter and, in the judgment of the Organization, are able and willing to carry out these obligations." The corresponding provision in Chapter III of the Dumbarton Oaks Proposals ran as follows: "Membership of the Organization should be open to all peace-loving States." By the time the text reached Committee 2 of Commission I at San Francisco, which was responsible for Membership, Amendment and Secretariat, the draft had undergone a change. It read: "Membership of the Organization is open to all peace-loving States which in the judgment of the Organization are able and ready to accept and carry out the obligations contained in the Charter."[5] The text in the course of discussions in Committee 1/2 was further modified and the final formula was thrashed out as it exists today. The transformation of the draft of the Dumbarton Oaks to the present one was necessitated in view of the delegates' dissatisfaction at the elusive phrase "peace-loving."[6] The term was generally deemed to be insufficient. To declare oneself, thought the delegates, "peace-loving" should not suffice to acquire membership in the Organization. As the Rapporteur of Committee 1/2 asked, which "nation has ever professed any other sentiment"?[7] It was felt that it would also be necessary to prove that a nation was (1) ready to accept and fulfil the obligations, and (2) that it was able to accept and fulfil them. Yet the term was retained to provide the Organization with an omnibus power to accept or reject a State's application. The Uruguayian delegate's observation that the term had

---

zation," *American Journal of International Law*, Vol. 43, 1949, pp. 679-704; Shigejiro Tabata, "Admission to the United Nations and Recognition of States," *Japanese Annual of International Law*, Vol. 5, 1951, pp. 1-14; Kelsen "Membership in the United Nations," *Columbia Law Review*, Vol. 46, 1946, p. 391.

[5] *UNCIO Docs*, Vol. 7, p. 41.

[6] *Ibid.*, pp. 11-43, 120-4, for the discussion; and for the Reports of the Rapporteurs, *ibid.*, pp. 287-332.

[7] *Ibid.*, p. 308.

no juridical connotation was cited approvingly by the Rapporteur in his earlier report.[8]

Faithful to the principle of universality, the delegation of Uruguay proposed—corresponding to the Argentine proposal in relation to the League of Nations—that all communities should be members of the Organization and that their participation should be made obligatory; that is to say, it should not be left to the choice of *any* nation whether to become a member of the Organization or to withdraw from it. Other delegations believed that universality in this sense was an ideal towards which it was proper to aim, but to which it was not necessary to adhere unswervingly. But there was unanimous belief that "adherence to the principles of the Charter and complete acceptance of the obligations arising therefrom were essential conditions to participation by States in the Organization."[9]

On the question of the conditions and criteria on which an applicant for membership should be judged, two principal tendencies were manifested in the discussion. On the one hand, there were some who declared themselves in favour of inserting in the Charter specific conditions which new members should be required to fulfil. On the other hand, others maintained that the Charter should not needlessly limit the Organization in its decision concerning requests for admission, and asserted that the Organization itself would be in a better position to judge the character of candidates for admission. The latter view prevailed. The Rapporteur reported finally that "the Committee *did not feel it should recommend the enumeration* of the elements which were to be taken into consideration."[10] He also made it clear that this "*does not imply*, however, that *in passing upon the admission of a new member, considerations of all kinds cannot be brought into account*."[11] The Report concluded with these words: "The text adopted sets forth more clearly than the Dumbarton Oaks proposals those qualifications for membership which the delegates deemed fundamental, and provides a more definite guide to the General Assembly and the Security Council on the admission of new members."[12]

[8] *Ibid.*, p. 290.   [9] *Ibid.*, p. 308.
[10] *Ibid.*, (Italics added.)   [11] *Ibid.* (Italics added.)
[12] *Ibid.*, p. 309. (Italics added.)

This report was approved by Commission I at the San Francisco Conference.[13] The Rapporteur of Committee I of Commission II, which also deliberated on admissions to the UN, reported:

> The Committee recommends that new members be admitted by the General Assembly upon recommendations of the Security Council. . . . In supporting the acceptance of this principle, several delegates emphasized that the purpose of the Charter is primarily to provide security against a repetition of the present war and that, therefore *the Security Council should assume the intial responsibility of suggesting new participating States.*[14]

The views quoted above created a sense of anxiety among the delegates that the Security Council might dominate the General Assembly in matters of admission. The issue was referred to an Advisory Committee of Jurists, which felt that "these texts *would not in any way weaken* the original text adopted by the Committee."[15] The Rapporteur of Committee 11/1l announcing accordingly added that the "Committee agreed that this interpretation should be included in its minutes as the one that should be given to this provision of the Charter, and on this basis approved the text as suggested."[16]

The passages cited above with emphasis show that the framers of the Charter of the UN intended to create a system of admission where "the admission of a new member would be subject to study." Secondly, such criteria was embodied in the Article which the delegates deemed "fundamental" and further enumeration was deliberately avoided. Finally, as to the respective sphere of competence of the Security Council and the General Assembly, the framers went to the extent of laying down expressly their wish as to how the relevant provision is to be interpreted—so as not to weaken the position of the General Assembly in this regard.

JUDICIAL AFFIRMATION OF THE LAW OF ADMISSIONS

The above conclusions were tested before the International Court

---

[13]Report of Rapporteur, Commission I, *UNCIO* Docs., Vol. 6, p. 299.
[14]*UNCIO* Docs., Vol. 8, p. 451. (Italics added.)
[15]*Ibid.*, p. 487. (Italics added.)   [16]*Ibid.*, p. 495.

of Justice in two advisory opinions. The facts leading to the advisory opinions were as follows.

The fears and precautions which the framers of the Charter exhibited while drafting Article 4, however, proved futile not long after the establishment of the UN. The procedure of admission to the UN became embroiled in the cold war manoeuvrings of the two Power Blocs. The criteria of peace-loving nature of applicants and their willingness and capacity to abide by the Charter obligations, were thrown overboard. The qualifications of States came to be judged on the basis of bloc affiliations.

The Charter of the UN—unlike the League Covenant which made the Assembly the sole authority to effect admissions of new members—places the power of admissions both on the Security Council and the General Assembly. "The admission of any such State" reads paragraph 2 of Article 4, "to membership in the United Nations will be effected by a decision of the General Assembly upon the recommendation of the Security Council."

A *decision* of the General Assembly and a *recommendation* by the Security Council are the two *sine qua non* for admission of new members into the Organization. The decision by the General Assembly according to paragraph 2 of Article 18, should be taken by a two-thirds majority of the members present and voting. And veto would apply to the recmmendation of the Security Council as the matter cannot be treated as procedural.

With the special position of the Security Council in the scheme of the Charter and the privileged status of the permanent members, the Council began to have the first and last say in the matter. The Security Council treated applicants in "package deals," the legality of which was tested before the ICJ through an advisory opinion.

Up to the time the General Assembly decided to request for the advisory opinion seventeen States had applied for admission. Of these Afghanistan, Iceland, Sweden, Siam, Pakistan, and Yemen were at that time outside the power blocs. The rest, viz. Albania, Mongolian People's Republic, Bulgaria, Hungary, Rumania (of the Soviet bloc), Ireland and Portugal (for their sympathies with the Nazis), Transjordan, Finland, and Hungary (for miscellaneous reasons) failed to receive recommendation of the Security Council. The Big Powers had agreed at Potsdam that Hungary, Rumania, Bulgaria, and Finland should be admitted to the UN. The Soviet Union insisted that Italy's admission could not take place until that promise was fulfilled.[17] Australia, the USA, and the UK were opposed to voting on the applications *en bloc*. The question of simultaneous admission was not new. The US had made similar proposals in regard to the applications of Albania, Mongolia, Afghanistan, Transjordan, Ireland, Portugal, and Sweden, although it "had misgivings about some of the applicants."[18]

In short, bloc affiliations became the primary criteria for admission into the UN. If the Soviet Union blocked the admission of countries within the Western bloc, the West saw to it that no Soviet bloc nation got admitted in the UN. So much so such countries became pawns (insofar as admission to the UN was concerned) in Big Power cold war diplomacy. The result, in an evenly-matched bi-polar world, was that there was a deadlock in UN admissions.

In an effort to resolve the conflict the matter was referred by the General Assembly to the International Court of Justice by a resolution proposed by Belgium and adopted on 17 November 1947.[19] The question posed was:

Is a member of the United Nations which is called upon, in virtue of Article 4, of the Charter, to pronounce itself by its vote, either in the Security Council or in the General Assembly, on the admission of a State to membership in the United Nations, juridically entitled to make its consent to the admission dependent on conditions not expressly provided by paragraph 1 of the said Article? In particular, can such a member, while it recognizes the conditions set forth in that provision to be fulfilled by the State concerned, subject its affirmative vote to the additional

[17]UN Doc. A/404, pp. 2-3; and UN Doc. S/204, 46, pp. 47-50.

[18]UN Doc. S/177, p. 5; *Security Council Official Records*, 1st Year, 2nd Series, No. 4, p. 42.

[19]Resolution 113 (II)B. Admission of New Members, *General Assembly Official Records*, 2nd Sess.

condition that other States be admitted to membership in the
United Nations together with that State?[20]

The question, in line with the present enquiry, might be framed
this way: Is the Organization, acting through the members, bound
strictly by the criteria laid down in Article 4 for effecting admission?
Has not the Organization—and, therefore, the members—any
implied powers to prescribe other qualifications over and above those
mentioned in Article 4?

Advisory Opinions of the ICJ

After a close scrutiny of the scope and content of the question
posed to it, the Court felt that the question was in effect
confined to the following point only: Are the conditions, stated
in paragraph 1 of Article 4, exhaustive in character in the sense
that an affirmative reply would lead to the conclusion that a member
is not legally entitled to make admission dependent on conditions
not expressly provided for in that Article, while a negative reply
would, on the contrary, authorize a member to make admission
dependent also on other conditions.[21] Reciting paragraph 1 of
Article 4 the Court found that the "requisite conditions are five
in number: to be admitted to membership in the United Nations,
an applicant must (1) be a State; (2) be peace-loving; (3) accept
the obligations of the Charter; (4) be able to carry out these
obligations; and (5) be willing to do so."[22]

After laying down that all these conditions were subject to the
judgment of the Organization, the Court proceeded to answer
whether those conditions were exhaustive or otherwise. The text
of this paragraph, said the Court, "by the enumeration which it
contains and the choice of its terms, clearly demonstrates the
intention of its authors to establish a legal rule which, while it fixes

---

[20] As to the history of the consideration of the question of admission leading to
the request for the advisory opinion see Yuen Li Liang, "Notes on Legal
Questions Concerning the United Nations, Conditions of Admission of a State
to Membership in the United Nations," *American Journal of International Law*,
Vol. 43, 1949, pp. 288-95.

[21] "Admission of a State to the United Nations (Charter, Article 4), Advisory
Opinion," ICJ *Reports*, 1948, p. 57.

[22] *Ibid.*, p. 62.

the conditions of admission, determines also the reasons for which
admission may be refused; for the text does not differentiate between
these two cases and any attempt to restrict it to one of them would
be purely arbitrary."[23] The natural meaning of the words used,
the Court argued, led to the conclusion that these conditions
constituted an exhaustive enumeration and were not merely stated
by way of guidance or example. The provision would lose its significance and weight if other conditions, unconnected with those laid
down, could be demanded. The conditions, said the Court, stated
in paragraph 1 of Article 4 must therefore be regarded not merely
as the necessary conditions, but also as the conditions which
sufficed.

It was urged upon the Court that the *travaux preparatoires*
show a different intent. In fact, the dissenting judges based their
argument primarily on the preparatory work. In a powerful joint
dissenting opinion judges Basdevant, Winiarski, Sir Arnold
McNair, and Read took a strong line to the effect that Article 4
"does not create a system of accession," and that "admission of a
new member is pre-eminently a political act, and a political act of
the greatest importance."[24] Citing the San Francisco documents
(chronicled earlier) the dissenting judges held "that a member of
the United Nations remains legally entitled . . . to put forward considerations foreign to the qualifications specified in paragraph 1
of Article 4."[25] Judge Zorcic, likewise, thought "that Article 4
does not contain exhaustive provisions, but on the contrary is a
guide on admissions, containing only the fundamental and indispensable qualities required of a candidate."[26] Judge M. Krylov,
too , arrived at the "inevitable conclusion" that "members have a
right of discretionary and political appreciation limited only by the
broad purposes and principles of the Charter and subject to the
legal requirement of good faith under paragraph 2 of Article 2."[27]

The majority of the judges, however, viewed the matter differently. The majority opinion was that the conditions enumerated
did not represent an indispensable minimum, in the sense that

[23]*Ibid.*   [24]*Ibid.*, p 85.
[25]*Ibid.*, p. 90.   [26]*Ibid.*, p. 99,
[27]*Ibid.*, p. 111,

political considerations could be superimposed upon them, and prevent the admission of an applicant which fulfilled them. "The spirit as well as the terms of the paragraph," the Court ruled, "preclude the idea that considerations extraneous to these principles and obligations can prevent the admission of a State which complies with them"[28] With regard to the implications of the *travaux preparatoires*, the Court, while holding that there was no occasion to resort to preparatory work in case the text of a Convention was sufficiently clear, nevertheless pointed out that if "the authors of the Charter had meant to leave members free to import into the application of this provision considerations extraneous to the conditions laid down therein, they would undoubtedly have adopted a different wording."[29] The Court maintained that it did not follow from the exhaustive character of paragraph 1 of Article 4 that an appreciation was precluded of such circumstances of fact as would enable the existence of the requisite conditions to be verified. It held that the Article did not forbid the taking into account of any factor which it was possible reasonably and in good faith to connect with the conditions laid down in that Article. The taking into account of such factors was implied in the very wide and very elastic nature of the prescribed conditions; no relevant political factor—that is to say, none connected with the conditions of admission—was excluded.[30] Referring to the argument that the question of admission involved a decision of a political character, the Court observed that the Charter had laid down definite limitations on the relevant organs' powers and criteria of judgment which allowed, in this case, for a wide liberty of appreciation.[31]

In the *Second Admission Case*[32] the Court, called upon to determine whether the General Assembly could make a decision to

---

[28]*Ibid.*, p. 63.

[29]For opposite conclusion, see the Joint Dissenting Opinion of Judges Basdevant, Winiarksi, Sir Arnold McNair, and Read: "In our opinion, while the Charter makes the qualifications specified in paragraph 1 of Article 4 essential, it does not make them sufficient. If it had regarded them as sufficient, it would not have failed to say so. The point was one of too great importance to be left in obscurity." *Ibid.*, p. 90.

[30]*Ibid.*, p. 63.   [31]*Ibid.*, p. 64.

[32]"Competence of the General Assembly for the Admission of a State to the United Nations," ICJ *Reports*, 1950, p. 2.

admit a State when the Security Council had transmitted no recommendation to it, gave a negative ruling in the most unambiguous language. The Court held that it required two indispensable things to effect admission of a new member: a "recommendation" of the Security Council and a "decision" of the General Assembly; that the recommendation should come before the decision; and that to admit a State in the absence of such a favourable recommendation would almost nullify the role of the Security Council in the exercise of one of the essential functions of the Organization.[33]

In propounding the law of admissions of international organizations the International Court of Justice was aiming at a precarious balance. On the one hand it severely restricted the scope of implied powers; and on the other the concept of international personality and the independent identity of the UN were further developed. A delicate balance was also struck between the Organization's collective judgment and the individual member's national interests.

A State seeking admission had to submit to a process of examination, an examination that involved a probe into its *bona fides*, its past behaviour, future intentions, its readiness to abide by the regime of law that the Organization created and its capacity to carry out its obligations. The Organization was granted a power of independent "judgement," "discretion," "liberty of appreciation"— subject only to the limitations placed upon it by its constituent instrument, its organic law. It is true, the judgment, discretion, etc., of the Organization means the judgment, discretion, etc., of the members that compose it. The members would seldom use the above faculties to jeopardize their own national interests or the interests of their allies, but if the collective will, the general consensus, as represented by a two-third majority vote in the General Assembly and acquiescence of the 5 permanent members in the Security Council, so demand the will of the individual member was subordinated to the will of the Organization.

[33]*Ibid.*, pp. 7, 9. The power of subjective appreciation granted to the Organization, within the framework of Article 4, is not in any way severely circumscribed. There is an abundant scope for discretionary authority, as can be seen in actual practice.

In fine, the admissions process of the UN theoretically could be characterized this way. Though the framers of the Charter were fairly clear in their mind that the requirements they were mentioning in Article 4 of the Charter were only "fundamental" and that extraneous considerations could not be ruled out, the ICJ felt that the language of the Article left no room for such interpretation. The enumerated criteria, in the opinion of the Court, was "exhaustive." But it did leave sufficient openings in phrases like "judgment," "discretion," "liberty of appreciation," etc. The result was that members were free to exercise discretion in matters of admissions, but their grounds for admission or refusal should be based squarely on the express qualifications of Article 4. The concepts of "statehood," "peace-loving" nature of a nation, its "ability" and "willingness" to be bound by Charter obligations, were too subjective and amorphous a criteria to restrict the enormity of discretion. This will be brought out clearly in the next section dealing with the practice of both the League and the UN.

THE LEAGUE AND UN PRACTICE OF ADMISSIONS

Conditions of Membership in the League

The League judged the applications for membership on the following criteria:[34]

(*a*) Was the application for admission to the League in order?

(*b*) Was the government applying for admission recognized *de jure* or *de facto* and by which States?

(*c*) Was the applicant a nation with a stable government and settled frontiers? What were its size and its population?

(*d*) Was it fully self-governing?

(*e*) What had been its conduct, including both acts and assurances, with regard to: (*i*) its international obligations; (*ii*) the prescriptions of the League as to armaments?

The first question is inconsequential. The second is irrelevant for the present discussion. Items (*c*), (*d*), and (*e*) create a wide discretionary power. The League under these enquiries exercised its "right of appreciation" with utmost pragmatism. As to the

[34]League of Nations, *Records of First Assembly*, Meetings of the Committees, Vol. 2, p. 159.

third criterion it might be said that the League viewed the matter realistically and admitted all nations which had a reasonably stable government and well-settled frontiers. Where, however, the League was faced with uncertainty it denied admission. The cases in point are those of Azerbaidjan, Georgia, and the Ukraine. Taking advantage of World War I the above States, which were part of the Russian Empire, asserted autonomy and sought recognition as independent States. Azerbaidjan had actually received *de facto* recognition in early 1920 from Great Britain, France, and Italy; but later in the year, the recognized government lost control of the situation.

The Comittee which was to report on qualifications of the applicants found that "Azerbaidjan does not appear to have a stable Government whose authority extends over the whole of the territory" and for this reason admission was denied, no member of the League voting for it.[35] The Ukraine was also denied admission on similar grounds.[36] Georgia's request, too, was rejected on the same grounds, though by a divided vote.[37]

The questionnaire, it may be noticed, required information about the size and population of the applicant State. This question assumed special significance when small States like the Principality of Lichtenstein, San Marino, and Monaco applied for admission to the League. Lichtenstein, though a sovereign State under international law, was so small and its resources so very meagre that it had deputed to other powers various of its functions such as the control of customs, the administration of posts, and diplomatic representation. The position of San Marino and Monaco was no better. The latter, however, raised less difficulty, for San Marino failed to furnish information which was essential for the consideration of its application, and Monaco withdrew its application. Lichtenstein posed special difficulty in that its case was being strongly championed by the Swiss government.[38]

A diplomatic formula was evolved by the special committee which was entrusted with the solution of the problem of diminutive

[35]League of Nations, *Records of the First Assembly*, Plenary Meetings, p. 664.
[36]*Ibid.*, pp. 561, 665.
[37]*Ibid.*, pp. 630-3.   [38]*Ibid.*, pp. 643-4, 667-8.

States. The Committee suggested three alternatives: (*i*) association with the League with full representation but without a vote; (*ii*) representation by some other State; (*iii*) admission to membership with full privileges to be exercised only where their special interests were involved.

The First Committee of the Second Assembly which considered the matter reported finally that experience should be awaited before any definite conditions were laid down.[39]

In regard to the fourth criteria, i.e. the status of the applicant, the League evolved a new concept of international personality. No more were independence and sovereignty the primary grounds on which the international status of a community was judged. Self-government became the hallmark. As Newton Rowell found, a "new principle was introduced into diplomatic practice" by the Covenant, "viz. that the condition of admission to the family of nations should be not independent and separate sovereignty, but full self-government."[40] The Dominion of Canada, the Commonwealth of Australia, the Union of South Africa, and India became original members of the League. These States enjoyed equal status with other members of the League, e.g. delegates from these nations were eligible for representation on the Council of the League; and their nationals could be elected as judges of the Permanent Court of International Justice.

The fifth criteria relating to the conduct of the applicant with regard to its international obligations and the prescriptions of the League as to armament corresponded to the conditions of Article 1 which required an admitted State to "give effective guarantees of its sincere intention to observe its international obligations," etc. Though the condition did not prove onerous in practice, the League nevertheless took particular care to investigate into the record of the applicant in this regard and in some cases did demand such guarantees. The cases in point are those of Bulgaria and Hungary. In the case of the former, the Conference of Ambassadors was

[39]League of Nations, *Records of the Second Assembly*, Plenary Meetings, p. 820.

[40]Newton W. Rowell, *The British Empire and World Peace*, Toronto, 1922, p. 178.

requested to supply information as to whether the Bulgarian Government had loyally carried out the Treaty of Neuilly-sur-Seine.[41] Hungary was admitted upon a solemn undertaking by its delegate that it would observe its international engagements, even though the military clauses of the Treaty of Trianon had been only partially carried out.[42]

In certain cases, declarations were made by the representatives of the States applying for admission. For example, the Finnish delegate, in a letter to Lord Robert Cecil, made a general declaration committing his government to take steps to effect the requisite reforms for the protection of minorities.[43] Estonia, Latvia, and Lithuania, likewise, were required to sign identical declarations with reference to their international obligations for the protection of minorities.[44] In 1921, almost a year after its admission to the League on a recommendation of the First Assembly Albania had to sign a declaration containing stipulations for the protection of minorities.[45] The government of Luxemberg gave an assurance in writing that it "will take the necessary measures to bring the constitutional laws of the country into harmony with the obligations involved in admission to the League of Nations."[46] The Abyssinian Government, too, was required to sign a declaration adhering to the obligations of paragraph 1 of Article 2 of the Convention of St. Germain of 10 September 1919, concerning the slave trade, and undertaking to conform to the principles set forth therein and in the Protocol concerning traffic in arms.[47] This brings us to the question of armaments and the League regulations appertaining to the same.

[41]For the report of the Conference of Ambassadors, see League of Nations, *Records of the First Assembly*, Plenary Meetings, pp. 600-1, 603-5.

[42]League of Nations, *Records of the Third Assembly*, Plenary Meetings, Vol. 2, pp. 122-3.

[43]League of Nations, *Records of the First Assembly*, Plenary Meetings, p. 585.

[44]League of Nations, *Records of the Second Assembly*, Meetings of the Committees, Vol. 2, pp. 533, 580, 583.

[45]League of Nations, Minutes of the 14th Session of the Council, pp. 115, 160; *Records of the First Assembly*, Plenary Meetings, pp. 568-9.

[46]League of Nations, *Records of the First Assembly*, Plenary Meetings, p. 586.

[47]League of Nations, *Records of the Fourth Assembly*, Plenary Meetings, p. 125.

A Permanent Advisory Commission on Military, Naval, and Air Questions was set up to investigate into the applicant's armament position. This Commission worked in co-operation with the Committee of the Assembly which was in charge of the admissions. In the case of some States the examination was rather prefunctory.[48] In some cases[49] the military and naval programmes were required to be submitted for scrutiny. The examination was more rigorous in the case of certain ex-belligerent States, e.g. Austria, Bulgaria, and Hungary.[50]

In the ultimate analysis, the process of admission to the League of Nations was extraordinary in the sense that States had to shed some of the traditional trappings of sovereignty, submit to a not-altogether exultory mode of investigation into the sensitive field of defence and had to give undertakings, sometimes written, over matters which were hitherto deemed to be within the reserved domain of sovereign States. The process, however, was not too exacting. Political commonsense and expediency rather than legal considerations played a predominant part in judging the applications for membership.[51] A semblance of legality was nevertheless maintained throughout.

The Admissions Practice of the United Nations

Major battles were fought in the United Nations more on the criteria of statehood and peace-loving nature of the States seeking admission than on the rest of the conditions. The concept of statehood especially received greatest attention. Since it would be highly unwieldy to generalize on all the admissions to the UN a few case studies will be undertaken with a bit of prefacing.

On the Concept of Statehood. The position under international law is that four criteria must be fulfilled before a State

[48]As, for instance, in the case of Albania. See League of Nations, *Records of the First Assembly*, Meetings of the Committees, Vol. 2, p. 214.

[49]As in the cases of Finland, Latvia, and Lithuania. See *ibid.*, pp. 231-2; *Records of the Second Assembly*, Plenary Meetings, pp. 334-9.

[50]League of Nations, *Records of the First Assembly*, Meetings of the Committees, Vol. 2, pp. 163-71, 218, 233-8; *Records of the Third Assembly*, Plenary Meetings, Vol. 2, pp. 122-3.

[51]Friendlander, *op. cit.*, p. 98.

can be called as such. The Montevideo Convention on the Rights and Duties of States, which comes nearest to the traditional concept, has it that "the State as a person of international law should possess the following qualifications: (a) a permanent population; (b) a defined territory; (c) government; and (d) capacity to enter into relations with the other States."[52]

Claims of statehood were made on numerous occasions: for admission into the UN, to appear before specific organs of the UN to participate in certain Specialized Agencies, to bring matters affecting peace and security to the notice of the UN, to be a party to the Statute of the International Court of Justice and to get admittance into other bodies catering to the general upliftment of nations. The UN, its organs, and the Specialized Agencies had to apply their judgment over these claims.

As the following analysis will reveal the policy of admission and the right to participation, with the concomitant acquiescence of the claims of statehood granted to such States, have more often than not been guided by pragmatic appreciation of reality than by a scrupulous observance of the norms of traditional international law.

Original Membership. The policy of pragmatic considerations subordinating traditional criteria of statehood can be discerned even before the UN was born. Participation of Byelorussia and the Ukraine at the San Francisco Conference, not to mention India and the Philippines,[53] was a certain indication of UN practice on admissions.[54] The position of Lebanon and Syria was also

---

[52]Article I, 49 Statute 3097, US *Treaty Series*, No. 881, 26 December 1933.

[53]India before attaining independence was enjoying some external independence within the British Commonwealth, had an outstanding war record, and was a member of the League, even before its independence, which was on 15 August 1947. The Philippines became independent on July 1946.

[54]It is true that a large amount of diplomatic bargaining was done over this issue by the Big Powers at Yalta and Crimea Conference and the Soviet republics were not allowed to enter the UN before a final bargain was struck as a *quid pro quo* to the Soviet acceptance of the voting formula. Nevertheless the fact remains that the Sponsoring Powers were creating a precedent by admitting States which were not States in the strict sense of the term under traditional international law. See Ruth B. Russell and Janette E. Muther, *A History of the United Nations Charter*, Washington, D.C., 1958, pp. 536-7.

anomalous, with French assertions that its responsibilities over these two countries at that time were not yet terminated.

Post-formation Admissions. Subsequent to the establishment of the UN however a semblance of adherence to the traditional norms of statehood was shown by UN organs. Much of the controversy regarding the criteria of statehood however turned around the elusive concept of "defined territory," "stable and effective government" and on the concept of "independence."[55]

The classic example of the controversy over the concept of "defined territory" can be found in the case of Israel's admission to the UN. The Arab States (particularly Syria, Egypt, Iraq, Lebanon, Saudi Arabia, and Yemen)[56] objected to Israel's admission on the ground that its borders were contested. In answer to this objection it was argued[57] that the territorial requirement must be construed in the light of the General Assembly resolution conferring territory upon Israel[58] and that it did not matter that certain details as to the delimitation of this territory remained unsettled. Philip C. Jessup, representing the US then, indicated in a spirited statement that both "reason and history" demand no precise delimitations of the boundaries.[59] Finally, Israel was admitted in 1949.

The defined "territory" criteria was invoked from time to time in the UN but the practice reveals that the UN adopted what the Tribunal in the *Dentache Continental Gas-Gesellschaft* vs. *Polish State*[60] had said: "In order to say that a State exists ... it

---

[55]A systematic and exhaustive analysis of the claims and counter claims around these concepts in the UN organs and in the Specialized Agencies can be found in Rosalyn Higgins, *The Development of International Law through the Political Organs of the United Nations*, London, 1963, pp. 17-57. The present section is based on this author's findings.

[56]*Security Council Official Records*, 3rd year, 385th Meeting, 3-4 (S/1131) and 316th Meeting, 19-20 (S/PV.386); *General Assembly Official Records*, 3rd Session, part 2, pp. 311-2 (SA/855); *ibid.*, *Ad hoc* Pol. Ctee. 267 (A/818); *ibid.*, pp. 181, 289; *ibid.*, pp. 107, 220, 222, 294-5, 305-6 respectively.

[57]For example, Uruguay, *General Assembly Official Records*, 3rd Session, *Ad hoc* Pol. Cttee., 297 (A/18); USSR, *Security Council Official Records*, 3rd year, 383rd Meeting, p. 22 (S/1093) and 386th Meeting, pp. 30-1 (S/1121).

[58]*General Assembly Official Records*, 2nd Session, res. 181 (II) 131.

[59]*Security Council Official Records*, 3rd year, 383rd Meeting, p. 1093.

[60]11 *Annual Digest*, 1929-30, No. 5, 1929, p. 15.

is enough that (its) . . . territory has a sufficient consistency even though its borders have not yet been accurately delimited."

The admission of Yemen and the Congo (Leopoldville), in spite of the fact that the former's boundaries were far from precise and the latter's sovereignty over the Katanga region was effectively being challenged by Moise Tshombe at the time of its admission (15th Session), show that the UN was guided by the criteria of consistency rather than accurate delimitation of borders.

In the last mentioned case however it was the concept of "stable and effective government" which received considerable probing. The Central Congolese government at that time was far from stable and effective, with the threat of Katanga secession, the Kasai rebellion, and a host of warring tribes creating confusion and chaos. But the General Assembly had no other choice except to bet on a horse and stick to the end.[61] Likewise the UN had a difficult time grappling with the unstable and ineffective governments in Ruanda and Burundi when they were admitted to the Organization.[62] It would appear that the UN took the view that internal dissensions were no concern of the Organization. So long as external intervention or influence was proved absent the States seeking admission must be obliged.

On the Concept of Independence. The concept of independence was raised in varied circumstances. For example, South Korea's application was attacked by Communist States on the ground that the South Korean regime was a puppet government imposed on the Korean people.[63] Mongolia's admission likewise

[61]*General Assembly Official Records*, 4th Emergency Special Session, 863rd Meeting, p. 102 (A/L. 292 Rev. 1).

[62]See for the "misgivings" as to the ability of these trust territories to maintain law and order if given independence on the scheduled date of 1 July 1962, General Assembly Res. 1746 (XVI) passed after considering the report of a Commission appointed for the specific purpose of ascertaining the preparedness of these territories for independence. Both the Commission and the General Assembly had grave doubts; nonetheless, these territories were admitted soon after independence. A/5147, Add. 1-2 and A/5148 respectively for their application; S/5149 and S/5150 for the Security Council recommendations and General Assembly resolutions 1748 (XVII) and 1749 (XVII) for their admission.

[63]*Security Council Official Records*, 4th year, 423rd Meeting, p. 7 (S/1281).

was rejected on the ground that it lacked independence.[64] The Mauritanian application was also objected to by Morocco on the same grounds.[65] Again, sometimes defence arrangements of newly independent States were considered by some delegations to compromise the applicant's sovereignty.[66] On occasions absence of diplomatic relations too was said to negate independence.[67] It might be said, in short, that though issues of admission were ultimately decided by political and diplomatic considerations, a semblance of adherence to the traditional norms of statehood was maintained but with the broadest and most liberal interpretation of these criteria.

It will now be examined as to how the admissions process has affected the traditional concept of recognition.

ADMISSION TO INTERNATIONAL ORGANIZATION AND THE CONCEPT OF RECOGNITION

The preceding section, it is believed, brings out sufficiently the way the admissions process of the League and the UN have affected traditional concepts of sovereignty, statehood, and independence. Another concept which receives the same treatment is recognition.

The rationale behind the concept of recognition itself has undergone a vital change in the modern methods of co-operation among nations. International law as a code of conduct applicable to a select band of civilized European States is no more a true description of this discipline. Recognition, consequently, is not a benevolent gesture of a few States of Christian community in relation

[64]*Security Council Official Records*, 2nd year, Spl. Supp. 13 (S/95). For Dr. Kerno's useful summary of the vicissitudes of these applications, see ICJ *Pleadings*, 1948, p. 42 in Conditions of Admission of a State to Membership in the United Nations case.

[65]*Security Council Official Records*, 15th year, 911th Meeting.

[66]See for instance, USSR and Poland objections over Jordan's application, *Security Council Official Records*, 1st year, 2nd Ser. Supp. 4, p. 136 (S/101); *General Assembly Official Records*, 2nd Session, 117th Meeting, pp. 1044-53 (A/471).

[67]As in the case of Transjordan, *Security Council Official Records*, 1st year, 2nd Ser. 56th Meeting, pp. 91-1 (S/101) and Supp. 4, 72 (S/101); 2nd year, Spl. Supp. 3, pp. 14-5 (S/101). For other examples, see Higgins, n. 55, pp. 17-57.

to another indicating an intention that the former condescends to treat the latter on an equal footing. Recognition in the modern sense indicates a State's willingness to have normal intercourse with the recognized State. This is not to say that a State withholding recognition of another is committing an unpardonable illegality, nor even to suggest that a State which fails to secure recognition of one or more particular States does not belong to the juridical community of nations. The conflict of individual interests of members of this community are well brought into relief when the process of admission to international organizations is focussed on the maze of politico-legal jungle that is the institution of recognition.

World War I resulted not only in the emergence of a number of new international persons but also in a new political order. With the the establishment of the League of Nations a number of problems in international law cropped up. One such problem was: what relation the acceptance of a new State's or government's representation by an international organization has with recognition of such a State or government by individual members of the Organization? The problem can be viewed from two standpoints. One is whether acceptance of admission to membership in an international organization presupposes its members' recognition of the new State. The other is whether acceptance of admission to membership or representation has the same legal effect as recognition. It hardly needs emphasis that the two questions have a vital bearing on the law of admission to international organization. If the first problem is answered in the affirmative the whole structure of the law of recognition is pulled down. And if the second postulate is found to be true then, too, the institution of recognition would need a considerable revamping.[68]

---

[68]On this problem, see M. Lachs, "Recognition and Modern Methods of International Co-operation," *British Yearbook of International Law*, Vol. 35, 1959, pp. 252-9; Shigejiro Tabata, "Admission to the United Nations and Recognition of States," *Japanese Annual of International Law*, Vol. 5, 1961, p.1; S. Rosenne, "Recognition of States by the United Nations," *British Yearbook of International Law*, Vol. 26, 1949, p. 437; and Malbone W. Graham, *The League of Nations and the Recognition of States*, Berkeley, 1933.

The League of Nations Debate

On 12 February 1920 the Secretary-General of the League informed the Council that the minister of Colombia had submitted to him a draft form of accession to the Covenant wherein:

Colombia desired to accede to the Covenant, but did not wish to find herself thereby committed to a recognition of the independence of Panama, a signatory of the peace treaty. Colombia had not yet recognized the independence of Panama, and a treaty upon this question between Colombia and the United States was even now awaiting ratification.[69]

After a brief discussion it was decided by the League Council that the Secretary-General should be authorized to draft an acknowledgement of Colombia's proposal of accession, without expressing any opinion on the point at issue.[70] The debate, however, did not end. The First Committee which deliberated on the question of admissions also faced the same problem. M. Politis, the eminent lawyer from Greece, maintained that admission might imply *de jure* recognition by all members. Lord Robert Cecil, on the other hand, claimed that the rules of admission as stated in Article 1 of the Covenant did not infringe the liberty of individual States in matters of recognition.[71] The question was referred to a committee of international jurists for an advisory opinion. The Committee, too, was divided in its opinion: "Two opinions had been expressed: one view held that admission to the League involved the recognition of the State requesting admission by all States members of the League; the other view was that it only entailed observation of the conditions expressly laid down by the Covenant."[72]

In the subsequent debate on the subject in the plenary meetings of the Assembly, M. Chagas of Portugal played a conspicuous part.

[69]League of Nations, *Process-Verbal of Second Session of the Council*, 4th Meeting, p. 5.

[70]*Ibid.*

[71]League of Nations, *Records of the First Assembly*, Meetings of the Committees, Vol. 2, p. 157.

[72]*Ibid.*, p. 160.

Contending that recognition *de jure* was an act which was individual
to the States which grant it, M. Chagas submitted a resolution with
the following citation:

> Whereas the *de jure* recognition of a State is an act by which
> individual relations are established between the recognizing
> State and the recognized State . . . and whereas such relations
> have been defined by traditional international law and are not
> necessarily quite the same as collective relations arising from
> membership of the League of Nations.[73]

The proposal fell through. Except the delegates from Rumania
and Poland none were prepared to commit themselves to M. Chagas'
view.[74] By far the best opinion was expressed by M. Poullet of
Belgium, who made a penetrating study of the problem when
he said:

> There is no question of requiring as a *sine qua non* for admission
> into the League recognition *de jure* by all the members of the
> League of Nations of the State asking for admission, but that
> nevertheless, it is not reasonable for a State which does not
> recognize *de jure* another State . . . to vote for the admission of
> the State which it does not recognize, because admission to the
> League implies the guarantee of Article 10 and is a more serious
> matter than the mere dispatch of diplomatic representatives to
> a foreign capital.[75]

The logical conclusion, argued M. Poullet, should be that if a State
had not recognized *de jure* another State seeking admission the
former could not vote for admission of the latter. By focussing the
attention on the obligations of the Covenant, especially the implications of Article 10, M. Poullet changed the entire course of
discussion to the right point at the right time.

It needs no penetrating study to see how enormous are these
"international obligations" on which "effective guarantees" are
sought for admission into the League. The Covenant requires the

---

[73]League of Nations, *Records of the First Assembly*, Plenary Meetings, p. 620.
[74]*Ibid.*, pp. 618-20.
[75]*Ibid.*, pp. 623-4.

applicant State to abandon the unlimited right of declaring war at its pleasure or according to its own individual judgment under Article 12; the State admits the right of the League to discuss its foreign policy under Article 11, it accepts arbitration in the disputes in which it is concerned under Article 13 or, alternatively under Article 15 the intervention of the Council; and under Article 16, it abandons its right to neutrality when another member of the League fails to observe its obligations under Articles 12, 13, and 15.

The above obligations are applicable not only to the State seeking admission but also to those which are within the Organization already. When States, members of the League, vote for admission into the League they show their willingness to abide by, if the similie is permitted, the rules of the game as envisaged by the Covenant. The relations that the Covenant establishes amongst the members of the League, *qua* members, are more extensive and more serious than does the institution of recognition between the recognizing and the recognized State. The provisions of the Covenant are not empty slogans; they are a code of conduct legally binding on all those States which signed the Covenant. As Fisher of Britain reminded:

> We must either treat the League seriously or not. If we treat the League seriously we must treat the Covenant seriously. . . . I earnestly ask the Delegates in this Assembly to consider, when they are voting on the admission of a new State, whether they are prepared to take the responsibility of advising their respective Governments to come to the assistance of that State in the hour of need.[76]

Despite reminders of the above nature, despite opinions of varied shades, the League proceeded to admit States on political expediency.[77] Membership was given to all kinds of States, though

[76]*Ibid.*, p. 633.

[77]See for the discussion on the States admitted to the League and the grounds on which admission was granted, Manley O. Hudson, "Membership in the League of Nations," *American Journal of International Law*, Vol. 18, 1924, P. 436; Lilian M. Friedlander, "The Admission of States to the League of Nations," *British Yearbook of International Law*, 1928, p. 84,

some of them were recognized *de jure* by only a small number of the members of the League. It was generally agreed that recognition by members of the League was not to be considered a *sine qua non* for admission. The controversy as to whether or not admission to the League *amounted* to recognition was not settled. The publicists of the generation picked up the thread of debate.

Manley O. Hudson after reviewing the process of admission thought "that a vote of admission into the League implies some degree of 'recognition' by the members of the League."[78] Lilian M. Friedlander, likewise, maintained that "admission to the League is, for the post-war world, what 'recognition of a sovereign State' was before 1920, and that the qualifications laid down in Article 1 of the Covenant . . . are the essential qualities of any independent State to-day."[79]   Edward J. Phelan, writing on "The Sovereignty of the Irish Free State," tried to prove that the Irish Free State was a full international person by the fact that it was admitted to the League. The qualifications, asserted Phelan, which a community must possess before it could be admitted to the League of Nations, were to be found defined in Article 1 of the Covenant. He went further and maintained that admission to the League "is the equivalent of the old 'recognition' . . . it is more definite and more impressive, because it . . . (is) collective."[80] Phelan, however, was aware that membership of the League alone did not confer effective international status, but his argument was "that only States which fulfil the qualifications required for membership of the League and which can accept the obligations involved in it are to-day full international persons."[81]

This way the two problems were merged. The question whether recognition by members of the League was an essential condition before admission came to be linked with the question whether admission amounted to recognition of the new member by the

[78]M.O. Hudson, *op. cit.*, p. 454.

[79]L.M. Friedlander, *op. cit.*, p. 100.

[80]*The Review of Nations*, Vol. 1, No. 3, March 1927, p. 45.

[81]*Ibid.*, p. 46. Professor Shiegejiro Tabata has neatly catalogued other writers who hold that admission to the League means recognition. (See, "Admission to the United Nations and Recognition of States," *Japanese Annual of International Law*, No. 5, 1961, pp. 7-8.

existing ones. By denying the former the latter question was not answered. Any conclusion in this connection must take into account the position under the UN.

Position under the United Nations

Paragraph 1 of Article 4 of the Charter, as has been seen earlier, prescribes certain qualifications that must be fulfilled by a State seeking admission to the UN. It has also been seen that these conditions have been pronounced by the principal judicial organ of the UN, to be exhaustive. It will be examined now if admission of any such State that fulfils the prescribed qualifications means recognition by the rest of the individual members of the Organization. The question came up quite early in the UN, though in an indirect way, in relation to the matter of Chinese representation. The problem was, what government (Kuomintang or Communist) was entitled to represent the State of China in the UN, where China, *qua* State, was already a member. Neither the provisions of the Charter nor the rules of procedure of the Security Council and the General Assembly threw much light directly on the problem.

On the initiative of Sir Benegal N. Rau, the then Representative of India to the UN,[82] a confidential memorandum on the legal aspects of the problem of representation in the UN was prepared by the Secretariat for the information of the Secretary-General, Trygve Lie, the text of which was later released to the press.[83] Deploring the linkage of the question of representation with the question of recognition by member States the Memorandum maintained that the two institutions had superficial similarities but were essentially different: "Recognition of a new State, or of a new government of an existing State, is a unilateral act which the recognizing government can grant or withhold."[84] On the other hand, "membership of a State in the United Nations and representation of a State in the organs is clearly determined by a collective

[82] See UN Doc. No. S/1047, *SCOR*, 5th year, Supp. for 1 January through 31 May 1950, p. 2.

[83] UN Doc. S/1466, *ibid.*, pp. 18-23.

[84] *Ibid.*, p. 19.

act of the appropriate organs . . . therefore . . . it would appear to be legally inadmissible to condition the latter acts by a requirement that they be preceded by individual recognition."[85]

To substantiate the first proposition the Memorandum referred to the unsettled controversy among scholars as to whether recognition was a high policy of power or a stabilized legal institution and cited a statement of the US representative, Austin. The US representative replying to the Syrian delegate's charge that the US recognition of Israel was premature and illegal, had declared:

> I should regard it as highly improper for me to admit that any country on earth can question the sovereignty of the United States of America in the exercise of that high political act of recognition of the *de facto* status of a State.
>
> Moreover I would not admit here, by implication or by direct answer, that there exists a tribunal of justice or any other kind, anywhere, that can pass judgment upon the legality or the validity of that act of my country.[86]

In support of the second proposition, viz. that admission to the UN was a collective act distinct from the individual act, that is, recognition, the Memorandum cited the practice of the League and the UN and arrived at the conclusion that (1) a member could properly vote to accept a representative of a government which it did not recognize, or with which it had no diplomatic relations, and (2) such a vote did not imply recognition or readiness to assume diplomatic relations.[87] The Memorandum mentioned instances where members of the League and the UN did cast a favourable vote for admission to the Organization of States which were not recognized by those members individually.

The point at issue, it is submitted, is not whether or not admission should be preceded by *de facto* or *de jure* recognition of the individual members of the Organization, nor even whether the practice at the League or UN was unbroken, but to see if "collective recognition" by a given number of members of a general

[85]*Ibid.*, p. 20.
[86]*Ibid.*, p. 19.
[87]*Ibid.*, p. 22.

organization amounts to "individual recognition" by the same members. The instances cited are not helpful for this inquiry. What is called in question is the argument that since admission of a new State into an organization is a collective act, whereas recognition of that State by any of the members "is an unilateral act which the recognizing government can grant or withhold," the two acts are different and mutually exclusive, and, *a fortiori* the former does not amount to an implied recognition either.

The above view is wrong on two counts. One, it takes the institution of recognition in the narrow sense of having diplomatic relations. Two, it ignores the legal effects of the two institutions.

It needs no elaborate argument to prove that recognition is more than mere willingness to establish diplomatic relations. It certainly is not an indicator to an all-pervasive direct or general intercourse. Recognition of a State means the recognizing State's willingness to treat the recognized State as one among the Comity of Nations and thereby demonstrating a desire to abide by the norms of international law which set the limits to the rights and responsibilities of the members of this Comity of Nations. Does admission, say, to the UN create such a bond, establish such legal relations? It does.

The Charter of the UN, signed by 125 States of the world, has as one of its stated purposes the establishment of "conditions under which justice and respect for the obligations arising from treaties and other sources of international law can be maintained"; another of its purposes is "to bring about by peaceful means, and in conformity with the principles of justice and international law, adjustment or settlement of international disputes." The above provisions make it clear that relations between members of the UN are regulated on the principles of international law. Paragraph 1 of Article 2, which prescribes the fundamental principles for the guidance of members as well as the Organization, stipulates that the Organization is based on "the principles of the sovereign equality of all its members," paragraph 4 forbids "the threat or use of force" which may endanger the "territorial integrity or political independence" of any other State. In addition to this the

Charter creates a host of duties and obligations that are binding on the members in their mutual relations both within and without the Organization. The lawbreaker is liable for suspension under Article 5 and for expulsion under Article 6. The expenses of the Organization are to be borne, as apportioned by the General Assembly, under paragraph 2 of Article 17. The members agree (Article 25) to carry out the decisions of the Security Council; they agree (Article 33) to seek solution to their disputes "by negotiation, enquiry, mediation, conciliation, arbitration, judicial settlement, resort to regional agencies or arrangements, or other peaceful means of their own choice." The members agree to place at the disposal of the Security Council armed forces, air and naval contingents and offer assistance and facilities such as rights of passage, in case the Security Council decides to take enforcement action under Chapter VII. Even action taken in pursuance of the inherent right of self-defence is to be "immediately reported" to the Security Council.

Membership, according to Article 52, of regional arrangements or agencies and the activities therein should not be inconsistent with the purposes and principles of the UN. All members pledge (Article 56) to take joint and separate action for the achievement of social, economic, educational, cultural reforms, and further, take a pledge to assure universal respect for, and observance of, human rights and fundamental freedoms for all without distinction as to race, sex, language or religion. Members responsible for non-self-governing territories and those administering trust territories undertake extensive obligations under Chapters XI, XII, and XIII. Members agree under Article 94 to comply with the decisions of the ICJ in any case to which they are parties.

The obligations enumerated above establish clearly that the relationship that comes into existence between a newly admitted State and the rest of the members of the UN is more serious, more extensive and more binding than that established between a recognized and a recognizing State. The question whether the obligations are being fully fulfilled is a question of politics; why they are not being respected is a question of sociology; and what is to be done to improve the position is a problem for the statesmen.

Even if the opinion of Hans Kelsen, that members have transferred to the UN their competence to grant recognition of States or governments by ratifying or adhering to the Charter, were not accepted, it might be said in conclusion that the law of admission to the UN has far greater significance, and has analogous, though not similar effects, as the law of recognition. This view is reiterated by eminent publicists like Hans Kelsen,[88] Herbert W. Briggs,[89] J. Charpentier,[90] Philip C. Jessup,[91] Quincy Wright,[92] and Shegejiro Tabata.[93]

There is one caveat that has to be entered, i.e. membership need not necessarily result in the effects which recognition produces in the municipal courts of members; also, the analogy does not hold good as far as withdrawal of recognition and its counterpart suspension and expulsion from the Organization is concerned.[94]

SUMMATION

The above cursory survey of the practice of admissions of both the League and the UN reveals that though the organizational discretion in this field was purpoted to be circumscribed by specific constitutional provisions, in fact, the express criteria were such that the organizations, consequently the member States, were free to stretch the same to cover very liberal ideas and notions. The discretion, in the case of the UN, was limited to the express criteria mentioned in Article 4 but the criteria themselves were so broad and amorphous that it amounted practically to no limitation.

Consider for instance the concept of "State." Does it mean an independent sovereign State? If so India, Byelourussia, the

[88] *Principles of International Law*, 1952, pp. 277-88.

[89] "Community Interest in the Emergency of new States: The Problem of Recognition," American Society of International Law, *Proceedings*, 1951, pp. 172-80.

[90] *Le Reconnaissance International et al l'Evolution du Droit des Gens*, 1956, pp. 330-1.

[91] *A Modern Law of Nations*, New York, 1949, pp. 44-51.

[92] "Some Thoughts about Recongition," *American Journal of International Law*, Vol. 44, 1950, pp. 550-9.

[93] "Admission to the United Nations and Recognition of States," *Japanese Annual of International Law*, No. 5, 1961, pp. 1-14.

[94] See on this point, *ibid.*, pp. 11-4.

Ukraine, and many other members were not in any traditional sense sovereign, independent States. But then they did enjoy certain amount of theoretical and practical international status at the time of the San Francisco Conference. It would have been unrealistic to deny these States membership in the Organization. Likewise the notion of stable territory was to be liberally interpreted; for, it would have been preposterous for the Organization to deny admission to a State just because a fraction of its frontiers was in dispute. The concept of independence also had to be liberally construed. Otherwise, there would have been no end to filibustering with charges and counter-charges of compromises of independence. In fact the whole controversy regarding admissions in the first decade of the existence of the UN was mainly based on the argument that States belonging to one camp or other had no independence, were satellites of the respective Big Power, and were simply unqualified as States which was the primary criterion in Article 4 of the Charter. If the argument had gained credence there would have been very few qualified countries for membership in the UN. Which State in this age of interdependence is totally independent? The traditional concepts of statehood, independence, sovereignty and stable frontiers, therefore, had to be liberally construed in practice.

What the ICJ was objecting to was the package deals among Great Powers. That could not have been fitted into the framework—broad though—of Article 4. By inference it was rejecting such grounds for refusing admission as the lack of diplomatic relations between the admission-seeking State and the member which cast a negative vote. The reasons, the Court inferred, had to be couched in the language of Article 4.

As regards the concept of recognition, it also underwent a drastic change. Though the issue of individual recognition was wisely separated from admission, or organizational recognition, admissions to UN as was shown in the relevant section of the present chapter entailed even graver relationships. Membership in the UN enjoins all signatories to the Charter in more serious responsibilities and relationships than the institution of admission is supposed to accomplish.

The criteria of Article 4 of the UN Charter i.e. "peace-loving," "State," "ability and willingness" to carry out Charter obligations, are broad indeed to accommodate almost every liberal interpretation and also to invoke a wide variety of grounds to refuse admission.   But paragraph 2 of the Article, as the Court pointed out, brooks no other interpretation than that a "recommendation" of the Security Council must precede the "decision" of the General Assembly for admitting a State into the Organization.

CHAPTER 6

SUBSIDIARY ORGANS OF THE UN
AND IMPLIED POWERS

THE UN CHARTER empowers its plenary organ, namely, the General Assembly, and the organ responsible for the maintenance of world peace and security, namely, the Security Council to establish subsidiary organs as they deem fit for the performance of their functions. Articles 22 and 29 make express provisions in this regard.[1]

In view of the extensive and varied functions assumed by these organs they have established a number of subsidiary organs. The General Assembly, for instance, established almost a hundred subsidiary organs during the first eight years.[2] They differ considerably in types of function, membership, duration and other respects. They range from the Atomic Energy Commission and the Disarmament Commission to Negotiating Committees for Extra-Budgetary Funds; from the Committee on International Criminal Jurisdiction to Joint Staff Pension Board; from UNICEF to UNRWA, etc. The subsidiary organs that invited greatest attention were the Interim Committee[3] and the Administrative Tribunal. Since the latter raised a number of issues relevant to our present enquiry it has been chosen as a case study. For a better understanding of the problems involved the establishment of the UN Administrative Tribunal must be seen in perspective.

[1] Article 22 reads: "The General Assembly may establish such subsidiary organs as it deems necessary for the performance of its functions." Article 29 provides identical powers in the case of the Security Council.

[2] See *Repertory of Practice of United Nations Organs*, Vol. I, New York, 1955, pp. 661-724, for a succinct summary of the nature, variety, and analytical examination of these bodies. The Security Council, under Article 29, similarly established several subsidiary organs varying in powers and functions in tune with the tasks. For a sample survey of such organs, see *Repertory of the Practice of the Security Council*, Supp. 1959-63, New York, 1965, pp. 99-120.

[3] See *ibid.*, pp. 45-8, for a discussion of the Interim Committee.

ESTABLISHMENT OF UN ADMINISTRATIVE TRIBUNAL

Though the origin[4] of international civil service can be traced back to more than hundred years, the importance and the problems attendant thereto were not realized until after the establishment of the League of Nations.[5] The post-World War II period especially has given rise to a whole body of law governing the relations between international civil servants and the organizations they serve. Described variously as "international administrative law," "internal law of international organizations," "domestic law of international organizations," and "integral law of international organizations," this aspect of the law of international organizations has, however, attracted comparatively little notice among scholars and publicists in the field.[6]

[4]International civil service is considered to have originated in modern history in 1856, with the establishment of the European Danube Commission. See L.C. Green, "The Status of the International Civil Service," *Current Legal Problems*, Vol. 7, 1954, p. 192; Josef L. Kunz, "Privileges and Immunities of International Organizations," *American Journal of International Law*, Vol. 41, 1947, pp. 828-62.

[5]Even now, as an important official of the UN Administrative Tribunal remarked to the writer some of the international organizations "throw the employees out" without due process.

[6]See on the subject bibliographies published by the UN in Doc. AT/DEC/1 to 70/Add., pp. 35-8 and AT/DEC/71 to 86, pp. 139-40. In addition to this compilation the following can be consulted usefully:

Wilfred C. Jenks, "Some Problems of an International Civil Service," *Public Administration Review*, Vol. 3, 1943, p. 93; J.E.S. Fawcett, "Place of Law in International Organization," *British Yearbook of International Law*, Vol. 36, 1960, p. 321; Casteneda, "International Organizations and Legal Progress—A Commentary," *Howard Law Journal*, Vol. 8, 1962, p. 152; Trygve Lie, *In the Cause of Peace*, New York, 1954; F.R. Scott, "The World's Civil Service," *International Conciliation*, No. 496, 1954; Dag Hammarskjoeld, "The International Civil Servant," *Current Notes on International Affairs*, June 1961, p. 39; E.J. Phelan, "The New International Civil Service," *Foreign Affairs*, Vol.2, 1932-33, pp. 307-14; Hammarskjoeld, "International Civil Servant in Law and in Fact," *Servant of Peace*, New York, 1962, pp. 329-53; "International Service," *ibid.*, pp. 80-5; Alan H. Schechter, *Internpretation of Ambiguous Documents by International Administrative Tribunals*, London, 1964; Wilfred C. Jenks, *The Proper Law of International Organizations*, London, 1962, pp. 25-132; "The Assembly, the Tribunal and World Court," *American Bar Association Journal*, Vol. 40, 1954, p. 1065; Maxwell Cohen "The United States and the United Nations Secretariat: A Preliminary Appraisal," *McGill Law*

Rationale behind the Special Status of International Civil Service

As early as 1856 members of staff of the European Danube Commission were guaranteed, under its constitution, what was then called "neutrality," to be respected even in time of war. The League Covenant, under Article 7, provided that "officials of the League when engaged on the business of the League shall enjoy diplomatic privileges and immunities." It is common practice today that officials of all major international organizations enjoy international immunities in various grades.[7]

The reasons behind this special status of international civil servants are not far to find. International organizations created by the concerted action of a set of sovereign States can hardly be subjected to the jurisdiction of the courts of a single State.[8] The officials are constantly sought to be kept independent of national control. An international organization has got to be detached in outlook if it has to serve the community interests of all its member States and not become a tool of one or a group of member States. For this reason the members who man the Organization are likewise expected to be impartial in their attitude and possess in general highest standards of integrity and competence. Positively, they should be imbued with, what Wilfred Jenks called, an "international outlook": "An awareness made instinctive by habits of the needs, emotions, and prejudices of the peoples of differently circumstanced countries, as they are felt and expressed by the peoples concerned, accompanied by a capacity for weighing these frequently imponderable elements in a judicial manner before reaching any decision to which they are relevant."[9]

The loyalty-to-the-organization-first principle was evolved slowly in the course of practice. The League of Nations, for

---

Journal, Vol. I, 1953, p. 169; W.R. Sharp, "Trends in United Nations Administration," *International Organization*, Vol. 14, 1961, p. 393; S. Sirpaul, "Developments in the Legal Machinery of the United Nations, "*International and Comparative Law Quarterly*, Vol. II, 1962, p. 573.

[7]Wilfred C. Jenks, *International Immunities*, London, Stevens, 1961.

[8]Friedman and Fatouros, "The United Nations Administrative Tribunal," *International Organization*, Vol. II, 1957, p. 14.

[9]Jenks, *Public Administration Review*, p. 95.

instance, did not prescribe international loyalty by its Covenant; it was evolved as its Secretariat developed.[10] The constitution of the European Danube Commission made no mention of the concept. But today it is a principle most firmly embedded in personnel policies of all international organizations.

Position under the UN Charter

Loyalty and Independence of Members of Staff. Article 100 of the UN Charter ensures the principles of loyalty and independence of the staff of the Organization. It States:

(1) In the performance of their duties the Secretary-General and the Staff shall not seek or receive instructions from any government or from any other authority external to the Organization. They shall refrain from any action which might reflect on their position as international officials responsible only to the Organization.

(2) Each member of the United Nations undertakes to respect the exclusively international character of the responsibilities of the Secretary-General and the staff and not to seek to influence them in the discharge of their responsibilities.

Paragraph 3 of Article 101 lays down a guideline to the Secretary-General: "The paramount consideration in the employment of the staff and in the determination of the conditions of service shall be the necessity of securing the highest standards of efficiency, competence, and integrity."

In pursuance of the above policy Staff Regulation 1 of the UN affirms: "Members of the Secretariat are international civil servants. Their responsibilities are not national but exclusively international. By accepting appointment they pledge themselves to discharge their functions and to regulate their conduct with the interests of the United Nations only in view."[11] Regulation 1.9 lays down that every member of the staff shall be administered an oath to the above effect.

---

[10]Scott, *op. cit.*, p. 286.
[11]IN Doc. ST/AFS/SGB/94, 1953.

Does international loyalty mean renunciation of national sentiment? It does not; all that is required of an international civil
servant is that he be able to subordinate his national sentiments
to his international duties. An indifference to national origins
is not the same as international loyalty.[12] The members of staff of
international organizations, in fact, are permitted to enjoy national
citizenship rights, such as voting in elections, and membership
in political parties. The preponderance of privileges members of
staff of international organizations have come to enjoy has sometimes attracted exaggerated charges, but by and large it is admitted
by even strong critics that the existence of a devotion to ideals
and activities beyond the horizon of a single State, among
individuals of all nationalities, is one of the most encouraging
discoveries of our age.[13]

Methods of acquiring Highest Standards of Efficiency. In
addition to the privileges and immunities granted to international
officials, which are meant for the benefit of the Organization as
distinguished from personal benefits, the highest standards of
integrity, efficiency, and competence are sought to be achieved
by granting to them fair conditions of service. So much importance
is attached to the latter that a new jurisprudence is being evolved
concerning the conditions of service of international civil service,
i.e. the law of international administrative tribunals.[14] In order to
assure scrupulous observance of terms of appointment and
conditions of service the UN has found it necessary to establish
an Administrative Tribunal with powers to compel compliance from
the administration as well as officials of the Organization to the
legal relations governing their employment.

Precedents and Parallel Bodies of the UN Administrative Tribunal
On the suggestion of the Preparatory Commission the General
Assembly adopted on 24 November 1949 the Statute of the

---

[12]Scott, *op. cit.*, p. 286.

[13]*Ibid.*, p. 317.

[14]Jenks, *The Proper Law of International Organizations;* Rahmatullah Khan,
"Judicial Control of the UN Secretary-General's Discretionary Powers in
Personnel Matters," *International Studies*, Vol. 7, 1965, p. 279.

Administrative Tribunal.[15] The UN Tribunal, based on a similar tribunal of the League of Nations, is not without precedent. A similar body was envisaged for the International Institute of Agriculture, whose statute was adopted in 1932, but it was never convened. Today comparable organs exist in several international organizations in the form of "appeal boards," which formally had a consultative function but in practice attained a status approaching that of a judicial body. Usually they are of a "paritary" character, i.e. both the personnel and the Organization are represented in them equally.[16] The International Court of Justice also functions as a tribunal to settle staff disputes; the members of the Registry of the Court can appeal, following a certain procedure, to the Court itself.[17]

The League of Nations, which originally had a procedure under which members of staff had a right to appeal to the Council, established a tribunal in 1927. On the demise of the League the tribunal was transferred to the International Labour Organization which now has jurisdiction over personnel problems of several other organizations.[18]

STATUS AND COMPETENCE OF THE UN ADMINISTRATIVE TRIBUNAL

The UN Administrative Tribunal,[19] as an examination of its Statute would reveal, was designed to be an independent, judicial,

[15]See Resolution 351A(IV) of 24 November 1949, amended by Resolution 7828 (VIII) on 9 December 1953 and by Resolution 957(X) on 8 November 1955.

[16]The UNESCO (before it joined the ILO system), the Organization for European Economic Co-operation, the Council of Europe, and the European Coal and Steel Community have such bodies.

[17]See Article 17 of the Staff Regulations for the Registry of the ICJ, ICJ *Yearbook*, 1946-47, p. 68.

[18]For a comprehensive treatment of the League Tribunal, see the Memorandum submitted by ILO in the "Effect of Awards of Compensation made by the United Nations Administrative Tribunal," *Pleadings, Oral Arguments Documents*, ICJ Advisory Opinion of 13 July 1954, pp. 48-52 (referred to hereafter as ICJ *Pleadings*, 1954).

[19]The UN Tribunal has jurisdiction, apart from its own staff relations, over those of the International Civil Aviation Organization, United Nations Relief and Works Agency, Palestine Refugees in Near East; comprehensive jurisdiction in respect of UN Joint Staff Pension Fund; and also over pension matters in respect of personnel of the International Labour Organization, the United

body created for the purpose of settling disputes between the administration and its employees. Barring appointment of members and revision of the Statute, in respect of which the General Assembly has full powers, the Tribunal is vested with considerable independence. This is evident from the following provisions of its Statute.

On matters of appointment and election of judges Article 3 of the Statute provides:

(1) The Tribunal shall be composed of seven members, no two of whom may be nationals of the same State. Only three shall sit in any particular case.

(2) The members shall be appointed by the General Assembly for three years, and they may be re-appointed.

(3) The Tribunal shall elect its President and its two Vice-Presidents from among its members.

Article 2 of the Rules of the Administrative Tribunal prescribes that the Tribunal shall elect each year at its plenary session a President, a first Vice-President, and a second Vice-President for that year. They are eligible for re-election. The elections are made by a majority vote.

The President directs the work of the Tribunal and of its secretariat; represents the Tribunal in all administrative matters; and presides at the meetings of the Tribunal. In his absence the first Vice-President looks after the above business, the second Vice-President alternating the first. No case is heard by the Tribunal except under the chairmanship of the President or one of the Vice-Presidents.

Article 2, paragraph 3, accords the Tribunal the right to decide its own competence: "In the event of a dispute as to whether the Tribunal has competence, the matter shall be settled by the decision of the Tribunal." Again, Article 3, paragraph 5, entrusts the Tribunal a large measure of freedom in matters of termination:

Nations Educational, Scientific and Cultural Organization, the Food and Agriculture Organization, the International Civil Aviation Organization, and the World Health Organization.

"No member of the Tribunal can be dismissed by the General Assembly unless the other members are of the unanimous opinion that he is unsuited for further service." Article 10, paragraph 2, finally, establishes the judicial character of the Tribunal: "Subject to the provisions of Articles 11 and 12, the judgments of the Tribunal shall be final and without appeal."[20]

In addition to the above, the Tribunal can grant hearings to third parties and can regulate other matters relating to the functioning of the Tribunal (Article 6). In deserving cases the Tribunal can suspend time-limits prescribed under Article 7 concerning petitions (Article 7, paragraph 5). It can decide to hold its sessions *in camera*, if circumstances demand it (Article 8).

As regards remedies, the Tribunal under Article 9, paragraph 1, can, if it finds the application well-founded: (*a*) rescind the decision contested; (*b*) order specific performance of the obligation invoked; (*c*) award compensation, equivalent to 2 years net base salary; (*d*) in exceptional cases, order payment of higher indemnity. In cases of violations of procedure prescribed by Staff Regulations and Rules, the Tribunal can under Article 9, paragraph 2, remand the case for institution or correction and order payment of compensation not exceeding the equivalent of 3 months net base salary for such loss as may have been caused by the procedural delay.

It is Article 2, paragraph 1 (combined, of course, with Article 10, paragraph 2, dealing with the finality of its judgments), which deals with the competence of the Tribunal, that tips the balance finally in favour of its judicial character. The paragraph reads:

The Tribunal shall be competent to hear and pass judgments upon applications alleging non-observance of contracts of employment of staff members of the Secretariat of the United Nations or of the terms of appointment of such staff members.

[20]Article 11 provides that in case of excess or failure of the Tribunal's jurisdiction or in the case of error of law, or a fundamental error in procedure resulting in a failure of justice, the parties can request a special committee, formed for the purpose, to seek an advisory opinion of the ICJ which shall be binding. Article 12 allows revisionary proceedings on the basis of the discovery of a fact of a decisive nature which at the time of the Tribunal handed down its judgment was not known to the party or the Tribunal.

The words "contracts" and "terms of appointment" include all pertinent regulations and rules in force at the time of alleged non-observance, including the staff pension regulations.

Competence

The question of the Tribunal's competence can best be appreciated in the context of the notorious US loyalty cases leading to an advisory opinion of the ICJ relative to the nature of the Administrative Tribunal and the binding effect of its awards.

In 1953 the services of a number of United Nations employees of American nationality who had declined to answer questions before a federal grand jury and a congressional committee investigating communist activities and subversion, were terminated by the Secretary-General.[21] Several of those dismissed appealed against this action to the UN Administrative Tribunal, alleging a breach of their employment contracts. In decisions handed down on 1 September 1953 the Tribunal found eleven of the claims well-founded, and ordered compensation in seven cases and reinstatement in four. When the Secretary-General subsequently declined to reinstate the four, as it was within his discretion to do so, they also were awarded compensation.

The awards ordered by the Tribunal in the eleven cases came to a total of $ 179,420. At the 1953 session of the UN General Assembly, an item covering this sum was included in the supplementary financial estimates submitted by the Secretary-General to the Assembly's Fifth (Administrative and Budgetary) Committee. This touched off an extensive debate on the propriety of such payments under the circumstances.[22] Eventually the Assembly decided, by a vote of forty-one to six with fifteen abstentions to seek an advisory opinion from the International Court of Justice on the

---

[21] See L.C. Green, "The Status of the International Civil Service," *Current Legal Problems*, Vol. 7, 1954, pp. 204-11, for the case leading to the Administrative Tribunal awards. An expert opinion was elicited from a Commission of Jurists supporting such action. See UN Doc. A/INF/51, 1952. For a summary, see Cohen, "The United States and the United Nations," *op. cit.*, pp. 180-5.

[22] See ICJ, *Pleadings*, 1954, pp. 202-18 for views expressed in the Fifth Committee, expertly summarized in the written statement submitted by the Secretary-General of the UN,

legal issues involved. In the meantime the item of $ 179,420 was removed from the supplementary estimates.

However, before going into an analysis of the advisory opinion of the ICJ it would be better to see if there are precedents on this matter in the history and jurisprudence of the League of Nations Administrative Tribunal. The following, therefore, is devoted to an examination of the same.

Precedents of the League of Nations Administrative Tribunal

During the League economic crisis in 1932 the issue was mooted whether the Assembly, by unilateral action, could legally reduce salaries of members of staff. After consideration by the Supervisory Commission which felt that it was not worth the financial saving "to disturb the staff and impair the sense of security and stability that earlier Assemblies sought to give them" the matter was discussed in the Fourth Committee.[23]

The Fourth Committee after an inconclusive debate decided to refer the issue to a Committee of Jurists.[24] The Committee of Jurists, consisting of such stalwarts as Basdevant, Max Huber, Sir William Malkin, and Pedroso, submitted its unanimous report on 8 October 1932.[25] The jurists held that the Assembly did not have the right to reduce salaries of the Secretariat, unless such a right had been expressly recognized in the contracts of appointment. Having reached the conclusion that the above obligation arises out of contractual rights, the jurists considered the question whether the Assembly possessed the right to derogate therefrom in the exercise of its budgetary authority. Their answer was in the negative:

> The Assembly . . . has taken measures to ensure that the rights of officials are respected. This was the object with which . . . it adopted the Statute setting up an Administrative Tribunal having jurisdiction to hear complaints alleging non-observance

[23]League of Nations, *Official Journal*, 13th year, No. 7, Minutes of the 67th Session of the Council, pp. 1237-8; *ibid.*, Special Suppl. No. 107, *Records of the 13th Assembly*, Meetings of Committees, Minutes of the Fourth Committee, p. 129.

[24]*Ibid.*, p. 51.

[25]*Ibid.*, pp. 206-8.

of the terms of appointments of officials (Article 2). Article 10 of this Statute shows clearly that, in the conception of the Assembly, its budgetary authority is not to serve the purpose of defeating the rights of officials. The Article states that any compensation awarded by the Tribunal shall be chargeable to the budget of the administration concerned. . . .

If the Assembly reduced the salaries of officials, the latter would have the right to have recourse to the Administrative Tribunal. The considerations set out above lead the Committee to think that the Tribunal would decide in favour of the officials.[26]

The opinion of the jurists was accepted by the Fourth Committee[27] and new procedures of appointment were adopted subsequently by the League inserting provisions in the Staff Regulations to the effect that appointments made after 15 October 1932 were subject to modification by the Assembly.[28]

The question of the binding effect of the decisions of the League Administrative Tribunal did not come up until after the outbreak of World War II. In December 1939 the League Assembly took steps, in view of the war, to retrench drastically the staff of the League Secretariat and that of the ILO. Officials were offered the choice of resigning or of having their appointments suspended. If they resigned they were offered a sum amounting to either six month's or one year's salary according to their length of service. If they elected suspension, they were offered an *ex gratia* payment of three months' salary. And those who did neither were served a month's notice or compensation *in lieu* of such notice. The Staff Regulations were accordingly amended reducing the period of notice from six months to one, and providing that the indemnity would be payable in instalments over a four-year period instead of in a lump sum.[29]

[26]*Ibid.,* p. 208.

[27]*Ibid.,* pp. 72-3.

[28]Article 30b is of the Staff Regulations of the League: Article 16a of the Staff Regulations of the ILO.

[29]See League of Nations, *Official Journal,* Special Suppl. No. 194, *Records of the 20th (Conclusion) and 21st Sessions of the Assembly,* p. 245; and *Records of the 20th Assembly,* Plenary Meetings, p. 45.

Eleven officials of the League and two from the ILO whose contracts were so terminated brought complaints before the Tribunal alleging that the action of the Secretary-General and the amendments under which that action was taken infringed their acquired rights under their previous terms of contracts and hence void. The Tribunal in a series of 13 judgments, in practically identical terms, found for the complainants.

The Tribunal based its conclusion on the grounds that the Staff Regulations "in their form as it was subsisting at the date of the contract of employment of the Applicant, formed a part of this contract," and that the applicants had "an acquired right to which amendments of the Regulations ... could not be applied without mutual agreement." The Tribunal held that the Assembly resolution of 14 December 1939 infringed those acquired rights the sanctity of which was safeguarded by Article 97 of the Staff Regulations. The Tribunal cited with approval the position in this regard of the Committee of Jurists in 1932. And it refused to accept the contention that the League was not in a position to honour the acquired rights of its staff.[30]

The developments and debates consequent to the above judgments of the League Tribunal make an interesting study. The matter was immediately referred by the acting Secretary-General to the Supervisory Commission which felt that "an acceptance of the findings of the Administrative Tribunal would put its decision above the authority of the Assembly, [and that] the Supervisory Commission could not take the responsibility of advising the Acting Secretary-General and the Acting Director of the International Labour Office to apply the judgments of the Administrative Tribunal."[31]

In April 1946 the Second (Finance) Committee which considered the matter referred it to a Sub-Committee of seven. The Sub-Committee in its report,[32] while upholding the Administrative

[30]See Annex II to the ILO Memorandum, *op. cit.*, for the text of judgment No. 35 in the case of *Zoppino* v. *ILO*, pp. 80-3.

[31]League of Nations, *Official Journal*, Special Suppl. No. 194, *Records of the 20th (Conclusion) and 21st Session of the Assembly*, p. 162.

[32]*Ibid.*, pp. 261-3.

Tribunal's competence to consider the application and interpretation of the decisions of the Assembly or other Staff Regulations, nevertheless, stated emphatically that it was one thing to interpret and apply and it was quite a different thing to say that it could question the validity of those decisions themselves and that it was subject to no overriding powers by the very body which had created it. It found it impossible to suppose that, in no circumstances, however pressing the necessity in the interests of the peoples of the world, could the League derogate from some contract to a private individual employed by it: "Only an excessively static legal view would justify the conclusion that the League was fettered in its own administrative organization by the rules of the private law of contract applicable to the employees of a trading or commercial undertaking."[33]

Commenting on the report Sir Hartley Shawcross, the Rapporteur of the Sub-Committee, pointed out that commonsense would dictate that since the League was not "a troupe of travelling actors or a tramway company, or a municipal corporation, and since it was an Organization of the sovereign States of the world, the issue should be considered in an entirely peculiar status of the League."[34]

The Sub-Committee placed great reliance upon the right of the Assembly to abolish the Statute of the Tribunal. What would happen to the "acquired rights" of the officials if the Assembly decided to make use of this power? Could there be any remedy? *Ubi jus ibi remedium.* The absence of remedies militated against the whole idea of acquired rights, it was argued. The Sub-Committee however did recognize that there might be a moral obligation ("the protection against its abuse is not a legal but a political one lying in the hands of the States members of the League") and recommended an *ex gratia* payment in respect of legal costs.

There was a vigorous dissent from the majority point of view. The minority view was that it was absolutely contrary to the notion of law and the sovereignty of law that the Assembly, the organ of one of the parties to the dispute, should have the right to oppose the execution of a judgment of which it did not approve. The lack

[33]*Ibid.*
[34]*Ibid.*, p. 261.

of remedies argument was countered with the position in international law where there are no remedies against States, yet the international community almost without exception accepts judicial or arbitral decisions.

In the discussion that followed Sir Hartley's presentation of the report to the Finance Committee, M. Kaeckenbeeck of Belgium drew attention to the serious consequences which might follow from the adoption of that attitude risking an impression that the standpoint of law was being completely abandoned in favour of political arbitrariness:

> By refusing to execute a judgment which displeased it, the League of Nations would be gravely violating the rules of law and of the sovereignty of law and such action would have extremely serious repercussions in an international organization in which constant efforts had been made to substitute law for force. The intention in transferring to the Tribunal the former judicial powers of the Council had, in fact, been to substitute judicial decisions for decisions of a political nature.[35]

Nevertheless, this opinion of the Sub-Committee was approved by the Finance Committee and accepted by the Assembly which refused to vote the funds necessary to satisfy the awards.

ILO Action Subsequent to League Tribunal's Awards

Two of the awards which had been disregarded by the Assembly related to officials of the ILO which had accepted the ruling of the Assembly in the matter. This ruling was reflected in Article XII of the Tribunal's Statute as adopted by the International Labour Conference on 9 October 1946. The Article read:

> In any case in which the Governing Body of the International Labour Office or the Administrative Board of the Pensions Fund challenges the decision of the Tribunal confirming its jurisdiction, or considers that a decision of the Tribunal is vitiated by a fundamental fault in the procedure followed, the question as to the validity of the decision given by the Tribunal

---

[35] See ILO Memorandum, *op. cit.*, pp. 85-7.

shall be submitted by the Governing Body, for an advisory opinion, to the International Court of Justice. . . . The opinion given by the Court shall be binding.[36]

ADVISORY OPINION OF ICJ ON THE EFFECT OF AWARDS OF THE ADMINISTRATIVE TRIBUNAL[37]

The question submitted to the Court was as follows: "(1) Having regard to the Statute of the United Nations Administrative Tribunal and to any other relevant instruments and to the relevant records, has the General Assembly the right on any grounds to refuse to give effect to an award of compensation made by that Tribunal in favour of a staff member of the United Nations whose contract of service has been terminated without his assent? (2) If the answer given by the Court to question (1) is in the affirmative, what are the principal grounds upon which the General Assembly could lawfully exercise such a right?"

The Court answered the question by examining whether the Tribunal was established either as a judicial body or as an advisory organ or as a mere subordinate committee of the General Assembly. Having found that it was intended to be a judicial body it had no difficulty in pronouncing that its judgments and awards were binding.

Only a brief reference to the provisions of the Statute of the Tribunal was sufficient to arrive at the above conclusion. Pointing out the terminology in Articles 2 and 10, "tribunal," "judgment," competence to "pass judgment upon applications," etc., the contrast between the Joint Appeals Board created by Staff Rule III.1, the independence of judges as ensured by paragraph 5 of Article 3, the Court ruled "that the Tribunal is established, not as an advi-

---

[36]See G.B./C.S.Q.II/P.V.6; Minutes of the Private Sitting of the 99th Session, September 1946, pp. 15, 37; and see *Record of Proceedings of the 29th Session of the International Labour Conference*, p. 229—for the consideration and adoption of this text respectively by the Staff Questions Committee, the Governing Body, and the International Labour Conference.

[37]The authorized citation is: "Effect of Awards of Compensation made by the U.N. Administrative Tribunal, Advisory Opinion of 13 July 1954: I.C.J. Reports, 1954, p. 47," which will be referred to hereafter, for short, as ICJ *Reports*, 1954.

sory organ or a mere subordinate committee of the General Assembly, but as an independent and truly judicial body pronouncing final judgments without appeal within the limited field of its functions."[38]

The Court then invoked the well established and generally recognized principle of law, "a judgment rendered by such a judicial body is *res judicata* and has binding force between the parties to the dispute."[39]

Elaborating further the reasons that led the Court to that conclusion the Court pointed out that when the Secretary-General concludes a contract of service with a staff member he does so in his capacity as the chief administrative officer of the UN thus engaging the legal responsibility of the Organization, which is the juridical person on whose behalf he acts. It stated further:

> If he terminates the contract of service without the assent of the staff member and this action results in a dispute which is referred to the Administrative Tribunal, the parties to this dispute before the Tribunal are the staff member concerned and the United Nations Organization, represented by the Secretary-General, and these parties will become bound by the judgment of the Tribunal.[40]

It follows, said the Court, that the General Assembly, as an organ of the United Nations, must likewise be bound by the judgment.

The finality of the judgments rendered thus has been established as a deliberate choice. The Court said that paragraph 2 of Article 10, which says that the Tribunal's judgments shall be final and without appeal, was adopted consciously. It quoted the opinion of the League rapporteur and that of the Fifth Committee of the UN General Assembly which drafted the statute of the Tribunal, to the effect that no provision for appeal was made in the interests of finality and to avoid vexatious proceedings. The UN rapporteur had also explained that it would have had adverse effect on the morale of the staff if appeal beyond the Administrative Tribunal

---

[38]*Ibid.*, p. 53.
[39]*Ibid.*   [40]*Ibid.*

delayed the decision in a case which had already been heard before organs within the Secretariat created for that purpose.[41]

It was contended before the Court that it would be absurd not to allow the General Assembly an implied power to review cases where the Tribunal had wrongly exercised its jurisdiction or when new facts of decisive importance have been discovered. To this the Court replied:

> In order that the judgments pronounced by such a judicial tribunal [functioning under a special statute and within the organized legal system of the UN] could be subjected to review by any body other than the Tribunal itself, it would be necessary, in the opinion of the Court, that the statute of that tribunal or some other legal instrument governing it should contain an express provision to that effect.[42]

The General Assembly, added the Court, could hardly act as a judicial organ—considering the arguments of the parties, appraising the evidence produced by them, establishing the facts and declaring the law applicable to them—all the more so as one party to the dispute was the United Nations itself.[43]

Arguments Concerning Implied Powers of the Organization to create a Judicial Tribunal

At one stage the very competence of the General Assembly to establish a judicial tribunal rendering binding judgments was challenged. The argument was that there is no express provision for the establishment of judicial bodies or organs. In such a situation can the Organization create such a body. The General Assembly, it was argued, had no implied powers to create such an organ. According to the *Injuries* case (which the Court also cited) "the Organization must be deemed to have those powers which, though not expressly provided in the Charter, are conferred upon it by necessary implication as being essential to the performance of its duties."[44]

[41]*Ibid.*, pp. 54-5.
[43]*Ibid.*
[42]*Ibid.*, p. 56.
[44]ICJ *Reports,* 1949, p. 182.

Can such a *necessary* implication be read in the provisions of the Charter to establish that a judicial tribunal is essential for the performance of its duties?

The Court found the necessary implication in the following provisions:

Under the provisions of Chapter XV of the Charter, the Secretariat, which is one of the principal organs of the UN, comprises the Secretary-General and the Staff. The Secretary-General is appointed by the General Assembly, upon the recommendation of the Security Council, and he is "the chief administrative officer of the Organization." The staff members are appointed by the Secretary-General under regulations established by the General Assembly. In the words of paragraph 3 of Article 101 of the Charter, as was noted earlier, the "paramount consideration in the employment of the staff and in the determination of the conditions of service shall be the necessity of securing the highest standards of efficiency, competence and integrity."

In the absence of any organ competent to adjudicate upon disputes that would arise inevitably between the staff and the Organization in view of the complex code of the latter's conditions of service, it would have been hardly consistent with the expressed aim of the Charter to promote freedom and justice for individuals, and with the constant preoccupation of the United Nations Organization to promote this aim, that it should afford no judicial or arbitral remedy to its own staff for the settlement of any dispute which might arise between it and them. The Court stated:

> In these circumstances the power to establish a tribunal, to do justice as between the Organization and the staff members, was essential to ensure the efficient working of the Secretariat, and to give effect to the paramount consideration of securing the highest standards of efficiency, competence and integrity. *Capacity to do this arises by necessary intendment out of the Charter.*[45]

Arguments on the Subordinate Position of the Tribunal

A more subtle argument before the Court was that while an

[45]*Ibid.*, p. 57. (Italics added.)

implied power of the General Assembly to establish an Administrative Tribunal might be both necessary and essential, nevertheless, an implied power to impose legal limitation upon the General Assembly's express Charter powers was not legally admissible. The argument was that the General Assembly cannot, by establishing the Administrative Tribunal divest itself of the power conferred by paragraph 1 of Article 17 of the Charter, which states that the "General Assembly shall consider and approve the budget of the Organization." Would it not, it was contended, contravene this provision to hold that the General Assembly had no power over items of appropriations relating to awards made by the Tribunal ?[46]

The Court countered the argument by stating that "the function of approving the budget does not mean that the General Assembly has an absolute power to approve or disapprove the expenditure proposed to it; for some part of that expenditure arises out of obligations already incurred by the Organization and to this extent the General Assembly has no alternative but to honour these engagements."[47]

The Court affirmed that the awards made by the Tribunal, in view of its judicial character and the principle of *res judicata* applying to its judgments, were of such a character.

The more serious argument advanced before the Court was that the Administrative Tribunal being a subsidiary, subordinate or secondary organ, could not bind by its judgments the General Assembly which established it. The argument assumed that by the establishment of the Administrative Tribunal, the General Assembly was creating an organ which it deemed necessary for the performance of its *own functions*.[48] The Court, however, made a distinction between the functions and powers of the General

---

[46]See US statement, *Pleadings*, 1954, pp. 136-9.

[47]ICJ *Reports*, 1954, p. 59.

[48]"The International Community was not ready in 1945, and is no more so today, to give blanket advance approval to uncontrolled proliferation of independent or quasi-independent agencies of interntional control. It is only if an organ is to be truly subsidiary that advance authorization for its establishment is found in the Charter of the United Nations," argued the US statement marshalling evidence from *travaux preparatoires*, see *Pleadings*, 1954, p. 153.

Assembly on the ground that the General Assembly had no judicial functions to perform. It said:

> By establishing the Administrative Tribunal, the General Assembly was not delegating the performance of its own functions: it was exercising a power which it had under the Charter to regulate staff relations. In regard to the Secretariat, the General Assembly is given by the Charter a power to make regulations, but not a power to adjudicate upon, or otherwise deal with, particular instances.[49]

As for the contention that no subordinate organ could bind its own parent body the Court found that the question could not be determined on the basis of the description of the relationship between the General Assembly and the Tribunal, that is by considering whether the Tribunal was to be regarded as a subsidiary, a subordinate, or a secondary organ, or on the basis of the fact that it was established by the General Assembly. It depends, said the Court, "on the intention of the General Assembly in establishing the Tribunal, and on the nature of the functions conferred upon it by its Statute. An examination of the language of the Statute of the Administrative Tribunal has shown that the General Assembly intended to establish a judicial body; moreover, it had the legal capacity under the Charter to do so."[50]

The Court agreed that the Tribunal was subordinate in the sense that the General Assembly could abolish the Tribunal by repealing its Statute, that it could amend the Statute for review of the future decisions of the Tribunal and that it could amend the Staff Regulations and make new ones. But it refused to uphold the contention that the General Assembly was inherently incapable of creating a tribunal competent to make decisions binding on itself. Great reliance was placed by the US Government on the League precedent mentioned earlier.[51]

The Court ruled, however, that the cases adjudicated upon by the Tribunal of the League, and the circumstances in which they

---

[49]ICJ *Reports*, 1954, p. 61.   [50]*Ibid.*, p. 61.
[51]See *Pleadings*, 1954, pp. 159-81. See also the Secretary-General's survey of the League of Nations historical precedent, *ibid.*, pp. 218-26.

arose, were different from those which led to the request for this opinion. Moreover, the cases arose under the Statute of the Administrative Tribunal of the League, and not under the Statute of the Administrative Tribunal of the United Nations, and the Assembly was acting under the Covenant and not under the Charter.

In view of the complete lack of identity between the two situations, and of the conclusions already drawn by the Court from the Charter and the Statute of the Administrative Tribunal and other relevant instruments and records, the Court held that it could not regard the action of the Assembly of the League in 1946 as an applicable precedent or as an indication of the intention of the General Assembly when the Statute of the Administrative Tribunal was adopted in 1949.[52]

Accordingly the Court, by nine votes to three, answered part 1 of the question in the negative. There was no necessity, therefore, to go into part 2. There was a vigorous dissent from Judges Alvarez, Hackworth, and Levi Carneiro.

The Dissenting Opinions

Alvarez's Dissent. Judge Alvarez began his dissent by his renowned theory of the "new international law." The last two social cataclysms and the liberation from colonial yoke of a number of countries, the mood of the emerging States on the example of the Russian revolution, argued Judge Alvarez, has opened up "a new *epoch,* a new *era.*" International law of this epoch "is no longer exclusively *juridical* and *individualistic*" but it "assumes a *political* and social character." It establishes "*a new regime of interdependence*" replacing the traditional individualistic regime.[53]

The Charter of the UN, according to Judge Alvarez, applies this social law in a number of its provisions particularly in Chapters IX to XIV. Finally, a further characteristic of the new international society is that it has been organized by the Charter of the United Nations. Then he proceeded to examine the framework of the UN: "The principal organs play the most important part in the new

[52]ICJ *Reports,* 1954, p. 62.
[53]*Ibid.,* pp. 69-70.

international society; almost all the activity of that society is concentrated in those organs. The only purpose of the subsidiary organs is to assist the principal organs to discharge their duties."[54]

From the above postulate he concluded, that the General Assembly was an "all-powerful legislative organ," a "supreme power ... bound only by the Charter which established it ... nothing above the Assembly except moral forces, particularly public opinion."[55] A logical and practical consequence of the foregoing is that any attempt to limit the power of the General Assembly would run counter to the realities of international life.

Whatever the realities of international life and the powers of the General Assembly, Judge Alvarez raised some baffling riddles. Invoking the implied powers of the Organization, which the Court had readily conceded in the *Injuries* case, he posed the question whether the General Assembly would have no such powers if the Tribunal had acted *ultra vires*, e.g. if it granted an amount of compensation which was higher than the amount claimed, or if the compensation had been awarded without valid grounds, or if the Tribunal had committed an *abus du droit*?[56]

Judge Alvarez also cited some concrete cases. One such case would be, when the Assembly considered that an application was well founded and the Tribunal found it inadmissible. Could it then be argued that the General Assembly was not entitled to sustain this application? Another case would be where a change might occur in the economic or social conditions between the date of the giving of the award and that of its performance, e.g. an abrupt fluctuation in the value of the dollar. Again, what if the General Assembly had no funds available for the purpose.

These are hard questions but the majority were not denying them. They conceded that the General Assembly could review the judgments though it could not function that way constitutionally, but their opinion was that it could not do so until it amended the Statute and inserted a provision to that effect.

[54]*Ibid.*, p. 70.
[55]*Ibid.*, p. 72.
[56]*Ibid.*, pp. 73-4.

Judge Hackworth's Dissent. Judge Hackworth termed the majority *dicta*, that since the Tribunals's judgments were final and *res judicata* their awards were binding, "an over-simplification of the problem."[57] Hackworth contended that the establishment of the Tribunal can be attributed only to the General Assembly's powers to create subsidiary organs for the performance of its functions. He stated emphatically: "Nowhere in the Charter can there be found any authorization, express or implied, for the establishment by the General Assembly of any other kind of organ be it judicial, quasi-judicial, or non-judicial."

Is this true? The fact is that the UN is given the power to establish subsidiary organs *as an organization* under paragraph 2 of Article 7 which says: "Such subsidiary organs as may be found necessary may be established in accordance with the present Charter."

Who creates these subsidiary organs? The General Assembly is expressly empowered under Article 22 to create such organs for the performance of its functions. The Security Council too can do so under Article 29, also "for the performance of its functions." The Secretariat and the other principal organs of the Organization also have functions to perform. What happens if *they* deem it necessary to establish a subsidiary organ for the performance of *their* functions. They have no such express powers. Have they any implied powers? The answer seems to be in the affirmative in view of the blanket provision under paragraph 2 of Article 7. This provision applies to the Organization as a whole. The Organization can establish subsidiary organs—there is no mention of the stock phrase, "for the performance of its functions"; instead, "in accordance with the present Charter," is inserted. This clause visualizes set procedures established for the purpose in due course. In fact, there are provisions establishing such express powers in the case, of the General Assembly and the Security Council. The Secretary-General also has functions to perform, as the chief administrative officer, like making appointments, under regulations made by the General Assembly and ensuring highest levels of efficiency and integrity.

[57] *Ibid.*, p. 77.

This is a field where two principal organs are endowed with jurisdiction for a single function. The General Assembly makes the regulations. The Secretary-General makes the appointments. Both the regulation-making power and the appointment-power have to combine to ensure the desired result.

Both the principal organs are given earmarked functions. The jurisdiction is concurrent. The two organs realize that the end cannot be achieved without establishing an organ to ensure fair-play and justice in the administration of the Secretariat. They combine to create one: the Administrative Tribunal is the result. But it cannot be subordinated to one organ alone. It has to be a watchdog to see if the paramount consideration is being kept in view in matters of appointments and in the effective discharge of the conditions of service. It can nullify an unfair appointment made by the Secretary-General or can render an unjust regulation made by the General Assembly void as vitiating the paramount requirement. The latter course is a drastic measure. The League Tribunal in 1946 however had recourse to it when the Assembly passed a resolution unilaterally altering the conditions of service.

It is not a case of the General Assembly or the Secretary-General creating a subsidiary organ for the performance of their functions. It is the case of the Organization creating a watchdog body to see if the two principal organs are performing their stated duties in good faith. And since the Organization is an abstract entity which cannot act except through one of its principal organs, the General Assembly is made use of. The principal organs have not only rights, powers, and functions to perform, but they have some duties too.

Since this particular duty pertains to a matter which is internal and administrative in nature, a judicial body is created within the framework of the UN.

This line of argument leads to one drastic result. It strikes at the root of the General Assembly's regulation-making power, and its powers to amend the Tribunal's statute or to abolish the Tribunal altogether. Is necessity for ensuring the paramount purpose made mandatory under Article 101 of the Charter so overriding as to place such a restrictive interpretation on the respective powers of the Secretary-General and the General Assembly? The Court obviously was not prepared to travel that far. It would indeed be radical but Article 101 could be certainly interpreted as imposing duties than conferring rights on these two bodies, in which case the power to abolish the Tribunal can hardly be viewed as a proper perpetuation of the duty enjoined on the two organs to ensure highest standards of efficiency, integrity, and competence.

Judge Levi Carneiro's Dissent. The key to Judge Carneiro's dissent is the statement that "the system of the United Nations regarded as a whole is of more importance than the literal meaning of a few words taken from the Statute and the Resolutions."[58]

He deducts from the above aphorism the following conclusions: the Assembly, as the first of the six principal organs mentioned in Article 7, dominates the whole Organization, decisively intervening in the formation of the other principal organs, with a considerable control, varying in degree, over their activities. It cannot surrender its prerogatives, nor can it irrevocably delegate them. Moreover it possesses certain implied powers [Article 11(*a*)]. He goes on to point out that the Tribunal is not truly independent, its members are not judges, that its judgments cannot enjoy more force than the ICJ judgments over which the Security Council is given an option of control, etc.

In view of the majority judges' opinion on each and every point raised above, which had been amply brought out in the preceding pages, no further comment seems to be warranted at this stage.

REPERCUSSIONS OF THE ADVISORY OPINION

The contingencies and cases to which the dissenting judges adverted to to claim for the General Assembly an appellate authority over the Administrative Tribunal were too serious to be ignored. But as the majority felt, one could not claim an implied appellate authority to any organ of the UN when the General Assembly had given, in the legitimate exercise of its powers, the Tribunal's

[58] *Ibid.,* p. 92

judgments and awards an express finality. The necessity therefore to create a body competent to rectify excessive exercise of
the Tribunal's jurisdiction was felt strongly. The General Assembly,
it was agreed with the Tribunal's observations, was constitutionally
not suited to sit as a judicial body—hearing parties, evaluating
evidence, and rendering judicial verdicts. Thus a committee was
proposed to review the Administrative Tribunal's judgments.

In tune with the foregoing feeling a double amendment was
adopted to the Tribunal's statute, once in 1953, when Article 9,
providing for the effects of the Tribunal's judgments, was amended
in order to give more freedom to the Secretary-General in matters
of temporary appointments;[59] and once again in 1955 when two
new articles were introduced in the Statute.[60] The effect of the
second amendment is that if a member State, the Secretary-General,
or the person in respect of whom a judgment has been rendered
by the Administrative Tribunal (including any person who has
succeeded to his rights on his death) objects to the judgment
on the ground that the Tribunal has exceeded its jurisdiction or
competence or that the Tribunal has failed to exercise jurisdiction
vested in it, or has erred on a question of law relating to the provisions of the Charter, or has committed a fundamental error in
procedure which has occasioned a failure of justice, such member
States, the Secretary-General or the person concerned may, within
thirty days from the date of the judgment, make written application
to the Committee asking the Committee to request an advisory
opinion of the ICJ. The Committee was authorized by the General
Assembly to make such requests to the ICJ.

The appeals procedure, described above, however, has not been
used in the UN till the date of writing. This speaks undoubtedly
of the balance and rectitude of the work of the Administrative
Tribunal. One thing that emerges clearly out of the foregoing
discussions is that the UN Administrative Tribunal has come to
be recognized as a judicial organ in the system of the UN created
for the purpose of rendering binding judgments between the UN
administration on the one hand and the members of the staff on

[59]General Assembly Resolution 782 (VIII)B of 9 December 1953.
[60]General Assembly Resolution 957 (X) of 8 November 1955.

the other. The Tribunal has emerged, once its legal status has been recognized, as the watchdog of the rights of the employees— the legal guardian, in Koh's phrase, of the international civil servant.[61]

SUMMATION

The foregoing analysis reveals that the doctrine of implied powers serves as a double-edged sword. It can be invoked to claim fresh fields of activity as well as to limit the sanctioned authority. The use to which it is put depends upon the needs of the Organization. If one takes a look at the subsidiary organs created by the General Assembly and the Security Council under Articles 22 and 29 respectively one will get a correct picture of the range and meaning of these provisions. The subsidiary organs in fact can (and do) serve as the eyes and ears of the Organization. The utility and effectiveness of the Commissions in Korea, Palestine, Lebanon, etc., cannot be overemphasized.

If the above mentioned subsidiary organs can be identified as the eyes and ears of the UN, the Administrative Tribunal serves as a conscience-keeper. And when once the Organization takes steps to establish such a body with full powers to pull it up if it fails to conform to its own contractual engagements, it can hardly claim powers to over-rule the tribunal's unpalatable findings.

Nevertheless, there is a possibility of such subsidiary organs transgressing their terms of reference. The International Court's observation in the *Expenses* case, viz. "the body corporate or politic may be bound, as to third parties, by an *ultra vires* act of an agent,"[62] as was pointed out earlier, must be understood in the limited context of financial liability. The Court was not pronouncing upon the larger problem of the legal effect of unconstitutional acts of international organization or their subsidiary organs. This is the subject of our scrutiny in the following chapter.

---

[61]Byung Chul Koh, *The United Nations Administrative Tribunal*, Baton Rouge, 1966.
[62]ICJ *Reports*, 1962, p. 168.

PART THREE

CRITIQUE

CHAPTER 7

LEGAL CONTROLS OF THE EXERCISE
OF IMPLIED POWERS

THE DEDUCTION FROM the previous chapters, if the nuances in each chapter are discerned properly, is that implied powers could be invoked not to claim powers over vast expanses of the field but only interstitially to fill lacunae in express authorizations and to accord such functional authority as is necessary for the effective performance of the purposes of the Organization. The question that hovered all along, yet skirted until now, is what is the guarantee that international organizations will not make such exertions into unknown fields and unauthorized areas? What are the legal controls over the excess of power and abuse of power?

To an extent, there are procedures for political control over alleged illegal activities of international organizations. This was dramatically exposed in the United Nations General Assembly at its 21st session. The Soviet Union, faced with the threat of losing voting rights in the Assembly as a penalty (under Article 19) for failure to pay up its budgetary assessments on account of UNEF and ONUC, brought the Organization nearly to a brink. States, especially super States, can be safely expected to put up such performances whenever they think that international organizations are treading on their sensitive toes. It is a question of the relative strength of the State concerned and the relative chargin with which the international community expresses itself. Prime Minister Wilson's clear denunciation of the UN Resolutions on Rhodesia as being "irresponsible"[1] is a case in point.

---

[1]Speaking in the House of Commons on 1 November 1968, the British Prime Minister stated that the UN had been passing "irresponsible resolutions" in the case of Rhodesia, "leaving us [Britain] to do the dirty work." *The Times*, London, 2 November 1968.

The above and a numerous other allegations of illegality made by statesmen and scholars[2] raise two sets of questions. One, what is the remedy available to State members of the United Nations Organizations vis-a-vis unconstitutional acts? What is the legal effect of such illegal acts? The questions are of considerable delicacy involving judicial craftsmanship. One would scan in vain the textbooks of international law and the Commentaries on the Charter of the United Nations for answers to these questions. Only recently some imaginative publicists have attempted to deal with this "basic legal dilemma," however "offering no concrete formula."[3] Even an author of such eminence and authority as R.Y. Jennings limits his analysis of the issue of nullity and effectiveness in international law to one of "raising questions rather than attempting to answer them."[4] E. Lauterpacht makes an able analysis of the "very heart of the role of law in international organization" and offers some tentative criteria.[5]

Acts of international organizations can be impugned on several counts: assertion of competence by an incompetent organ; excess of power; abuse of power; serious departure from fundamental rules of procedure; wrongful exercise of discretionary powers, etc. In the context of the present enquiry only excess and abuse of implied powers by international organizations shall be dealt with.

In the present unorganized society of States the problem has hardly received any clear formulation. However, in the sphere of international arbitration the issue has been solved to an extent. The "Model Rules on Arbitral Procedure" adopted by the Inter-

---

[2] The most recent being, C.G. Fenwick, "When is There a Threat to the Peace? Rhodesia," *AJIL*, Vol. 61, 1967, pp. 753-5; see also Rahmatullah Khan, *Kashmir and the United Nations*, Delhi, 1969.

[3] Hans W. Baade, "Nullity and Avoidance in Public International Law: A Preliminary Survey and a Theoretical Orientation," *Indiana Law Journal*, Vol. 38, 1963-64, p. 497.

[4] R.Y. Jennings, "Nullity and Effectives in International Law," *Cambridge Essays in International Law*, London, 1965, p. 64.

[5] E. Lauterpacht, "The Legal Effect of Illegal Acts of International Organizations," *ibid.*, p. 88.

national Law Commission in 1958 can be said to have codified the existing law on the subject.[6] Article 35 provided as follows:

> The validity of an award may be challenged by either party on one or more of the following grounds: (*a*) that the Tribunal has exceeded its powers; (*b*) that there was corruption on the part of a member of the Tribunal; (*c*) that there has been failure to state the reasons for the award or a serious departure from a fundamental rule of procedure; (*d*) that the undertaking to arbitrate or the compromise is a nullity.

As regards unconstitutionality of acts of international organizations, especially the excess or abuse of implied powers, one necessarily has to go back to the *Expenses* Opinion.

EXPENSES OPINION

The Court, it might be recalled had evolved the doctrine of institutional effectiveness whereby "when the Organization takes action which warrants the assertion that it was appropriate for the fulfilment of one of the stated purposes of the United Nations, the presumption is that such action is not *ultra vires* the Organization."[7] As the UNEF and ONUC operations were clearly appropriate for the fulfilment of the stated purpose of maintaining international peace and security, the Court adopted an ingenious argument to meet the further contention, namely, that the General Assembly was not competent to mount and conduct such operations. According to the Court:

> If the action was taken by the wrong organ, it was irregular as a matter of that internal structure, but this would not necessarily mean that the expense incurred was not an expense of the Organization. Both national and international law contemplate cases in which the body corporate or politic may be bound, as to third parties, by an *ultra vires* act of an agent.
>
> In the legal systems of States, there is often some procedure for determining the validity of even a legislative or governmental

[6]*Yearbook of the International Law Commission,* Vol. 2, 1958, p. 78.
[7]ICJ, *Reports,* 1962, p. 168.

act, but no analogous procedure is to be found in the structure of the United Nations.[8]

The above doctrine was sufficient to dismiss the objections on the validity of expenses incurred on UNEF and ONUC. Nevertheless, the Court did examine the validity of the resolutions pertaining to these operations, and upheld their "charterability." In the fortuitious circumstance of the General Assembly being competent to undertake the above mentioned operations the Court was not called upon to stretch the point of functional division further. If it really had found that the General Assembly was not competent to undertake such functions, or alternatively, if it were faced with the exercise of a function which was outside the jurisdiction of the General Assembly, the Court probably would have hesitated before evolving such a far-reaching doctrine.

Such were the thoughts that impelled Judge Sir Gerald Fitzmaurice to make rather strong reservations on the plurality opinion's mainstay. In his opinion the notion of the irrelevance of the spheres of competence could not be pressed too far:

> It is certainly correct in one sense, namely, that internal irregularities would not affect liabilities definitely incurred by or on behalf of the Organization, in relation to third parties outside the Organization or its membership. But what is really in question here is the relationship of the member States *inter se*, and vis-a-vis the Organization as such, and there can be no doubt, that in principle at least, expenditures incurred in excess of the powers of the expending body are invalid expenditures. The question is, are they invalid if they merely exceed the powers of the particular organ authorizing them but not those of the Organization as a whole? It is true that there are cases, both in the domestic and in the international legal spheres, where all that matters (except on the purely internal plane) is that a certain act has in fact been performed, or not performed, as the case may be, and where the reasons for, or channels through which the the performance or non-performance has taken place are im-

[8]*Ibid.*

material. But in the present case, the question of the financial obligations of member States in relation to the Organization is a question moving on the internal plane; and if an instrument such as the Charter of the United Nations attributes given functions in an exclusive manner to one of its organs, constituted in a certain way other and different functions being attributed to other and differently constituted organs this can only be because, in respect of the performance of the functions concerned, importance was attached to the precise constitution of the organ concerned.[9]

Also, Sir Gerald was hesitant to recognize that the majority has any authority to impose binding decisions on a reluctant minority in all cases. In the context of impositions of assessments on protesting members, he was even willing to concede that "member States retain a last resort right not to pay."[10] He did not, however, indicate what this right consisted of and under what conditions it could be exercised.

In an unusually thorough examination of the problem of nullity, Judge Morelli distinguished the acts which were voidable and those which were absolute nullity. In the opinion of Judge Morelli, Public International Law could not be construed to contain such finer distinctions as void, voidable, invalid, and non-existent acts, in the absence of review machinery of a compulsory character.[11] It was necessary, therefore, according to Judge Morelli,

to put a very strict construction on the rules by which the conditions for the validity of acts of the Organization are determined, and hence to regard to a large extent the non-conformity of the act with a legal rule as a mere irregularity having no effect on the validity of the act. It is only in especially serious cases that an act of the Organization could be regarded as invalid, and hence an absolute nullity. Examples might be a resolution which had not obtained the required majority, or a resolution vitiated by a manifest *exces de pouvoir* (such as, in particular,

[9]*Ibid.*, p. 200.
[10]*Ibid.*, pp. 203-4.
[11]*Ibid.*, pp. 221-3.

a resolution the subject of which had nothing to do with the purposes of the Organization).[12]

The burden of Judge Morelli's argument was that it was not necessary for the Court to go into the question of validity of the UN resolutions on which UNEF and ONUC were based, and "that the failure of the act to conform to the rules concerning competence has no influence on the validity of the act, which amounts to saying that each organ of the United Nations is the judge of its own competence."[13]

In his dissenting opinion President Winiarski picked up Judge Morelli's above argument to enter a strong refutation. He stated categorically:

It has been said that the nullity of a legal instrument can be relied upon only when there has been a finding of nullity by a competent tribunal. This reasoning must be regarded as echoing the position in municipal or State law, in the international legal system. In the international legal system however, there is in the absence of agreement to the contrary, no tribunal competent to make a finding of nullity. It is the State which regards itself as the injured party which itself rejects a legal instrument vitiated, in its opinion, by such defects as to render it a nullity. Such a decision is obviously a grave one and one to which resort can be had only in exceptional cases, but one which is nevertheless sometimes inevitable and which is recognized as such by general international law.[14]

The issue of nullity of acts of international organizations thus remained unresolved in the *Expenses* Opinion. Nevertheless, the case dramatically presented the problem of judicial control of acts of international organizations. Judge Morelli's view that organs of the United Nations are competent to decide their own competence, Judge Fitzmaurice's statement that member States have a last resort right to refuse to be bound by the majority decision

---

[12]*Ibid.*, p. 223; see also *ibid.*, pp. 216, 221-3.
[13]*Ibid.*, p. 105.
[14]*Ibid.*, pp. 227, 232.

about assessments, and Judge Winiarski's exposition on the lack of determination agencies for acts performed by international organizations, make a weired and challenging mixture of the realities of international life. The situation becomes even worse, if one remembers the abstruse and intricate task of ascertaining whether or not a particular act falls within the discretionary powers of an organization.

The difficulty of adjudging the constitutionality of acts of international organization comes out in greater relief if one takes recourse to another advisory opinion of the ICJ concerning the Inter-Governmental Maritime Consultative Organization (IMCO), which received comparatively scanty attention in academic circles.

THE IMCO ADVISORY OPINION

On 23 March 1959 the IMCO Assembly requested the ICJ for an advisory opinion on the constitution of the Maritime Safety Committee. The question posed was: "Is the Maritime Safety Committee of the Inter-Governmental Maritime Consultative Organization, which was elected on 15 January 1959, constituted in accordance with the Convention for the Establishment of the Organization ?"[15]

The issue before the Court in concrete terms could be formulated in the following manner. Has the Assembly in not electing Liberia and Panama to the Maritime Safety Committee, exercised its electoral power in a manner in accordance with the provisions of Article 28(a) of the Convention of 6 March 1948 for the establishment of the Inter-Governmental Maritime Consultative Organization. According to this Article:

> The Maritime Safety Committee shall consist of fourteen members elected by the Assembly from the members, governments of those nations having an important interest in maritime safety, of which not less than eight shall be the largest ship-owning nations, and the remainder shall be elected so as

[15]The official citation is "Constitution of the Maritime Safety Committee of the Inter-Governmental Maritime Consultative Organization, Advisory Opinion of 8 June 1960," ICJ, *Reports*, 1960, p. 151.

to ensure adequate representation of members, governments of other nations with an important interest in maritime safety, such as nations interested in the supply of large numbers of crews or in the carriage of large numbers of berthed and un-berthed passengers, and of major geographical areas.[16]

According to the representatives of the governments of Liberia and Panama, for the purposes of Article 28(*a*) the eight largest ship-owning nations should be determined by reference to the figures of gross registered tonnage as they appeared in the *Lloyd's Register of Shipping Statistical Tables, 1958*. The Governments of the United States and the United Kingdom, however, contended that the Assembly had a discretionary power to elect eight members, not necessarily the first eight found in the *Lloyd's Register*. In the elections held on 15 January 1959, Liberia and Panama failed to be elected, and protested strongly against the procedure of election. Hence, the reference to the Court.

It was contended before the Court that the Assembly was entitled to refuse to elect Liberia and Panama, by virtue of a discretion claimed to be vested in it under Article 28(*a*). The substance of the argument, as formulated by the Court, was as follows: The Assembly was vested with a discretionary power to determine which members of the Organization had "an important interest in mari-time safety" and consequently in discharging its duty to elect the eight largest ship-owning nations, it was empowered to exclude as unqualified for election those nations that in its judgment did not have such an interest. Furthermore, it was submitted that that discretionary power extended also to the determination of which nations were or were not "the largest ship-owning nations."[17]

The Court refused to accept this argument on the grounds that "the natural and ordinary" meaning of the relevant article coupled with its drafting history would not brook such an interpretation. It ruled:

What Article 28(*a*) requires the Assembly to do is to determine which of its members are the eight "largest ship-owning nations"

[16] *Ibid.*, p. 154.
[17] *Ibid.*, p. 158.

within the meaning which these words bear. That is the sole content of the question in relation to them. The words of the Article "of which not less than eight shall be the largest ship-owning nations" have a mandatory and imperative sense and precisely carry out the intention of the framers of the Convention.[18]

As respects the argument that the Assembly had a discretionary authority enabling it to choose the largest ship-owning nations, uncontrolled by any objective test of any kind, whether it be that of tonnage registration or ownership by nationals or any other, the Court ruled that it was not compatible with the mandatory provisions of the Article. "To give to the Article such a construction," affirmed the Court, "would mean that the structure built into the Article to ensure the predominance over the committee of 'the' largest ship-owning nations in the ratio of at least eight to six would be undermined and would collapse."[19]

It was urged upon the Court that the "largest ship-owning nations" criteria could not be confined to merely registered tonnage, and that the names and nationalities of the owners or shareholders of shipping companies should also be taken into account. But the Court felt such a method of evaluating the ship-owning rank of a country was neither practical nor certain and that it found no basis in international practice. Having thus reached the conclusion that the determination of the largest ship-owning nations depended solely upon the tonnage registered in the countries in question, the Court pronounced by nine votes to five: "That the Maritime Safety Committee of the Inter-Governmental Maritime Consultative Organization, which was elected on 15 January 1959, is not constituted in accordance with the Convention for the Establishment of the Organization."[20]

President Klaestad wrote a dissenting opinion wherein he sought to prove that the criteria contained in the clause "an important interest in maritime safety" accorded the Assembly a discretion

[18]*Ibid.*, p. 165.
[19]*Ibid.*, p. 166.
[20]*Ibid.*, p. 171.

which was predominant over the other provisions of the Article. Also the term "election" as found in the Article, according to President Klaestad, was "not compatible with any automatic test which imposed itself on the electing body in such a manner that no freedom of choice is left to that body."[21] The Article, in his opinion, could only mean that of the members which the Assembly had found to have an important interest in maritime-safety, not less than eight should be the largest ship-owning nations.

Judge Morena Quintana also wrote a dissenting opinion on similar lines, emphasizing particularly that the power of election given by the Article to the Assembly was incompatible with a mandatory obligation to designate a particular country.[22]

The case presents thus a prennial problem of interpretation of discretionary authority of international organizations. It highlights the fact that even in express provisions the discretionary power could be construed variously. If this is the position with regard to express authority the position wherein international organizations seek to draw upon powers by implication must necessarily be more complex. The complexity gets compounded if one has to interpret what is "necessary" for the effective performance of the Organization and what is the "necessary intendment" of the Charter.

ACADEMIC DEBATE

The problem received considerable attention in the *Institute de Droit International* in 1951.[23] Professor Wengler who prepared a report on the question of judicial appeal against the decisions of international organs circulated a questionnaire, no. 9 of which was as follows: "Does any rule of international law exist which excludes from challenge the decisions of international organs whose validity is not contested in due time, or ought one to admit the principle

[21]*Ibid.*, p. 174.
[22]*Ibid.*, pp. 177-8.
[23]E. Lauterpacht, *op. cit.*, pp. 192-4, has succinctly summarized the debates in the *Institute de Droit International* concerning this matter, on which this section is based.

that legally defective decisions are absolutely null, in the absence of a decision to the contrary?"[24]

A number of replies were received pertaining to this particular question. Professor de Luna while admitting that no rule excluded the challenge of decisions of international organs, however, conceded the principle that defective judicial decisions were absolutely null and could be challenged at any time.[25] Professor Verdross also affirmed the same principle, but pointed out that no means of redress existed.[26] Professor Wengler agreed with this opinion. There was considerable controversy as to the question of time-limit.[27] Professor Verzijl drew a distinction between those procedural defects which did, and those which did not, lead to nullity. He left the matter to a tribunal to decide. In the opinion of Professor Verzijl each case of validity, or otherwise must be contested in good time, and that no fixed rule, no presumptions of legality or nullity existed. He concluded:

... only essential defects should be taken into consideration because it is exactly the opposition of interested States to decisions legally rendered *bonafide* by an international body which is one of the grave flaws in the international community. *Lites finiri oportet.* This general approach to the problem naturally leads to a limitation of the possibility of redress (or of a second judicial instance) as a general maxim of a future *jus constituendum.*[28]

On the basis of these replies Professor Wengler drew up a fresh draft, Article 1 of which provided as follows:

... In the absence of judicial redress against the decisions of an international organ and the absence of provisions rendering them definitive, the validity of these decisions can be contested at any time and before any instances according to the general rules of international law, if the organ has violated the rules deter-

[24]*Annuaire de Institute de Droit International,* Vol. 44-I, 1951, p. 293.
[25]*Ibid.,* p. 347.
[26]*Ibid.,* p. 350.
[27]*Ibid.,* pp. 262, 266-7.
[28]*Ibid.,* pp. 354-8.

mining its competence procedure, or the contents of its decisions.[29]

The *Expenses* opinion could be said to have improved the positions taken in the *Institute de driot International*. The International Court took the definite view that in the absence of a *prima facie* nexus between the act and the purposes of the Organization the presumption was in favour of legality. The other question, pertaining to the time-limit within which an illegal act of an international organ could be impugned still remained unresolved. It seems fair to adopt the opinion of Professor Verzijl that the invalidity of that impugned act must be contested in good time. It would be a source of uncertainty if no such reasonable time-limit was fixed. The issue of time-limit could best be appreciated if one remembers the rationale behind the schemes of nullity which was clearly described by Judge Morelli in his individual opinion in the *Expenses* case:

> The rules under which in any legal system the problem of the validity of legal acts is considered face two different requirements. On the one hand there is the requirement of *legality*, that is to say, conformity of the act with the legal rule. Exclusive consideration of that requirement would have as its consequence the denial of any value to an act not in conformity with the legal rule. On the other hand, however, there is the requirement of *certainty*, which would be seriously jeopardized if the validity of a legal act were at all times open to challenge on the ground of its non-conformity with the legal rule.[30]

The only question that remains to be tackled is one of third-party determination or a review machinery. In the course of practice amongst international organizations a few instances could be found where a review machinery has been provided. But before that it must be mentioned that there is a tendency, evidenced both in the *Institute's* discussions and in the individual opinions of the *Expenses* case, to oversimplify, assimilate and equate the com-

[29]*Ibid.*, Vol. 45-I, p. 266.
[30]ICJ, *Reports*, 1962, p. 221.

pulsory character of such machinery with the review machinery of a non-compulsory character. All international organizations directly or indirectly can refer matters of interpretation of their constituent instruments to the International Court of Justice. Member States which feel aggrieved owing to any act or omission of international organizations can move the concerned organs to obtain judicial verdicts from the World Court. It is a question, again, of the enormity of the act or omission and the intensity of the feeling in the membership of the organization. A small minority, of course, has no opportunity of such judicial redress. Even here, one must admit, that a minority consisting of States of such stature as the Soviet Union and France, could, and did, seek such advisory opinions and still hold their own. Precisely to avoid such unpleasant contingencies international organizations must evolve review machineries to ascertain the validity of questionable and questioned acts. Arrangements were made in at least three instances, to a narration of which we turn next.

PRACTICE OF INTERNATIONAL ORGANIZATIONS

Specific provisions could be found in the constituent instruments connected with the following international organizations for the purpose of determining the effect and illegality of acts and omissions of these organizations. These are the Treaties establishing the three European Communities; the abortive Havana Charter establishing the International Trade Organization and the provisions of the statutes of various administrative tribunals. Since the last category of international bodies has been dealt with in the preceding chapter, only the first two categories would be mentioned here.

The European Communities[31] established a comprehensive method of judicial control over the acts of various organs of the community. Under Article 173 of the Treaty establishing the European Economic Community the Court of Justice is accorded jurisdiction to supervise the legality of the acts of the Council and Commission for the

---

[31]Gerhart Beber, *Judicial Control of the European Communities*, London, 1962.

following acts: "Lack of jurisdiction, substantial violations of basic procedural rules, infringements of this Treaty or of any rule of law relating to effect being given to it or of misuse of powers." The Article also provided for a time-limit and clearly established as to who could initiate proceedings. Under Article 174 the Court is authorized to declare the impugned act null and void if the complaint is found well-founded.

The International Trade Organization also provided under Article 96 a procedure to control acts of the Organization. The provision was as follows:

(*i*) The Organization may, in accordance with arrangements made pursuant to Article 96(2) of the Charter of United Nations, request from the International Court of Justice advisory opinions on legal questions arising within the scope of the activities of the Organization.

(*ii*) Any decision of the Conference under this Charter shall, at the instance of any member whose interests are prejudiced by the decision, be subject to review by the International Court of Justice by means of a request, in appropriate form, for an advisory opinion pursuant to the Statute of the Court. . . .

(*iii*) Pending the delivery of the Opinion of the Court, the decision of the Conference shall have full force and effect; provided that the Conference shall suspend the operation of any such decision pending the delivery of the opinion, wherein the view of the Conference damage difficult to repair would otherwise be caused to a member concerned.

(*iv*) The Organization shall consider itself bound by the opinion of the Court on any question referred by it to the Court. In so far as it does not accord with the opinion of the Court, the decision in question shall be modified.[32]

SUMMATION

The preceding analysis points to the following generalization. The problem of establishing machinery for review of acts

[32]For text, see Clair Wilcox, *A Charter for World Trade*, New York, 1949, p. 227.

of international organization goes to the core of the law of international institutions. The issue remained unresolved in the *Expenses* Opinion. The IMCO Advisory Opinion shows that given the will and sense of fair play international organizations could make use of the existing machinery, namely, the International Court of Justice.

That, however, does not mean that there is a review machinery of compulsory character. In the absence of such machinery the view that international organs remain the final arbiters of their acts, is a oversimplification of the problem. Any legal system that does not provide for redress of unconstitutional acts of its actors is bound to suffer a grave handicap, and remains, to that extent, defective. Foresight and imagination requires that such machinery for redress is either established in cases where it does not exist, or strengthened where it exists in a non-compulsive character.

The further question of the *effect* of illegal acts of international organizations warrants deeper research and understanding. The scope and frame of reference of the present study does not permit such an intensive probe. Tentatively the provisions of the abortive International Trade Organization, cited above, could be recommended to meet the contingency.

CHAPTER 8

CONCLUSIONS

OUR THEORETICAL DEDUCTION in Part I of the present study, has been that the UN could, in view of its objective international personality, assume unrestricted *legal* capacity under international law. Its capacities emanated not only from the express provisions of the Charter but also from all those implied and ancillary powers which sprang from, and were incidental to, the specific powers. The framework, it was found, was the stated purposes and objectives, and all means which were plainly adapted to that end and which consisted with the letter and spirit of the Charter were constitutional, any minor lapse in the internal competency notwithstanding.

However, it was shown that the doctrine of implied powers, and its logical extension, the doctrine of institutional effectiveness propounded by the International Court over a series of advisory opinions, would not provide the Organization with a *carte blanche*. The Court's dicta, it was asserted, had built-in checks and balances, or auto-limitations, both legal and political. On an examination of those dicta it was found that the Organization could assume only those functions which were "essential to the performance of its duties," and that they should arise by "necessary intendment" out of the Charter. It was suggested inferentially that the UN, even with the help of those tools of interpretation, was incapable, both legally and politically, of achieving the dreaded proportions of a super State. In fact, the likelihood in the current international context seems to be the other way round: the financial crisis seems to have rendered it substantially impotent, at least in the peace-keeping area.

The above conclusions were amply borne out in the course of practice. As brought out in Part II the potentialities of the implied powers and the doctrine of institutional effectiveness in practice were considerable and the limitations not a few.

The chapter on peace-keeping powers revealed a peculiar pheno-menon in practice. The machinery created under Chapter VII of the Charter was still-born. The UN failed to be effective even in the limited sphere it was constitutionally capable of being effective (in view of the requirement of unanimity of permanent members). The cold war and the early attempts by the power blocs to use the UN as an instrument of their national policies paralysed the UN.

The search for alternative peace-keeping organs in the UN, the Uniting for Peace procedure, and the Organization's later evolution as an instrument of preventive diplomacy could be viewed as the development of the implied powers of the UN. The General Assembly's broad powers under Articles 10 and 14 of the Charter in matters of world peace, by necessary implication, involved securing cease-fires, creating supervisory organs, and establishing interpository forces (UNEF). So also the Security Council's powers under Chapters VI and VII authorized it by implication to create truce commissions (Palestine, Kashmir, etc.) and para-military forces, with less than enforcement powers and more than interpository functions (the Congo and Cyprus operations). These by implications were found to be "necessary" instrumentalities that were legitimately required to perform one of the "essential" duties of securing international peace, a primary, "stated" purpose of the Organization.

The creation and operation of the instrumentalities do suffer the general debilities that are characteristic of the organs that create and operate them. The operations of the Security Council suffer the threat of permanent member veto and those of the General Assembly, because of the hortatory character of its resolu-tions, are inhibited at every stage by the necessity of consent of the concerned parties. But the fact remains that operations of the police, interpository and fire-brigade character, can be characterized as those actions legal bases for which can be found not in the express provisions of the Charter but in the necessary meanings of those provisions. In other words, it can be said that the UN has in the course of practice, developed some functions legal sanctity for which can be found in its implied powers.

As regards treaty-making, the controversy about the inter-relationship between international personality and treaty-making power reveals the supremacy of the express purposes and functions in order that implied powers in this direction could be deduced. We can visualize a case of the constituent instrument of an international organization which really has no functions that need the employment of treaties for effective perpetuation. Also, there can be a case where an organization possesses the necessary objective personality and needs utilizing treaties for carrying out its functions, but the constituent instrument does not contain any provision granting it treaty-making power. Logic and practical necessity demands that the first be denied the implied treaty-making power and the second be deemed to possess such powers. The true criteria to deduce any such power is the necessity for having recourse to treaty technique which must be essential for the performance of its duties.

In practice, it has been seen in the relevant chapter, international organizations have had recourse to treaties with minimal inhibitions and with practically no objections whatsoever. As it was para-phrased at that time, on the basis of practice, objective inter-national personality was not coterminous with treaty-making power, but that the latter could not be deemed to exist without objective international personality. There are several international organizations listed in Peaslee,[1] for instance, the Inter-African Pedological Service, the Inter-American Children's Institute, the International Office of Epizootics, the International Wool Study Group, etc., which act either as clearing houses of information or as co-ordinating centres of national policies of neighbouring countries. It would be highly farcical to grant them treaty-making powers in the absence of express provision to that effect. On the other hand, it would be equally preposterous to withhold such powers from organizations like the United Nations, the Inter-national Labour Organization, the World Health Organization, the International Maritime Consultative Organization, the Inter-national Civil Aviation Organization, etc., which have been entrust-

[1] Amos J. Peaslee. *International Governmental Organizations, Constitutional Documents,* Hague, 1961.

ed with important functions to perform. It is therefore necessary to look into the stated purposes and functions to draw an implication of treaty-making power. International personality alone cannot supply the necessary basis for reading into the constituent instrument of an international organization an implied power of treaty-making.

The doctrine of institutional effectiveness in this context serves a very useful purpose. When it is established that the Organization has an express or implied treaty-making power the authority which negotiates, concludes and ratifies such treaties, becomes a matter of internal significance, and any minor lapse in this process would not strip the treaty of its legal validity. It was seen at the end of Chapter 3 that the organs and officials of international organizations, though conforming to the basic requirements of authorization by competent organs, have been in practice taking a liberal attitude to traditional norms of treaty law, such as, for instance, the requirement of signature. The treaty practice of international organizations on the whole conforms to the doctrinal development in this regard.

The section on expulsion, suspension, and forced withdrawal reveals that implied powers in this connection, though available in extreme cases of grave and persistent violations, are not very conducive to a healthy development of international organizations. The dilemma between taking a crude step against a grave violator and inaction amounting to admission of impotency is painful indeed. This is one of the rare situations where legal validity would lead to not very happy results.

International organizations, therefore, have had recourse to varieties of punishment. Some have expelled even in the absence of express provision (for example, Cuba from the Organization of American States), some have forced withdrawal (for example, Czechoslovakia from the International Monetary Fund and the International Bank for Reconstruction and Development, South Africa from the International Labour Organization, etc.,) and some have excluded partially from some of their activities and organs (for example, Portugal and South Africa from the Economic Commission for Africa of the Economic and Social Council). Of course, as was seen in Chapter 4, the organizations were legally competent to take any of these steps. But partial exclusion seems to be the best practical remedy.

Pragmatism demands that the violation of the law must be punished not by total exclusion, outlawry being the municipal equivalent, but a punishment which subjects the culprit to the constant gales of world reprobation. Justice warrants the punishment to be commensurate with the violation. Excluding a member from commissions, committees, and other important organs in keeping with the gravity of the wrong done would be an ideal form of punishment. The formula of the International Wheat Agreement, it bears repetition, which through selective sanctions reduces the rights and privileges of the member conerned in proportion to its offence, is a remarkable innovation.

The viability of the doctrines of implied powers and institutional effectiveness grinds to a halt when it comes to express provisions, the natural and ordinary meaning of which do not allow for the free play of powers by implication. Express prohibition being too glaring an obstacle in the exercise of implied powers, international organizations sometimes have sought to read into express provisions an implication that does not exist. This happened in the case of the UN which, hamstrung over its admissions procedure owing to power bloc horse-trading for membership of their respective candidate nations, sought legal advice from the International Court of Justice.

The Court was faced with the dilemma of reconciling the wishes of the framers to the actual provision that emerged in the Charter and at the same time drawing up limitations to the claims of powers by implication. Article 4 clearly laid down certain criteria which should be taken into consideration when admitting a State into the Organization. Should it be treated as an exhaustive enumeration? The *travaux preparatoires* pointed to the negative conclusion; but the actual provision in the Charter did not mention anything about it.

The Court naturally viewed the matter in terms of effects. What would happen if the Court conceded that the list was not exhaustive? The criteria that a member seeking admission would be a "State," "peace-loving," "willing" and "able" to undertake the obligations of the UN, etc., were thoroughly flexible. Who was to decide whether the new member was a State; whether it was peace-loving, and so on. Of course, the majority of the members of the Organization. If they thought Monaco was a State and peace-loving, willing and able to carry out the obligations which fall on every member, then there was none to challenge their decision. If the majority felt China was not peace-loving then also there was no remedy. It was wholly a matter of subjective appreciation. The member States had the widest latitude for their discretionary powers.

To give scope over and above the discretionary powers granted under Article 4 was unnecessary. The member States might have anything in mind within the range of the criteria employed in that Article. The function definitely was a political act—and political act of the highest importance, as the dissenting judges emphasized—but every discretionary power, including, political, had guiding or controlling norms. Article 4 provided such norms. A member might at heart have some other consideration, but to object to the membership it should employ the terminology contained in the express provision.

The restrictive interpretation excluded possibilities of "package deals" which occasioned the Advisory Opinion in the *First Admissions* case; and it also excluded such other considerations as the new government's method of coming into power—a matter purely internal in effect. On the other hand a liberal interpretation would have opened up a Pandora's box, for the same reasons.

The *Second Admissions* case threw light on the Court's earlier view of the spheres of competence of important organs of the UN. It is interesting to speculate the effect of the Court's views in this and the *Expenses* opinion. Would the Court have held that, since the issue was one of internal competence the General Assembly could act without the recommendation of the Security Council? It is a difficult hypothesis. The Court in the *Expenses* case was faced with the problem of finances and the Organization's capacity to incur lawful expenses. In the *Administrative Tribunals* case it was deciding upon the Secretary-General's capacity to engage the credit of the Organization and the capacity of the plenary organ to deny the commitment. In the *Second Admissions* case, however, the Organization's capacity to decide the composition of its membership in a particular manner was at issue. Violation of the set procedure would have struck at the basic guarantees and fundamental status of the permanent members of the Security Council. A positive recommendation from the Security Council was a *sine qua non* of the admissions procedure. Either there was a recommendation or no recommendation. Recommendation was not a duty. It was only a favour. The members of the Security Council had a power and privilege to refuse admission on the basis of Article 4 of the Charter.

In the case of putting into motion the peace-keeping machinery under Chapter VII, the members of the Security Council, as guardians of world peace, have a duty to perform. If they fail to act they fail in their duty. When there is a deadlock and the other organ, i.e. the General Assembly, has a right and justification to invoke its implied or secondary powers in this regard and act or recommend action. The General Assembly's success in action and recommendations, of course, depend on the consent and willingness of the concerned parties and member States.

No such necessity exists in the case of the admissions process. The admissions procedure of the UN is not automatic. The Organization has wide discretionary powers within the meaning of Article 4. Moreover, universality is not a mandatory principle, only a desirable goal.

The establishment, status, and powers of the UN Administrative Tribunal brings to light the limiting aspects of the doctrine of implied powers. The doctrine can be used to augment the powers and to lay claim on a wide range of activities for international organization and at the same time the doctrine can be employed to place severe restrictions on its own powers—both in the interest of institutional effectiveness. In order that the employment relations in the Organization be based upon the firm foundation of the rule of law, the Organization establishes an administrative tribunal with powers to render binding and final judgments between the administration and its employees. It has powers to establish an advisory body, an appeals board, a paritary organ, or a judicial tribunal, with varying shades of functions, representation and powers.

It can do this by the necessary intendment out of its constituent instrument which prescribe high standards of service and expects loyalty to the Organization. These cannot be achieved without guaranteeing to its employees a measure of independence, certain privileges and immunities and above all security of tenure and fair conditions of service. The constitutional instruments and conventions, both bilateral and multi-lateral, on privileges and immunities ensure the necessary independence, privileges and immunities. Any of the enumerated bodies can ensure that the contractual obligations assumed by the Organization, in order to assure for its employees security of tenure and fair conditions of service (reduced to writing in the voluminous Manuals and periodical Bulletins), are adhered to. But an advisory body, an appeals board and even a paritary organ, apart from their hortatory as opposed to mandatory character, suffer from one fundamental defect: totally or partially the judge and the defendent are the same, which fact flies in the face of one of the basic tenets of natural justice.

The UN, therefore, adopted a statute that envisions almost total independence for its Administrative Tribunal. The appointment powers and the powers of abolition or amendment are common features found even in the truest of democracies where the judiciary and the executive are severely separated. That was the best method of securing the declared objective of highest standards of efficiency, integrity, and competence in the internal administrative machinery of the UN. The implied powers were thus used in this instance to restrict the powers of the Organization in the direction of arbitrariness, prejudice, and caprice.

Can the Organization claim in the same breath an implied power to reject the decisions of the Tribunal, not on the ground of the legal invalidity of the judgments for reasons of excess of jurisdiction, etc., but on the simple ground that it can refuse to be bound by the act of its own subordinate, subsidiary or whatever body the Tribunal is. The invocation of the implied powers in this case wolud have stultified the very purpose of the establishment of the Tribunal.

The International Court of Justice refused to countenance such a use of implied powers. Implied powers could be used to effectively carry out the stated purposes, express or implied functions and the declared objectives of the Organization, and not to jeopardize the effective performance of its duties. If the Tribunal's judgments could be picked and chosen for performance, the effect would be very opposite of security and fairness in the conditions of service of employees, which again, will result in the failure of securing highest standards of efficiency in the administration—a paramount goal according to paragraph 3 of Article 101 of the Charter.

The members of the Tribunal are not infallible. There might be genuine cases of mathematical mistakes or a lack of essential evidence which are unearthed subsequent to the judgment. In such cases a revisionary power is given to the Tribunal and in graver contingencies the parties are authorized by amendment to the Statute, following the Court's opinion in the *Administrative Tribunals* case, to go to the International Court for an advisory opinion which would be binding.

The general conclusion of the present study, therefore, might be laid down thus: that objective international personality of the United Nations combined with its stated purposes and the extremely important functions it performs, make it necessary to interpret its provisions liberally in order that the Organization functions effectively; that the doctrines of implied powers and institutional effectiveness are only tools employed to achieve the above goal; that neither the objective personality nor the said doctrines are capable of being used, both legally and politically beyond the framework of its purposes and principles.

This, however, does not mean that there is no necessity for evolving means of review of acts of international organization. The Specialized Agencies and other Inter-Governmental Organizations would do well to extend to the ICJ jurisdiction to review their contested acts. The United Nations being the upholder of international law would do itself a great service if it evolves a review machinery of its own on the lines of the Administrative Tribunal, or if it takes resort more often to the ICJ—as the League used to do—where a particular act gave rise to acute controversy.

BIBLIOGRAPHY

NOTE ON PRIMARY SOURCES

It is otiose and even presumptuous to attempt to list out primary source material for a subject as this. Suffice it to say that the Charter of the United Nations, the Covenant of the League of Nations, the General Assembly Official Records, the Security Council Official Records, the United Nations Treaty Series, the League of Nations Treaty Series, the League of Nations Official Journal, the Documents of the United Nations Conference on International Organization, San Francisco, the International Law Commission Reports and Year Books, and the Repertory of Practice of United Nations Organs have been the store-houses of information and data for this study.

The following Advisory Opinions of the International Court of Justice have been freely made use of :

Conditions of Admission of a State to Membership in the United Nations (Article 4 of the Charter), ICJ *Reports*, 1947-48, p. 57.

Reparation for Injuries Suffered in the Service of the United Nations, ICJ, *Reports*, 1949, p. 174.

Competence of the General Assembly for the Admission of a State to the United Nations, ICJ *Reports*, 1950, p. 4.

Effect of Awards of Compensation made by the United Nations Administrative Tribunal, ICJ *Reports*, 1954, p. 4.

Judgments of the Administrative Tribunal of the ILO, Order of 5 December 1955, ICJ *Reports*, 1955, p. 127.

Certain Expenses of the United Nations (Article 17, paragraph 2 of the Charter), ICJ *Reports*, 1962, p. 150.

Constitution of the Maritime Safety Committee of the Inter-Governmental Maritime Consultative Organization, ICJ *Reports*, 1960, p. 150.

SECONDARY SOURCES

Books and Monographs

BEBR, GERHART, *Judicial Control of the European Communities*, London, 1962.

BOWETT, D.W., *Law of International Institutions*, London, 1963.

CHEN, T.C., *The International Law of Recognition*, London, 1951.

Commission to study the Organization of Peace, 10th Report. *Strengthening the United Nations*, Arthur N. Holcombe, Chairman, New York, 1957.

FRYE, WILLIAM R., *A United Nations Peace Force*, New York, 1957.

GOODRICH, LELAND M. and HAMBRO, EDVARD, *Charter of the United Nations*, Boston, 1949, 2nd ed.

GOODRICH, LELAND M. and SIMONS, ANNE P., *The United Nations and the Maintenance of International Peace and Security*, Washington, D.C., 1955.

GRAHAM, M.W., *The League of Nations and the Recognition of States*, Berkeley, Cal., 1933.

GUETZKNOW, HAROLD, *Multiple Loyalties : Theoretical Approach to a Problem in International Organization*, Princeton University, 1955.

HARLEY, JOHN EUGENE, *The League of Nations and the New International Law*, New York 1921.

HIGGINS, ROSALYN, *The Development of International Law Through the Political Organs of the United Nations*, London, 1963.

HILL, MARTIN, *Immunities and Privileges of International Officials*, Washington D.C., 1947.

HUDSON, MANLEY O., *The Permanent Court of International Justice*, 1920-1942, New York, 1943.

JENKS, WILFRED C., *The Headquarters of International Institutions*, London, 1945.
——, *The Common Law of Mankind*, London, 1958.
——, *The Proper Law of International Organizations*, London, 1962.

JESSUP, PHILIP C., *Transitional Law*, New Haven, 1956.
——, *The International Problem of Governing Mankind*, London, 1947.
——, *The Use of International Law*, Ann Arbor, 1959.

KELSEN, HANS, *The Law of the United Nations*, London, 1950.
——, *Recent Trends in the Law of the United Nations : A Supplement*, London, 1951.

KING, JOHN KERRY, *The Privileges and Immunities of the Personnel of International Organisations*, Denmark, 1949.

LAUTERPACHT, E., (ed.) *The United Nations Emergency Force*, New York, 1960.

LAUTERPACHT, SIR HERSH, *The Development of International Law by the International Court*, London, 1958.
——, ed., *International Law Reports*, (1919-1956) Vols. 22 London, 1919-1958. (1919-1931/32) called *Annual Digest of Public International Law Cases*, 1933-34 (1949) called *Annual Digest and Reports of Public International Law Cases*.
——, *Recognition in International Law*, London, 1947.

LISKA, GEORGE, *International Equilibrium*, Cambridge, Mass., 1957.

MCNAIR, ARNOLD DUNCAN, LORD, *The Law of Treaties, British Practice and Opinion*, New York, 1938.

MILLER, DAVID HUNTER, *The Drafting of the Covenant*, New York, 1928.

NEKAM ALEXANDER, *The Personality Conception of the Legal Entity*, Cambridge, 1938.

OPPENHEIM, L., *International Law, A Treatise*, Seventh edition by Sir Hersch Lauterpacht, 2 Vols. London, 1952.
——, Eighth edition by Sir Hersch Lauterpacht, London, 1955.

PURVES, C., *The International Administration of an International Secretariat*, London, 1945.

REUTER, PAUL, *International Institutions*, New York, 1958.

ROSENNE, SHABTAI, *The International Court of Justice*, Leyden, 1957.

ROSNER, GABRIELLA, *The United Nations Emergency Force*, New York, 1963.

RUSSELL, RUTH B. and JEANNETTE E. MUTHER, *A History of the United Nations Charter*, Washington, D.C., 1958.

SCHNEIDER, J.W., *Treaty-Making Power of International Organisations*, Geneva, 1959.

SCHWARZENBERGER, GEORG, *Committee on the Charter of the United Nations, Report on Problems of a United Nations Force, International Law Association,* Hamburg Conference, 1960.

——, *Second Report on the Review of Charter of the U.N. International Law Association,* Dubrovnik Conference, 1956.

——, *International Law,* Vol. 1, London, 1949, 2nd ed.

SINGH, NAGENDRA, *Termination of Membership of International Organisations,* London, 1958.

STONE, JULIUS, *Legal Controls of International Conflict,* New York, 1954.

——, Second Impression, Revised with Supplement, 1953-58, New York, 1959.

TOUSSAINT, CHARMIAN EDWARDS, *The Trusteeship System of the United Nations,* New York, 1956.

WALTERS, F.P., *A History of the League of Nations,* 2 Vols., London, 1952.

WATKINS, JAMES T. and J. WILLIAMS ROBINSON, *General International Organization, A Source Book,* Princeton, NJ., 1956.

WEBSTER, SIR CHARLES, *Sanctions : The Use of Force in an International Organisation,* London, 1956.

WEISSBERG, GUENTER, *The International Status of the United Nations,* London 1961.

WILSON, FLORENCE, *The Origins of the League Covenant,* London, 1928.

WRIGHT, QUINCY, ed., *The World Community,* Chicago, 1948.

Articles and Periodicals

AMERICAN BAR ASSOCIATION, "The Assembly, the Tribunal and World Court," *American Bar Association Journal,* Vol. 40, 1954, p. 1065.

ANONYMOUS, "The United Nations Under American Municipal Law ; A Preliminary Assessment," *Yale Law Journal,* Vol. 55, 1945-46, p. 778.

ARMSTRONG, HAMILTON FISH, "The U.N. Experience in Gaza," *Foreign Affairs,* Vol. 35, 1957, p. 600.

AUFRICHT, HANS, "Personality in International Law," *American Political Science Review,* Vol. 37, 1943, p. 90.

——, "Principles and Practices of Recognition by International Organization," *American Journal of International Law,* Vol. 43, 1949, p. 679.

BAADE, HANS, "Nullity and Avoidance in Public International Law : A Preliminary Survey and a Theoretical Orientation," *Indiana Law Journal,* Vol. 39, 1963-64, p. 497.

BRANDON, MICHAEL, "Analysis of the Terms 'Treaty' and 'International Agreement' for purposes of Registration under Article 102 of the United Nations Charter," *American Journal of International Law,* Vol. 47, 1953, p. 49.

——, "Legal Status of the Premises of the United Nations," *British Yearbook of International Law,* Vol. 28, 1951, p. 96.

BROCHES, ARON, "International Legal Aspects of the Operations of the World Bank," *Recueil des Cours,* Vol. 98, 1959-III, p. 297.

CLAUDE, INIS, L. JR., "The U.N. and the Use of Force," *International Conciliation* No. 532, 1961.

——, "United Nations Use of Military Force," *Journal of Conflict Resolution* Vol. 7, 1963, p. 117,

COHEN, MAXWELL, "The United Nations Emergency Force : A Preliminary View," *International Journal*, Vol. 12, 1957, p. 109.

——, "The United Nations Secretariat—Some Constitutional and Administrative Developments," *American Journal of International Law*, Vol. 49, 1955, p. 295.

CORBETT, P.E., "What is the League of Nations?" *British Yearbook of International Law*, Vol. 5, 1924, p. 119.

CURTIS, GERALD L., "The United Nations Observation Group in Lebanon," *International Organization*, Vol. 18, 1964, p. 738.

DETTER, T.I.H., "The Organs of International Organizations exercising their Treaty-making Power," *British Yearbook of International Law*, Vol. 38, 1962. p. 421.

DRAPER, G.I.A.D., "The Legal Limitations upon the Employment of Weapons by the United Nations Force in the Congo," International and Comparative Law Quarterly, Vol. 12, 1963, p. 387.

EAGLETON, CYLDE, "International Organisation and the Law of Responsibility," *Recueil des Cours*, Vol. 76, 1950, p. 319.

FAWCETT, J.E.S., "The Legal Character of International Agreements," *British Yearbook of International Law*, Vol. 30, 1953, p. 381.

——, "The Place of Law in International Organization," *British Yearbook of International Law*, Vol. 36, 1960, p. 321.

FITZMAURICE, SIR GERALD, "The Law and Procedure of the International Court of Justice : General Principles and Substantive Law," *British Yearbook of International Law*, Vol. 27, 1950, p. 1.

——, "The Law and Procedure of the I.C.J. 1951-54 : General Principles and Sources of Law, " *British Yearbook of International Law*, Vol. 30, 1953.

FRIEDLANDER, LILIAN M., "The Admission of States to the League of Nations," *British Yearbook of International Law*, Vol. 9, 1928, p. 84.

GOODRICH, LELAND M., "The United Nations and Korea," *Journal of International Affairs*, Vol. 6, 1952, p. 115.

——, "The Maintenance of International Peace and Security," *International Organisation*, Vol. 19, 1965, p. 429.

——, "Expanding Role of the General Assembly," *International Conciliation*, no. 471, 1951.

GOODRICH, L.M. and ROSNER, GABRIELLA E., "The United Nations Emergency Force," *International Organization*, Vol. II, 1957, p. 413.

GREEN, L.C., "The Nature of the 'War' in Korea," *International Law Quarterly*, Vol. 4, 1951, p. 462.

——, "The Status of the International Civil Service," *Current Legal Problems*, 1954, p. 192.

——, "Membership in the United Nations," *Current Legal Problems*, Vol. 2, 1949, p. 258.

GROSS, LEO, "Was the Soviet Union Expelled from the League of Nations?" *American Journal of International Law*, Vol. 39, 1945, p. 35.

——, "Expenses of the United Nations for Peace-Keeping Operations : The Advisory Opinion of the International Court of Justice," *International Organisation*, Vol. 17, 1963, p. 1.

HAAS, ERNST B., "Types of Collective Security — An Examination of Operational Concepts, "*American Political Science Review,* Vol. 49, 1955, p. 40.

HAHN, HUGO J., "Euratom : The Conception of an International Personality," *Harvard Law Review,* Vol. 71, 1958, p. 1001.

HALDERMANN, JOHN W., "United Nations Territorial Administration and the Development of the Charter," *World Rule of Law Booklet Series,* No. 25, Durham, N.C, 1964, p. 95.

HARRIMAN, A., "The League of Nations, A Rudimentary Superstate," *American Political Science Review,* Vol. 21, 1927, p. 137.

HOFFMAN, STANLEY, "Sisyphus and the Avalanche : The United Nations, Egypt and Hungary," *International Organization,* Vol. 11, 1957, p. 446.

——, In Search of a Thread : The U.N. in the Congo Labyrinth," *International Organization,* Vol. 16, 1962, p. 331.

HUDSON, MANLEY O., "The Bank for International Settlements," *American Journal of International Law,* Vol. 24, 1930, p. 561.

——, "Membership in the League of Nations," *American Journal of International Law,* Vol. 18, 1924, p. 436.

JENKS, C. WILFRED, "Expulsion from the League of Nations," *British Yearbook of International Law,* Vol. 16, 1935, p. 155.

——, "Some Constitutional Problems of International Organizations," *British Yearbook of International Law,* Vol. 22, 1945, p. 11.

——, "Co-ordination : A New Problem of International Organization, A Preliminary Survey of the Law and Practice of Inter-Organisational Relationships," *Recueil des Cours,* Vol. 77, 1950, p. 151.

——, "Co-ordination in International Organisation: An Introductory Survey," *British Yearbook of International Law,* Vol. 28, 1951, p. 29.

——, "The Legal Personality of International Organisations," *British Year book of International Law,* Vol. 22, 1945, p. 267.

——, "The Status of International Organisations n Relation to the International Court of Justice, *Transactions, Grotius Society,* Vol. 32, 1946, p. 1.

R.Y. JENNINGS, "Nullity and Effectiveness in International Law," *Cambridge Essays in International Law,* London, 1965, p. 64.

JESSUP, PHILIP C., "Great Lakes — St. Lawrence Deep Waterway Treaty," *American Journal of International Law,* Vol. 26, 1932, p. 814.

——, "The subjects of a Modern Law of Nations," *Michigan Law Review,* Vol. 45, 1947, p. 383.

——, "U.S. Position on the Free Territory of Trieste," *Department of State Bulletin,* Vol. 19, 1948, p. 225.

——, "Force under a Modern Law of Nations," *Foreign Affairs,* Vol. 25, 1946.

JOHNSON, HOWARD C., and GERHART NIEMEYER, "Collective Security — The Validity of an Ideal," *International Organisation,* Vol. 8, 1954, p. 19.

KELSEN, HANS, "Collective Security and Collective Self-Defence under the Charter of the United Nations," *American Journal of International Law,* Vol. 42, 1948, p. 785.

——, "Membership in the United Nations," *Columbia Law Review,* Vol. 46, 1946, p. 391.

——, "The Free Territory of Trieste under the United Nations," *Yearbook of World Affairs,* Vol. 4, 1950, p. 174.

KUNZ, JOSEF L., "The Secretary-General on the Role of the United Nations," *American Journal of International Law*, Vol. 52, 1958, p. 300.

LACHS, MANFRED, "Recognition and Modern Methods of International Co-operation," *British Yearbook of International Law*, Vol. 35, 1959, p. 252.

LAUTERPACHT, SIR HERSCH, "Restrictive Interpretation and the Principle of Effectiveness in the Interpretation of Treaties," *British Yearbook of International Law*, Vol. 26, 1949, p. 48.

——, "The Subjects of the Law of Nations," *Law Quarterly Review*, Vol. 63, 1947, p. 438.

——, "The Subjects of the Law of Nations," *Law Quarterly Review*, Vol. 64, 1948, p. 97.

E. LAUTERPACHT, "The Legal Effects of Illegal Acts of International Organizations," *Cambridge Essays in International Law*, London, 1965, p. 88.

LIANG, YUEN LI, "The Legal Status of the United Nations in the United States," *International Law Quarterly*, Vol. 2, 1948, p. 577.

——, "Notes on Legal questions Concerning the United Nations, Conditions of Admission of a State to Membership in the United Nations," *American Journal of International Law*, Vol. 43, 1949, p. 288.

LISSITZYN, OLIVER J., "United Nations Administrative Tribunal : Effect of Awards. International Court of Justice, Advisory Opinion, July 13, 1954," *American Journal of International Law*, Vol. 48, 1954, p. 655.

MCMAHON, J.F., "The Court of the European Communities, Judicial Interpretation and International Organization," *British Yearbook of International Law*, Vol. 37, 1961, p. 320.

MCDOUGAL, MYRES and GARDNER, RICHARD, "The Veto and the Charter: An Interpretation for Survival," *Yale Law Journal*, Vol. 60, 1951.

MILLER, E.M., "Legal Aspects of U.N. Action in the Congo," *American Journal of International Law*, Vol. 55, 1961, p. 1.

MUNRO, SIR LESLIE, "Can the U.N. Enforce Peace," *Foreign Affairs*, Vol. 38, 1960, p. 209.

OPPENHEIM, L., "Le Caractere Essential de la Societe des Nations," *Revue Generale de Droit International Public*, Vol. 26, 1919, p. 234.

PARRY, CLIVE, "The Treaty-Making Power of the United Nations," *British Yearbook of International Law*, Vol. 26, 1949, p. 108.

——, "The Legal Nature of the Trusteeship Agreements," *British Yearbook of International Law*, Vol. 27, 1949, p. 164.

PEARSON, LESTER B., "Force for U.N.," *Foreign Affairs*, Vol. 35, 1957, p. 395.

PENFIELD, WALTER SCOTT, "The Legal Status of the Pan American Union," *American Journal of International Law*, Vol. 20, 1926, p. 257.

POTTER, PITMAN, B., "The Classification of International Organisations," *American Political Science Review*, Vol. 29, 1935, p. 212.

——, "Membership and Representation in the U.N.," *American Journal of International Law*, Vol. 49, 1955, p. 234.

Research in International Law under the Auspices of the Harvard Law School, "Draft Convention on the Law of Treaties, *American Journal of International Law, Suppl.*, Vol. 29, 1935, p. 653.

ROSENNE, SHABTAI, "United Nations Treaty Practice," *Recueil des Cours*, Vol. 86, 1954, p. 275.

——, "Recognition of the States by United Nations," *British Yearbook of International Law*, Vol. 26, 1949, p. 437.

RUDZINSKI, ALEKSANDER W., "Admission of New Members : The UN and the League of Nations," *International Conciliation*, No. 480, 1952.

SAYRE, FRANCIS B., "Legal Problems Arising from the United Nations Trusteeship System," *American Journal of International Law*, Vol. 42, 1948, p. 263.

SCHACHTER, OSCAR, "The Development of International Law through the Legal Opinions of the United Nations Secretariat," *British Yearbook of International Law*, Vol. 25, 1948, p. 91.

——, "The Quasi-Judicial Role of the Security Council and the General Assembly," *American Journal of International Law*, Vol. 58, 1964, p. 690.

SCHIMITOFF, C.M., "The International Corporation—Legal Organisation of a Planned World Economy," *Transactions, Grotius Society*, Vol. 30, 1944, p. 165.

SEYERSTED, FINN, "United Nations Forces : Some Legal Problems," *British Yearbook of International Law*, Vol. 37, 1961, pp. 351, 447.

——, International Personality of Inter-governmental Organizations: Do their capacities really depend upon their constitutions?" *Indian Journal of International Law*, Vol. 4, 1964, p. 1.

SIRPAUL, S., "Developments in the Legal Machinery of the United Nations", *International and Comparative Law Quarterly*, Vol. 11, 1962, p. 573.

SLOAN, BLAINE, F., "The Binding Force of the 'Recommendation' of the General Assembly of the United Nations," *British Yearbook of International Law*, Vol. 25, 1948, p. 1.

SOHN, LOUIS, B., "Authority of the United Nations to establish and maintain a Permanent United Nations Force," *American Journal of International Law*, Vol. 52, 1958, p. 229.

——, "Expulsion or Forced Withdrawal from an International Organization," *Harvard Law Review*, Vol. 77, 1964, p. 1381.

STUART, GRAHAM, H., "The International Lighthouse at Cape Spartel," *American Journal of International Law*, Vol. 24, 1930, p. 770.

TABATA, SHIGEJIRO, "Admission to the U.N. and Recognition of States," *The Japanese Annual of International Law*, No. 5, 1961, p. 1.

THOMPSON, KENNETH W., "Collective Security Re-examined," *American Political Science Review*, Vol. 47, 1953, p. 753.

TUCKER, ROBERT W., "The Interpretation of War under Present International Law," *International Law Quarterly*, Vol. 4, 1951, p. 27.

VOORHEES, D., "The League of Nations : A Corporation, not a Super-State," *American Political Science Review*, Vol. 20, 1926, p. 847.

WEINSTEIN, J.L., "Exchanges of Notes", *British Yearbook of International Law*, Vol. 29, 1952, p. 205.

WENGLER, WILHEIM, "Agreements of States with other parties than States in International Relations." *Revue Hellenique de Droit International*, Vol. 8, 1955, p. 113.

WILLIAMS, SIR JOHN FISCHER, "The Status of the League of Nations in International Law," *International Law Association*, 34th Conference, Vienna, 1926, p. 675.

WOLFERS, ARNOLD, "Collective Security and the War in Korea."

and "Collective Defence Versus Collective Security," *Discord and Collaboration*, Baltimore, 1962, pp. 167, 181.

WOOD, HUGH MCKINNON, "The Dissolution of the League of Nations," *British Yearbook of International Law*, Vol. 23, 1946.

WRIGHT, QUINCY, "The Jural Personality of the United Nations," *American Journal of International Law*, Vol. 43, 1949.

——, "Responsibility for Injuries to United Nations Officials," *American Journal of International Law*, Vol. 43, 1949.

——, "International Organisation and Peace," *The Western Political Quarterly*, Vol. 8, 1955.

——, "United States intervention in the Lebanon," *American Journal of International Law*, Vol. 53, 1959.

——, "Legal Aspects of the Congo Situation," *International Studies*, Vol. 6, 1962.

——, "Peace-Keeping Operations of the United Nations," *International Studies*, Vol. 7, 1965.

INDEX